Roots of a Region

Roots of a Region
Southern Folk Culture

John A. Burrison

University Press of Mississippi   Jackson

www.upress.state.ms.us

The University Press of Mississippi is a member
of the Association of American University Presses.

Front cover photos, left to right: Top row: Decoration Day, Central Cemetery,
Flatridge, Virginia (author); Hmong story cloth by May Tong Moua, Lilburn, Georgia
(photo by William F. Hull, courtesy, Atlanta History Center); street preacher
Raymond Willis, Atlanta, Georgia (author). Second row: Burlon Craig's "groundhog"
pottery kiln, Vale, North Carolina (author); African American quilt by Annie Howard,
Madison, Georgia (photo by William F. Hull, courtesy, Atlanta History Center);
dogtrot house, Oakhurst, California (photo by Laura Maish and Bill Storage). Third
row: face jug by Thomas Chandler, Edgefield District, South Carolina (courtesy,
McKissick Museum, University of South Carolina); pottery rooster by Charlie West,
White County, Georgia (author); wall graffiti, Atlanta, Georgia (author). Bottom row:
sweet tea, Harold's Barbeque, Kennesaw, Georgia (photo by Andy Sharp, courtesy,
Atlanta Journal-Constitution); Cajun Mardi Gras, southwest Louisiana (photo by T. J.
Smith); *The Banjo Lesson* by Henry O. Tanner (courtesy, Hampton University Archival
and Museum Collection, Hampton, Virginia)

Library of Congress Cataloging-in-Publication Data
Burrison, John A., 1942–
  Roots of a region : Southern folk culture / John A. Burrison.
     p. cm.
  Includes bibliographical references and index.
  ISBN-13: 978-1-934110-20-1 (cloth : alk. paper)
  ISBN-10: 1-934110-20-5 (cloth : alk. paper)
  ISBN-13: 978-1-934110-21-8 (pbk. : alk. paper)
  ISBN-10: 1-934110-21-3 (pbk. : alk. paper) 1. Southern States—Social life and
customs. 2. Regionalism—Southern States. 3. Material culture—Southern States.
4. Folk music—Southern States. 5. Folklore—Southern States. 6. Oral tradition—
Southern States. I. Title.
  F209.B87 2007
  306.0975—dc22
                              2007014682
British Library Cataloging-in-Publication Data available

CONTENTS

ACKNOWLEDGMENTS

For help with illustrations, permissions, and research, my thanks
to: Sheila Kay Adams, Beth Agnew, Janet Barrickman, Anna
Berkes, Beth Bilderback, Jennifer Bean Bower, Erika Brady, Brian
Cullity, Joseph Earl Dabney, Jane Ross Davis, Gail DeLoach, Laura
Drummond, Steve Engerrand, Laura Foster, Cathy Fussell, Jerry
Gandolfo, Sally Gant, Henry Glassie, Stacey Hayes, Chester Hewell
family, Matt Hinton, David Holt, Laurel Horton, Rob Hunter,
John Inscoe, Kathleen Ketterman, John Kollock, Richard Laub,
Nelson Morgan, Nicole Mullen, Daisy Njoku, Lee Orr, David Perry,
George Pickow, Katherine Pringle, Pam Prouty, Jean Ritchie, Peter
Roberts, Margo and Art Rosenbaum, Tony and Marie Shank, T. J.
Smith, Malinda Snow, Bill Storage, Gary Stradling, Chris Swanson,
Rebecca Vitt, Vicky Wells, Allen Woodall, and Terry Zug.

I also express my appreciation to: Matthew Roudané, Randy
Malamud, Greg George, Marta Hess, Lori Howard, and Tammy
Mills of Georgia State University's Department of English for
support with this project; Mike Krajewski for musical transcription
of Lillie West's ballads; and Craig Gill, editor-in-chief, University
Press of Mississippi, for his encouragement.

Roots of a Region

Introduction

A Pennsylvania Yankee
in Governor Lester Maddox's Court

I'm goin' to Georgia, I'm goin' to roam,
I'm goin' to Georgia to make it my home.
—From the southern folk song "Going to Georgia"[1]

"*Tell about the South. What's it like there. What do they do there.*" Shreve
McCannon makes this plea to his Harvard roommate, Mississippian
Quentin Compson, in William Faulkner's novel *Absalom, Absalom!*[2]
Shreve, the ultimate northerner—a Canadian—is enthralled by
Quentin's tale of the Sutpen family, and what better audience for
this unmistakably southern tale than a sympathetic outsider full of
curiosity about the region.

It was as such a curious northerner that I came to Atlanta in
1966, trying not to have too many preconceptions, eager to learn
about my newly adopted region (while ostensibly coming to teach at
Georgia State University). From the southern perspective, at least,
I was a Yankee; from my perspective as a Pennsylvanian, I thought
of Yankees as New Englanders (the label, in truth, is relative; to the
English, all Americans are Yanks). But, as one who had grown up in
Philadelphia and made only a few forays below the Mason-Dixon
Line, I was certainly an outsider.

While mining Georgia State's library recently for publications to
inform this book, I faced an intimidating wall of volumes about the
South, most by natives of the region. What could I hope to contribute to the millions of words already written? The autobiographical

patchwork that follows is meant to explain my interest in the South and thus help the reader understand what I, as a folklorist and (at least initially) an outsider, might be able to add to an understanding of the region.

Before detailing my own attraction to the South, I'd like to mention a few earlier links with my home state to suggest an affinity that otherwise may seem unlikely. Southerners, of course, had to come from somewhere, and during the eighteenth and early nineteenth centuries Pennsylvania was a significant source for southern settlement, especially of the mountains and Piedmont. The Great Philadelphia Wagon Road, terminating at Augusta, Georgia, followed the old Iroquois Warriors Path along a valley trough in the Appalachians, providing access to the southern backcountry. And as we'll see later, the Delaware Valley, including the Philadelphia area,

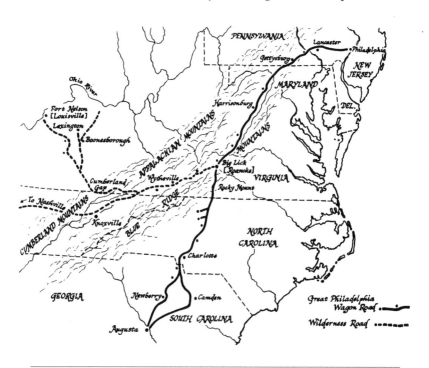

The Philadelphia Wagon Road, terminating at Augusta, Georgia, after providing access into the upland South from Pennsylvania via the Shenandoah Valley. Map by Tom Hill, in Joseph Earl Dabney, *Mountain Spirits*, Scribner's, 1974.

The old White County Courthouse, Cleveland, Georgia, a Pennsylvania Federal-style building said to have been modeled on Philadelphia's Independence Hall. It was built 1859–1860 by E. P. Williams with slave labor. Illustration by John Kollock, used by permission of artist, © 1976 in his *These Gentle Hills*, Copple House Books.

Jar attributed to Philadelphia potter Andrew Duche while in Savannah, Georgia, ca. 1740. Lead-glazed earthenware. H. 13". Courtesy, Museum of Early Southern Decorative Arts, Winston-Salem, North Carolina; in John A. Burrison, *Brothers in Clay*, University of Georgia Press, 1983.

generated features of American frontier culture such as the log cabin that were carried southward.

Fellow Philadelphians who preceded me by two centuries include naturalist William Bartram (in Georgia 1773–76, and in whose name a trail following his travel route has been established) and Georgia's earliest-known potter, Andrew Duche, who worked at Savannah (1738–43) before fleeing the colony as a rabble-rousing malcontent. A much later connection is a famous painting, *The Banjo Lesson*, by African American artist Henry Ossawa Tanner of Philadelphia, possibly inspired by a scene he witnessed while based in Atlanta (1889–90).[3]

Beginnings: Southern Folklore Beckons

My only real memory is of the fear. The rest of the event I recovered as a young adult from my parents. According to them it happened when I was about five (which would have been 1947) at Arden, Delaware. Now a suburb of Wilmington, Arden began as a utopian single-tax community and artists' colony modeled on an English village. We spent the summers at my grandfather's cottage there, and in the backyard on Saturday nights we hosted hootenannies, or folk music gatherings, organized by our cousin Billy Pressman and attended by luminaries of the early folk song revival who were based on the East Coast.

I remember waking on the night in question to the startling realization that I was alone in the cottage; calls to Mom and Dad were not answered, and I began to scream my head off, not realizing

Louisiana-born folk singer Leadbelly (Huddie Ledbetter) with his twelve-string Stella guitar, ca. 1940. *New York World-Telegram and Sun Newspaper* Photograph Collection, Library of Congress; courtesy, History Image.

that they were just outside, absorbed in the hootenanny. Finally, one of the guests came inside to see what all the fuss was about. The big black man lifted me onto his lap and sang to me (without his twelve-string guitar), whereupon I was calmed and promptly fell asleep. His lullaby was "Good Night, Irene," and the man was Huddie Ledbetter, better known as Leadbelly, the ex-con from Louisiana and Texas, then living in New York, who would become the subject of three books and a movie.[4] I was not old enough for the event to fully impact my consciousness, but it did foreshadow the path I was to take in life.

Not everyone is so fortunate as to find a true mentor in his or her chosen field. I encountered mine in my sophomore year at Pennsylvania State University when I took Samuel Bayard's ballad course. Like many teenagers of the late 1950s I'd been involved in the folk music revival, taking guitar lessons from George Britton of Philadelphia and visiting folk-music coffeehouses there like Ed and Esther Halpern's Gilded Cage. We listened to records by slick revivalists like the Kingston Trio and attended concerts when we could, but few of us had heard performances by authentic traditional singers who'd absorbed their music from their communities. It was this interest in folk music, in any case, that drew me to Professor Bayard's course.

As Sam stood in front of us on that first day of class, I thought I detected a mischievous twinkle in his eye as he paused frequently in his introductory lecture to refresh himself—with snuff! From pocket after pocket of his rumpled gray suit he produced an unending variety of snuff boxes, each containing a different flavor of powdered, fermented tobacco. He would tap the lid thrice with a knuckle, pop it open, grab a generous pinch and inhale deeply, brusquely flicking the remainder on the floor. Returning the box to its designated pocket, he'd then pull out a handkerchief to dust the underside of his beak-like nose, returning to his subject as if nothing out of the ordinary were happening. The students, at first mesmerized, soon exploded in a buzz of whispers. I was as intrigued as they by this odd behavior, but I was also becoming absorbed in his discussion of the importance of oral literature in earlier society and his experiences recording folk songs and music at the upper edge of the Southern Appalachian Mountains.

Exploring resources in Penn State's library for my term paper, I stumbled across Allen Eaton's *Handicrafts of the Southern Highlands*, published in 1937 and illustrated by New York photographer Doris Ulmann. His descriptions and her dignified portraits of craftspeople triggered in me a further attraction to Appalachian folk culture (one of their subjects, the teenaged potter Lanier Meaders, would become the touchstone for my first book, *Brothers in Clay*, after I moved to Georgia). It took a while for this first exposure to the academic study of folklore to sink in, but when it did it hit like a ton of bricks.

The following semester I took a course on news writing and, for a human-interest story assignment, interviewed Professor Bayard about his experiences collecting folk songs and music in the 1930s and '40s in southwestern Pennsylvania and adjoining West Virginia. My journalism instructor liked the piece and encouraged me to seek publication, but there didn't seem to be a happy medium between scholarly periodicals such as the *Journal of American Folklore* and revivalist magazines like *Sing Out!* So I naively set out to publish my own folklore magazine there in the town of State College. This meant establishing a relationship with a local printer, soliciting and writing ads for local businesses to cover expenses, renting an electric typewriter, typing the camera-ready text while doing the layout and pasteup myself, and writing the lead articles while soliciting others from a growing network of contacts.

Called *Folkways*, the magazine began unrealistically as a monthly and soon became an annual. The second issue focused on Appalachian folklore, with a feature on Kentucky mountain ballad singer Jean Ritchie based on correspondence with her (and resulting in a generous gift of her records that I treasure and still use in the classroom). That issue also included a story on the mountain dulcimer by makers Leonard Glenn and his son, Clifford, of Watauga County, North Carolina. In the process I purchased Leonard's "most expensive" (curly maple) model for thirty-five dollars, which now hangs on my office wall next to a beautiful fretless banjo by Clifford. The third and last issue of *Folkways* contained ads from national businesses and was distributed at key East Coast locations. This magazine, and the contacts it led to in the folklore world, launched me into graduate folklore study at the University of Pennsylvania.

It was an early autumn day in 1965, the first day of classes in my second year of study in Penn's Department of Folklore and Folklife. I was walking home past the late-Victorian houses of West Philadelphia, and the back of my neck began to tingle as I heard increasingly rapid footfalls behind me. When a hand clapped my shoulder, I was reminded of my many escapes from street gangs on my way to and from grade and high school in the same neighborhood. I wheeled to confront my assailant, and there stood a lanky young man of faintly Mediterranean appearance. The friendly smile under his walrus moustache led to an introduction: "I noticed that we were sitting in the same classroom and were walking home in the same direction. I'm Henry Glassie. I just moved to Philadelphia with my family and don't have any friends here. Could you come to my place for supper tomorrow night?"

The plaintive tone and piercing dark eyes left no room for refusal, so the next night, at his rented row house just a few blocks from my family home, I acquired a lifetime friend who was on his way to becoming one of the world's great folklorists. Raised in Washington, D.C., Henry has family roots in Virginia, and he did much of his early fieldwork in the South. That year was filled with nights of like-minded conversation, parties with a clique of fellow grad students (which included ballad-singing round-robins), and field trips into the Pennsylvania countryside in the Glassiemobile (Henry's Volkswagen bus) which resulted in the discovery of ballad singer Eva Girvin of Mt. Nebo, near Lancaster, a migrant from the North Carolina mountains. I learned as much about folklore through my bond with this gregarious humanist as from my professors; his scholarship continues to set the standard in the field. With Henry's guidance, I would join that generation of folklorists who made the leap from oral literature and music to material culture.

The phone rang too early on a Sunday morning in the spring of 1966. I rolled from my narrow bed, in the upstairs rear apartment of my family home where I lived while in graduate school, and answered it, my head still full of sleep. It was Helen Sewell, a good friend and fellow Penn folklore grad student. "Remember that job I told you about?" she teased in her southern accent, forcing me to recall her description of the teaching position she'd secured for herself at Georgia State University in her hometown of Atlanta. It was a rare opportunity to develop an undergraduate folklore curriculum in a state that had seen virtually no professional folklorists: a dream job in uncharted territory. "Well," she continued, "the job could very well be yours if you're interested."

Helen explained that she'd just become engaged to a Philadelphia lawyer and would be staying in that city. But she'd signed a contract with Georgia State, ordered books and journals for the library, and scheduled new courses for the upcoming academic year. The Department of English would be anxious to follow through with the position, and so long as I wasn't a felon, passed muster in a hastily arranged visit and interviews, and signed an oath of allegiance to the state of Georgia, I had an inside track. A new life, and the only full-time job I've ever had, awaited me.

One of the most memorable images from my early days in Atlanta is that of Lester Maddox, who became governor of Georgia in 1967, entertaining visitors to the new, white-columned Governor's Mansion by riding his bicycle backwards. Maddox was a different breed of politician from those I'd known up North: a segregationist who got the white vote by selling his Pickrick Restaurant near Georgia Tech rather than allow blacks to eat there (the pick handle he threatened them with becoming his symbol of defiance and calling into question Atlanta's New South motto, "The City Too Busy to Hate")—but then, once in office, appointing more African Americans to important state positions than any Georgia governor before him and opening his office for a weekly "Little People's Day" to hear grievances from anyone, black or white.[5] What was this recently-arrived northerner to make of this apparent contradiction? And my

Governor Lester Maddox riding his bicycle backwards in the state capitol, Atlanta, Georgia, 1970. Photo by Dwight Ross Jr.; courtesy, *Atlanta Journal-Constitution.*

wonderment was not a matter of bemused detachment: as a state employee, I'd suddenly become a part of this strange new world.

But in my first year in a state that had seen little folklore research, I could not afford to dwell on its politics. My calling was to make up for lost time by engaging (and engaging my students) in fieldwork. Given my training and early interest in folk music and song, it was the recording of those forms of expression that I emphasized at first, adding to them the emerging area of material folk culture, especially architecture, being pioneered by my friend Henry Glassie.

During my second week in Atlanta I heard a young night-shift elevator operator in the downtown building that housed my rented office whistling "Careless Love," a blues tune I recognized. We struck up a conversation, and he subsequently introduced me to an older fellow-worker, Luther Johnson. When both stopped by my office one night at my invitation, it became apparent that Mr. Johnson would be a prize folklore informant. Born on a dairy farm in DeKalb County, Luther was then living in northwest Atlanta. He'd been a prizefighter as a young man, claimed to have sparred with World Heavyweight Champion Joe Louis, and ran five miles every day; at age fifty-two, he still had a powerful physique. Luther could recite many of the plants his part-Indian father had used to prepare medicines. He also recalled magical cures and superstitions, but did not believe most of them: "Well, they believed witches was coming [at night], so they put down mustard seeds—you know, that was a million, million seeds. They was told that the witch would have to pick up all them seeds before he cross it [the threshold]. So they would spread them down in the door[way]. Well, that was enough to show them then it wasn't true: when they'd wake up, the seeds would still be down there. But they claimed the witch couldn't pick them all up and left."

Luther's father and grandfather were preachers, and he inherited an ability for preaching his peculiar biblical philosophy and for singing spirituals and gospel songs, his favorite and most personal type of song. But he didn't reject secular folk songs as "sinful," and could sing the blues as well:

In the wee midnight hours, long to-wards the break of day,
In the wee midnight hours, long to-wards the break of day;
Sure, the blues slip up on you, drive your mind away.

Blues, well you've hurt me, why do you stay so long, (2)
You come to me yesterday, stay with me all night long.

I told my baby I believe I'll go back home, (2)
'Cause the way that I am treated, I feel like I'm all alone.[6]

Luther also told "ha'nt" (ghost) stories as personal experiences:

This is true: I was walking home; I was going visiting, you know, at my friend's house. And on the way home the church was lit up real

Blues harp (harmonica) virtuoso Luther Johnson, Atlanta, Georgia, 1966. Photos are by author unless otherwise noted.

bright. I thought they was having service up there. When I got even with the church, the lights went out! Since I heard them talking about those things I just figured it was a haunted church. That never did frighten me, I just continued and went on. And several more seen the church lit up like that the same as I did. If it's imagination, it was a mighty large one!

And something else. My father loved to possum hunt. So did I; used to go with him. Moonlight night, you know; that time of year no leaves on the trees much. And so, when you see a dark spot up in the tree, you know they's a possum up there when the dogs "tree." Gets up there, shake the tree: sand fall! No possum; sand, just sand fall all down on the ground. So, I haven't been possum hunting much more since!

Luther's real talent, though, lay in playing the "blues harp," which he picked up from his uncle while taking breaks from work in the fields. When I gave him money to buy a harmonica at a nearby pawn shop, he brought back an Atta Boy–brand instrument and "drowned," or soaked, it in water so that the wooden partitions separating the holes swelled out, which he then cut off flush with the mouthpiece. That facilitated his creation of the slurred blues notes, achieved with a combination of breathing and tongue, teeth, and lip placement. Cupping the "harp" in both hands, he could expertly mimic a fox chase or a train chugging and whistling.

Soon after Luther visited one of my classes to demonstrate his gifts (when I recorded the "ha'nt" tales above), he left his job in the office building and I lost track of him. Years later, as I was walking down the street toward Georgia State, I was clapped on the back from behind with such force that it nearly knocked me over. Sure enough, it was Luther, grinning from ear to ear; he hadn't forgotten me. We exchanged news, and as we parted for the last time, his handshake let me know that this mighty man had not lost any of his power.

In that first year (1966–67), my students recorded some five hundred songs and tunes, enough to begin the Georgia Folklore Archives, the only intensive statewide effort to document Georgia's folk traditions (most of this material has since been transferred from my office to the Atlanta History Center, where it's being computer-catalogued). That same year, usually accompanied by a student or two and in one case an entire class, I recorded nineteen musicians and singers. All but Luther and blues fiddler Elbert Freeman of Monticello, in middle Georgia, were located in the hills and mountains of north Georgia. One of these was multi-instrumentalist Sam Hawkins of Matt, Forsyth County (thirty-five miles north of Atlanta), who merited many return visits. I was also documenting folk architecture in those same Appalachian uplands that had so intrigued me as a college student. The following account of one research trip illustrates my initial dual interests in folk music and architecture.

It was a wet Saturday afternoon in the summer of 1967 when student Joe Treadway and I drove along a muddy dirt road, his car brushing the dripping, overhanging boughs of roadside trees. Miserable as the weather was, these mountains near Clayton, in Rabun County—less than ten miles below the North Carolina line—still held a brooding beauty. We were on an offshoot of Germany Road, winding through a community known as Little Germany, an early settlement of Pennsylvania Germans. Looking off to the right through the glistening foliage, I spotted a rooftop and the characteristic "stripes" of a log structure below the ridge road we were on. It took us a while to find an entrance to the small hollow.

The access road was so mushy that we had to abandon the car a quarter of a mile from the house. Armed with a camera and battery-powered tape recorder, and unprotected from what was now a driving rain, we sloshed up the road until we could see the house distinctly. It would have taken a lot to excite me under those conditions, yet my heart was beginning to beat quickly. Joe whistled under his breath and exclaimed, "What the hell is it?" There before us was a tiny log cabin, the most minuscule I've ever encountered, consisting of a crudely V-notched 12' x 16' main room with small side and rear shed additions and a medieval-looking, steeply pitched roof. It was like something out of a Grimm brothers' folktale.

There probably was no more isolated situation in all of Appalachia, yet the sound of commercial country music could be heard from inside, indicating a radio powered by the line we saw snaking to a metered box. There at the door to greet us, with an assortment of mongrels, cats, and chickens, was a character as unreal as the fairy-tale cottage she lived in. Mrs. Carrie Kilby, a gnarled, four-feet-tall mountain woman, invited us in with only a cursory explanation on our part, offering us a seat by the wood-burning stove. There was barely room to move with three of us in the little room. After my questions about the community (to which she replied that she knew of no German descendants, having lived there all her life and being of "Arsh"—Irish, most likely Scotch-Irish—ancestry herself), we asked if she knew of any "old-timey" musicians or singers around yet. "Oh yeah, I pick the banjer," she replied, without the usual hesitation and show of modesty. "I used ta could pick any song that was ever wrote."

While she searched for her banjo, we surveyed the room. The only new thing in sight was the plastic-cased radio. The log walls were covered inside with brown cardboard ("pasteboard," as Carrie called it) from shipping cartons and decorated with a calendar and religious pictures. Pieced quilts lay crumpled on two beds, but there

Banjo player Carrie Kilby and her tiny log cabin, Little Germany, Georgia, 1967.

was no linen. A naked bulb hanging from the ceiling was the only artificial illumination. The collapsing fieldstone chimney was no longer usable, hence the stove. On the mantle hung a turkey wing, once used to brush ashes from the hearth. The rear shed served as a kitchen, the narrow side shed as a storage closet. There was no barn, but a corn patch and garden plot outside established this as a still-active subsistence farm.

Carrie found her old factory-made banjo, missing two strings and the fifth-string tuning peg. With the promise of "any song that was ever wrote," Joe and I were not going to be daunted by an incomplete instrument. We told her that we'd drive into Clayton, buy the necessary items, and return. I don't think she believed us, for an hour later, when we found our way back from town with a peg and full set of strings, she seemed pleasantly surprised that we'd gone to such trouble to hear her play. I restrung the banjo, and while Carrie attempted to tune it I tramped out again in the rain to fetch the tape recorder's takeup reel, which I'd neglected to bring from the car. On my return, Carrie was speechless with frustration because she couldn't get the instrument in tune, and Joe was cursing under his breath for not bringing along his own Vega banjo. Then, for a few magical moments, the instrument stayed roughly in tune, and Carrie, playing in a jerky, pre-bluegrass style, shouted out a few rousing stanzas of the ballad "John Henry." By the time we could set up the recorder, though, the banjo was hopelessly out of tune again, throwing all of us into a black mood.

For a time we waited for Carrie's husband, Ed, to come home from wherever he'd gone that day so that he could help us, but it was getting "dusky dark," and Joe and I were nervously anticipating the drive back to our weekend headquarters, the Smith House in Dahlonega, over fifty miles of slippery, hairpin roads. After saying our reluctant good-byes, we waded up the path (now a creek) toward the car with our soggy equipment, when a plaintive sound sent chills up our spines. Carrie, who had moved out to the dripping porch of the log cabin that was even too small for her, had gotten the banjo temporarily back in tune and was picking and singing:

A short life of trouble,
A few words to part;
A short life of trouble,
Poor girl with a broken heart.[7]

We paused when she called for us to return, but we were closer to the car than to the house, and dashing to open the car doors, we started our cautious trip back to Dahlonega. On a later visit to the area I inquired about the Kilbys and learned that they'd left for parts unknown after the cabin, which must have had stood in that cove for well over a century, burned to the ground.

While this adventure left me unsuccessful in recording Carrie's musical repertoire, it does hint at my rich experiences as a folklorist in the South. I am privileged to have known artists such as Carrie

Kilby, Luther Johnson, and the scores of others, many of them accomplished craftspeople, I was to meet in subsequent years. These exemplars of tradition have shared their lives with me, and the best way I know to repay them is to pass on in these pages what I've learned. Economically speaking, the South may once have been the poorest region of the country, but it was, and still is, the richest in folk culture.

I. The Core of the Culture

Folk Traditions and the Big Regional Picture

> Properly understood, folk tradition is a society's lifeline to its collective identity. . . . [T]o understand southern folk culture in all its complexity is to understand something very fundamental—the essential character of southerners.
> —Charles Joyner, *Shared Traditions: Southern History and Folk Culture*[1]

The overarching theme of this book is the importance of folklore (a term used interchangeably here with *folk traditions, folk culture,* and *folklife*) in shaping and expressing the culture of the American South.[2] A community-shared resource of accumulated knowledge, folklore is learned informally, preserved in memory and practice, and passed on through speech and body action to others in any group whose members have a common bond. Acquiring games from other children on the playground and watching older family members cook in the kitchen are familiar examples of this folk learning process. An enactment of the past in present behavior, folklore is essentially conservative, but given the fluid nature of face-to-face communication and the tendency of the human links in this chain of transmission to adapt their inherited traditions to suit personal needs and the times in which they live, folklore constantly changes—while remaining constant.

The physical isolation of farms and plantations of the frontier and antebellum South, and the impoverishment of the post–Civil War South, supported a mindset that put a premium on the ways of the ancestors. This centrality of folk traditions in southern life is

Henry Ossawa Tanner's 1893 painting *The Banjo Lesson* illustrates the folk learning process and may have been inspired by a scene the Philadelphia artist observed in the South. Courtesy, Hampton University Archival and Museum Collection, Hampton, Virginia.

attested in literature by such antebellum authors as Augustus Baldwin Longstreet, Harden E. Taliaferro, William Tappan Thompson, and George Washington Harris, and by postbellum writers such as Mark Twain, Joel Chandler Harris, Charles W. Chesnutt, and George Washington Cable.[3] For example, Taliaferro, whose pen name was "Skitt," published a wealth of folklore he acquired growing up in the North Carolina mountains in the 1820s. He presents the following tall tale as narrated by Larkin Snow, whose "ambition consisted in being the best miller in the land, and in being *number one* in big story-telling":

> "You see," said Larkin, "a passel uv fellers cum frum 'bout Rockford, Jonesville, and the Holler to have a fox-hunt, and kep' a-boastin' uv thar fast dogs. I told 'um my little dog Flyin'-jib could beat all thar dogs, and give 'um two in the game. I called him up and showed him to 'um, and you mout a hearn 'um laugh a mile, measured with a 'coonskin and the tail throwed in. I told 'um they'd laugh t'other side o' thar mouths afore it were done. They hooted me.

"We went out with 'bout fifty hounds, and, as good luck would hev it, we started a rale old Virginny red fox, 'bout three hours afore day, on the west side uv Skull Camp Mountain. . . . Not fur from Shipp's Muster-ground they passed me, and Flyin'-jib were 'bout half a mile ahead on 'um all, goin' fast as the report of a rifle gun. Passin' through a meader whar thar were a mowin'-scythe with the blade standin' up, Flyin'-jib run chug aginst it with sich force that it split him wide open frum the eend uv his nose to the tip uv his tail. Thar he lay, and nuver whimpered, tryin' to run right on. I streaked it to him, snatched up both sides uv him, slapped 'um together, but were in sich a hurry that I put two feet down and two up. But away he went arter the fox, scootin' jist in that fix. You see, when he got tired runnin' on two feet on one side, he'd whirl over, quick as lightnin', on t'other two, and it seemed ruther to hev increased his verlocity. He cotch the fox on the east side uv Skull Camp, a mile ahead uv the whole kit uv 'um."[4]

Travel writings, rural-life reminiscences, and county histories further document the role of folk culture in the South and complement the findings of twentieth-century folklorists. But the best way to appreciate the meaning of folk traditions to those who practice them is through their own words:

I keep up the slave songs that they learned in church, and the play songs too, and the stories, the riddles and things. . . . When I'm singing something that my old foreparents knew, if their spirits came around me, I believe they would be rejoicing.
—Bessie Jones, Georgia Sea Island Singers of St. Simons, Georgia[5]

I knew that no matter how far apart we might scatter the world over, that we'd still be the Ritchie Family as long as we lived and sang the same old songs, and that the songs would live as long as there was a family.
—Jean Ritchie, ballad singer of Viper, Kentucky, and Port Washington, New York[6]

National Heritage Fellow and Georgia Sea Island Singer Bessie Jones in performance, 1978. Photo by David Holt, www.davidholt.com.

I realized that there were only two older basketweavers who could do rivercane doubleweave baskets. For some time it had been my desire to learn the art of the doubleweave in order that it might be retained for future generations of the Cherokee craftworkers. The income is most important to me, as sales of my baskets have done much to help my family enjoy a better way of life.

—Eva Wolfe, basketweaver of Big Cove, North Carolina[7]

What we are doing today is actively practicing, as a way of life, a folk-art tradition. Without someone continuing the tradition, it would probably perish. . . . I want to keep the tradition alive, because I have immense respect for old-time potters. It's part of our heritage, and it's important for us to remember it.

—Michael Crocker, potter of Lula, Georgia[8]

We got a tradition of the old people's ways. . . . A lot of people make quilts just for your bed, for to keep you warm. But a quilt is more. It represents safekeeping, it represents beauty, and you could say it represents family history.

—Mensie Lee Pettway, quilter of Rehoboth, Alabama[9]

Before public education, mail-order catalogs offering affordable mass-produced goods, automobiles, radio, television, and computers connected southerners to the outside world, they depended on folk traditions for their values, survival skills, and quality of life. Folklore further provided the comfort of continuity with a familiar past, functioning as a cultural shock absorber when the old order collapsed following the Civil War. Modernization of the region makes the practice of folklore now more a matter of choice than necessity, supplying a sense of connection to a place and group, and even a livelihood for some.

Fuzzy Boundaries: Defining the South Geographically

No region of the United States has a more stereotyped identity than the South. Hoop-skirted belles vie with barefoot hillbillies and cotton-picking sharecroppers in popular mythology. These distortions do, however, reflect an important reality: the role of the land—both as terrain and as the basis for an agrarian way of life—in shaping the culture.

Where does the South begin and end?[10] Although the Civil War and its aftermath surely heightened the region's separateness from the rest of the country, a strictly historical approach based on membership in the Confederacy is not entirely satisfactory in establishing the region's limits, for Kentucky would be left out, as would border states such as Maryland, West Virginia, and Missouri that are to some extent culturally southern. But a strictly cultural approach is also problematic, for in clearly nonsouthern states there are "little Dixie" enclaves that have built upon southern traditions (e.g., Chicago's urban blues scene, rooted in the Mississippi Delta, and African American folk preaching in California).[11]

Ironically, the most southerly extremes of the geographic region—south Texas and south Florida—are the least culturally southern; but inland Florida still maintains features of southern culture, as illustrated by the following recent news item from Columbia County, in the northern part of that state (and the location of Stephen Foster Folk Culture Center State Park), reporting the use of a well-known southern food as a weapon: "According to police in Lake City . . . Felisha Ann Copeland, 31, on learning of her

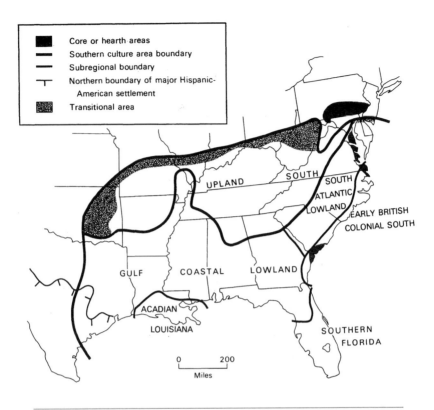

The American South and its cultural subregions. Map by Richard Pillsbury, in William Ferris and Charles Reagan Wilson, eds., *Encyclopedia of Southern Culture*, © 1989 by University of North Carolina Press, used by permission of publisher.

ex-husband's new girlfriend, dumped a pot of boiling grits in his lap while he was seated, naked, on the toilet of the home they still share. He suffered severe blistering."[12]

Central to the formation of a distinctly southern culture was the plantation system with its enslaved labor force; the region's character owes much to its large African American presence.[13] Defined in this way, it can be argued that the South extends as far west as east Texas. Popularly regarded as the South's upper limit, the political boundary of the Mason-Dixon line, which runs along the Pennsylvania-Maryland border, not coincidentally corresponds to markers of a shift from northern to southern speech observed by linguistic geographers.[14]

Topographically and ethnically based diversity makes this region far from homogeneous, however. The upland South (the Appalachian and Ozark mountains), which barely participated in the plantation system, nevertheless shares certain features with the lowlands (e.g., plural forms of the pronoun *you*); the Cajun and Creole cultures of south Louisiana, with their French roots, contrast with the more typical northern part of that state yet are still identifiably southern. This dynamic tension between a unified southern identity and affiliation with smaller communities is crucial to understanding the region's character.[15]

What Makes the South Different: Overview

As significant as folk culture was, and still is to some southerners,[16] its contribution to a regional identity is shared with broader cultural features and historical experiences that distinguish the South from the rest of the United States. These markers of southernness were strongest before a watershed period of change between the two world wars, but have not completely vanished today with increasing national homogenization. Some of these characteristics led to folk-cultural traits discussed in subsequent chapters, and all are reflected in the region's folklore. A review of this "big picture," however familiar to some readers, may help to contextualize the folklore discussed later; for each theme, I've incorporated specific traditions to demonstrate how folk-cultural roots spread through the soil of southern life.

Economy

As President Calvin Coolidge succinctly put it, "The chief business of the American people is business,"[17] and the business emphasized by southerners, beginning with the arrival of the English at Jamestown in 1607, has been agriculture, arising from the region's longer growing season and the gentleman-farmer aspirations of many of its influential early settlers. The agrarian way of life that developed is in contrast to the industrialization that has marked much of the North since the late eighteenth century.

Southern farms varied from small subsistence holdings typical of the uplands to large plantations, concentrated in the lowlands, that emphasized a cash crop. The first cash crops were tobacco ("sotweed") in Tidewater Virginia and Maryland, and rice and indigo in coastal South Carolina and Georgia. Some long-staple, or Sea Island, cotton also was grown in the latter states, but large-scale cultivation of up-country, or green-seed, cotton, which can thrive inland, did not become feasible until the 1793 invention of the cotton gin by Connecticut Yankee Eli Whitney.

The initial supply of indentured servants did not satisfy the demand for a large labor force; hence the institution of slavery became a feature of plantations and larger farms, moving the South toward its precipitous secession from the Union.[18] The majority of whites, however, were neither planter-aristocrats nor poor, but a rural middle class—what historian Frank Owsley called the "Plain Folk of the

Field hands weighing cotton near LaGrange, Georgia, 1933. Courtesy, Georgia Archives, Vanishing Georgia Collection, Trp-187.

Henry Bolton weaving white-oak baskets, a traditional craft integral to cotton farming, Wilkes County, Georgia, 1902. Photo by J. W. Stephenson; courtesy, Georgia Archives, Vanishing Georgia Collection, Wlk-126.

Old South."[19] In some sections, arable farming gave way to pastoral cattle grazing, and in either case, hunting and fishing significantly supplemented what was raised.

This shared southern experience of living off the land may seem romantic to those of us who don't end each day covered with sweat and dirt, but the region's folklore reveals the reality of a life hard-won from nature. Storyteller Frank Reid, who kept a 115-acre farm in the Georgia foothills, humorously depicted the farmer as little more than a beast of burden in his tale about "the old man who had a two-steer cart, but just one steer, a little bull. And he went up on the side of the mountain to get him some wood; had to yoke himself up with the bull! And as they came back towards the house, the bull

Storyteller and weather prognosticator Frank Reid, Loudsville, Georgia, 1970. Photo by Charles H. Bryson for Georgia Folklore Archives, Georgia State University.

started to run away. The old man hollered at his wife (her name was Stacie); he hollered, 'Head us, Stacie, head us!' Says, 'We're running away, damn us!' Well, they finally stopped, and she went out to get him out of the yoke. He says [breathing heavily], 'Unyoke the bull; I'll stand.'"[20]

"Mr. Frank" plowed with a mule, raising corn, sweet potatoes, and other garden produce; his wife, Pearl, milked their cow twice a day and churned butter, most of which she sold. Their farming life was neither glamorous nor simple; they applied a matrix of technical knowledge learned from elder family members and neighbors—that is to say, through folklore. And a critical piece of that farming lore was knowing how to foretell the weather. Mr. Frank gained a reputation as a prognosticator after correctly predicting the March snows that blanketed the mountains in 1960. Here are a few of his signs:

> The hair on a yearling's back in the fall, if it grows great long hair, it's more apt to be a bad winter. And the same way on a squirrel: if they have lots of hair, sign of a rough winter. And the shuck on corn: if it's a heavy shuck, it's a sign of a rough winter. And the fogs in August has something to do with it: if you keep [a record of] the number

of foggy mornings, there's apt to be a snow for each foggy morning (we're supposed to have five this winter). Three big frosts in the winter will be followed by a rain; three big dews in the summer will be followed by a rain. But now, all these signs, they can fail, they don't hit every time; generally speaking, though, you do depend on it.[21]

Following a pattern established in frontier days, southern farms were self-contained or solitary (known in Germany as an *Einzelhof*, but also common in the "Celtic fringe" of the British Isles) and often separated from each other by miles to form loosely knit "settlements," in contrast to the typical northern farming community modeled on the English village cluster. The resulting limited contact with neighbors and the outside world, as suggested earlier, fostered reliance on folklore as an inherited knowledge base for both livelihood and recreation, while heightening the importance of the family as the chief mechanism for passing on these traditions.

History

So much has been written about the Civil War and its aftermath in the South that only a few key points relating to folklore need be raised. This episode, which I rarely heard mentioned up North, is still, a century and a half later, a traumatic experience for some southerners, spoken about as if it occurred only yesterday; the Atlanta History Museum devotes a ten-thousand-square-feet gallery to its permanent exhibition *Turning Point: The American Civil War*. The impression left by the war on the psyche of later generations of southerners is reflected in a group of Confederate songs that continued to be sung into the twentieth century, such as "The Unreconstructed Rebel":

I'm just a Rebel soldier
And that is all I am,
And for your Land of Freedom
I do not give a damn;
I'm glad I fought agin it,
I only wish we'd won,

And I don't ask no pardon
For anything I done.[22]

The war also generated folk stories that are still being told in the South:

One time there was this Rebel soldier that went up on top of this hill overlooking this Yankee camp, and he says, "I kin lick any five Yankees you got in your camp!"

So they sent five of them up the hill, and in a little while here they all come back down just beat all to pieces—that Rebel had tore them up.

So he said, "I kin lick any ten soldiers you have got down there; send them up and I'll whup them!"

So ten of them went up; and in a few minutes all ten came back down the hill just beat to pieces; he had whupped all ten of them, boy.

And he say, "I can whup any twenty-five of you; just send twenty-five up and I kin whup them!"

So twenty-five of them went up, and in a minute all twenty-five came back down the hill just beat to hell.

So he said, "Why don't you send fifty up?!"

So fifty of the Yankee soldiers went up the hill, and in a minute here they come back down, just battered and tore all to pieces.

And he says, "I kin whup any hundred; any hundred you got down there, I kin whup them!"

And one of the previous fifty that went up there, he says to them, "You better be careful, men, that's a trick; there's two of them up there!"[23]

The war's impact on traditional crafts is not so obvious as with song and story.[24] By 1860 the South was experiencing industrial growth and becoming less dependent on factory-made goods from the North and overseas. But the war required southern factories to shift to military production, and the Union blockade reduced the flow of imports to a trickle, pushing handcrafting to the forefront in

Cup attributed to
Ferguson and Dial
Pottery, Jackson (now
Barrow) County, Geor-
gia, made ca. 1863
in lieu of imported,
factory-made table-
ware blockaded by
the Union. Alkaline-
glazed stoneware. H.
3½". Collection of Mr.
and Mrs. William W.
Griffin.

such media as clay and cloth. As a particular example, brothers-in-
law William Ferguson and Jonathan Dial of Jackson (present-day
Barrow) County, Georgia, whose careers as potters began with dark,
ash-glazed stoneware for food storage, advertised in an 1863 issue of
the *Southern Watchman* (published in nearby Athens) an expanded
range of wares to fill the void in mass-produced white tableware created by the blockade:

> In addition to Jars, Jugs, and such other ware as we have formerly
> kept, we are now trying to supply the demand for other useful house-
> hold articles. We are making Bowls and Pitchers, Dinner and Soup
> Plates, Cups and Saucers, Mugs, Coffee and Tea Pots, Bake Pans,
> [and] Chambers.

An editorial endorsement of their operation in the same issue stated
that it "is doing much to supply the people with a substitute for
earthenware. . . . It is true they are not as smooth and handsome
as the articles we have been used to, but are decidedly better than
none. This establishment and others of a like character, ought to be,
it strikes us, exempt from conscription." In Ferguson's case at least,
the editor's plea seems to have been heeded, for the note beside his
name in the 1864 militia census reads: "Potter. Exempted, justice of
peace." Another Georgia potter, Jesse Bradford Long of Crawford
County, in his fifties when the war broke out, served as a home

guard captain and produced chamberpots and other wares for Confederate hospitals.[25]

Women contributed to the cause by making quilts for hospitals and fund-raising raffles.[26] Some also took patriotic pride in returning to hand spinning and weaving for both military and domestic clothing, as expressed in the song "The Homespun Dress" (sung to the tune of "The Bonnie Blue Flag"):

> Hurrah! Hurrah!
> For the Sunny South so dear!
> Three cheers for the homespun dress
> The Southern ladies wear!
>
> Now northern goods are out of date,
> And since old Abe's blockade,
> We Southern girls can be content
> With goods that's Southern made.[27]

Hard times after the war encouraged the continuation of such hand skills, and a handcraft revival in the early twentieth century, focused in Appalachia, opened up an outside market as a means of economic development in the region.[28]

Mindset

Beginning with W. J. Cash's pioneering *The Mind of the South*, historians, sociologists, and popular writers have wrestled with the notion of a peculiarly southern way of behaving and thinking, what could be called a regional mindset.[29] From positive traits like hospitality (a reality that I, and early travel writers who often belittled their hosts for a lifestyle not in accord with their own, encountered over and over again) and courtesy (a vestige of the old courtliness and "good breeding" that I still see in my students) to such negative traits as resorting to violence as a means of resolving conflict,[30] portraits of the "typical" southerner, however generalized, have emerged. And central to these portraits are attitudes about race.

Folklore reflecting race relations is found on both sides of the color line, although blacks were understandably cautious about overtly sharing their feelings with their white neighbors. In the 1930s, Lawrence Gellert recorded such songs of complaint as the following in the Carolinas and Georgia on the condition that he preserve the African American singers' anonymity:

Down in Georgia, meanest place in the world,
White folks chasing niggers like chasing a squirrel.
In Atlanta, Georgia; in Atlanta, Georgia:
If you don't get lynched you will sure get pinched [arrested],
In Atlanta, Georgia.

It's the same thing all over the South,
It's the same thing that I'm talking about.
In Atlanta, Georgia; in Atlanta, Georgia,
If you don't get lynched you will sure get pinched,
In Atlanta, Georgia.[31]

Racial tensions are also expressed in folk narratives; the following not-very-funny folk joke told by a young white southerner acknowledges the region's reputation for racism:

Two black men are hitchhiking on the side of a busy, two-lane highway. And they've been walking, and walking, and they're both tired. So Jones says to Leroy, "Leroy, I'm sooo tired; can't we find us a car and get a ride with somebody?"

And Leroy goes, "Yeah, I think I have a plan. Jones, you go out there and lay down in the road, lay crossways, so whenever a car comes, they gonna have to stop. Then I'll run up and tell them you sick or something, and we'll get us a ride."

And Jones goes, "Yeah, that sounds like a good plan; I'll go lay out in the road."

So here comes this car, and Leroy says, "Jones, I sees a car coming!" And here comes this big Cadillac, vroom—bump, bump—right over Jones! Leroy says, "I just don't understand this. But," says, "Jones, here comes another car." This time, a great big Chevrolet from Michigan—vroom, bump, bump—right over Jones again. And Leroy says, "You know, this plan just ain't working."

So here comes a Mercedes, Florida license plate—mmmm, bump, bump—right over Jones. And Jones, still laying out in the road kinda messed up now, lifts up his head and says, "Leroy, are you sure this plan's gonna work?"

Leroy says, "Yeah, yeah; just lay back down." Now here comes a great, big Eldorado from California: mmmm, bump, bump. And then an LTD from Texas: mmmm, bump, bump. Both of them run right over Jones.

So now, Leroy hears in the distance this old rattle-trap car making a lot of noise. And he says, "Jones, we gonna get this one; I know they're gonna stop for us this time!" Jones isn't saying a word by this time. And here comes this old Ford jalopy coming up the highway, going about twenty-five miles an hour. And Leroy's saying, "We're gonna get it this time; we're gonna get us a ride!"

And the car comes up: bump, bump, erk [the "erk" sound is the car braking, then backing up]! Bump, bump, erk! Bump, bump, erk! Bump, bump, erk! That car was from Alabama.[32]

As this jest suggests, though, color is hardly a concern exclusive to the South, as shown by New England's early history of slavery and mercantile-maritime role in the slave trade, not to mention its treatment of Native Americans. So there's nothing strictly southern about racial prejudice.

What *is* southern is the eighty years of institutionalized racial segregation under the so-called Jim Crow laws (1877–1955),[33] and, less obviously, a code of role-playing for both races that had its origins in the plantation system, when whites had to rationalize enslaving fellow humans and blacks had to survive the "peculiar institution." This code still reverberates in the interactions of some southerners; its complexity was hinted at on my first day in Atlanta when a middle-aged gentleman, perceiving from my speech that I was a newcomer, helpfully offered this insight: "Son, there's one thing you need to understand about us white southerners: we may hate the nigras as a race, but the colored woman who nursed me—I love her like my own mama."[34]

Politics

With the end of Reconstruction in 1876, Abraham Lincoln's Republican Party had little support in the South, and the Democratic Party, controlled by an elite minority, dominated the political scene. The only challenge to this essentially one-party system was Populism, which rose to prominence in the South and Midwest in the 1890s. This progressive movement appealed to the working-class majority, mainly small farmers and millhands, and although it remained a force in the South for less than three decades and soon split along racial lines, it gave rise to a colorful species of demagogue represented by South Carolina's "Pitchfork Ben" Tillman, Louisiana's Huey Long, Alabama's George Wallace, and Georgia's Tom Watson and Eugene Talmadge.[35]

Integral to the speaking rallies of such politicians were the sure-fire vote-getting folklore genres of traditional food (usually barbeque) and music. Georgia folk musician Fiddlin' John Carson, who cut the first successful country music record in 1923, entertained in the campaigns of Watson, Talmadge, and Talmadge's son, Herman, the latter rewarding him, after becoming governor, with a sinecure as elevator operator at the state capitol. In support of Eugene's 1932 bid for governor, Carson wrote and recorded a song, "Georgia's Three-Dollar Tag," featuring Talmadge's campaign pledge to lower the cost of an automobile license plate. Its refrain asked the still-applicable question "Tell me how long must we wait / Until we get old Georgia in good shape?"[36]

Nor was Carson the only politically active folk musician in the South; "Fiddlin' Bob" Taylor, who was twice governor of Tennessee, heard John play as a boy and supposedly gave him his nickname.[37] Guitarist, gospel singer, and songwriter ("You Are My Sunshine") Jimmie Davis was two-time governor of Louisiana; and more recently, West Virginian "Fiddlin' Bob" Byrd's traditional musicianship helped him win votes in his campaigns for the United States House of Representatives and Senate.

Religion

One of the first things I noticed about Atlanta was how many churches there were in the city, and how many of them were Protestant. This, I soon discovered, was a reflection of the larger region, where Protestant Christianity, often interpreted in a fundamentalist and evangelical way, is by far the dominant faith (south Louisiana, with its large, French-derived, Catholic population, being an exception).[38] Especially in the rural and small-town South, as Georgia author Flannery O'Connor learned after moving to Milledgeville from more cosmopolitan Savannah,[39] a Catholic or a Jew could feel mighty lonesome, and many southerners still have a microview of religious diversity (e.g., Baptist versus Methodist, and the many splinter sects therein). "White" in the South once meant white Anglo-Saxon Protestant; limited experience with other religious and ethnic groups could lead to intolerance, as with the anti-Semitism stirred up in Georgia by Tom Watson in his newspaper, *The Jeffersonian*, against Leo Frank in the famous 1913 Mary Phagan murder case that caused a mob to lynch what was very likely an innocent man.[40] On the positive side, genuine Christian values may help account for the hospitality and courtesy mentioned earlier.

Some folklore connections to southern religion are obvious: the folk preaching mentioned earlier, spirituals and gospel songs in both black and white traditions, and a whole subgenre of folk jokes known as preacher tales, which humanize—by humorizing—an otherwise respected figure:

> This Baptist preacher died one time and went to heaven. Got up to the Golden Gates and met Saint Peter. He asked him to give his name and his occupation. So he told him he was a Baptist minister, and had pastored the Baptist Church for thirty-five years, and told what a great number of people that he had baptized under the fellowship of the church. So Saint Peter said, "All right, just have a seat over there."
>
> And about that time another fellow came in; Saint Peter told him to give his name and occupation. Said he was a Methodist preacher, and he'd pastored the Methodist Church for thirty-five years and told what a great number he'd brought into the fellowship of the Methodist Church. Saint Peter said, "All right, just have a seat."
>
> About that time another guy come in. Saint Peter asked him to

Brother Raymond Willis, elder of Bibleway Temple of God, takes his evangelical message to the streets of downtown Atlanta, Georgia, 2006: "Repent!"

give his name and occupation. He told his name; told him he's a taxi driver, had been driving a taxi for eleven years. Saint Peter just opened the gate and said, "Go on in."

These two preachers jumped up and said, "Now, wait a minute!" Said, "Here we are both preachers; there's seventy years of service for the two of us. And we have to wait, and this taxi driver gets to go on in?"

And Saint Peter said, "Yeah, he scared more Hell out of people in that eleven years than y'all have in the seventy years you've been pastoring churches."[41]

Then there are folk sects, perhaps the most intriguing—if atypical—of which is the serpent-handling branch of the Pentecostal-Holiness movement.[42] The oldest living southern folk-religious practice, though, is pre-Christian: the Green Corn ceremony of the Yuchis, Creeks, and Seminoles in Oklahoma and Florida has roots that may go back a thousand years or more.[43]

Speech and Food

Two of the strongest markers of southern identity for those living outside, as well as inside, the region are forms of folk-cultural expression.[44] Food will be discussed in subsequent chapters, and speech is best left to the linguistic geographers who study the subject scientifically.[45] There's one thing, though, I'll venture to say about southern speech. Since many of us recognize a southern "accent"—whatever part of the South the speaker is from—when we hear it, there must be dialect features shared by the entire region. Equally significant, though, are class/education-based and subregional differences, including distinct speech "islands" (e.g., Gullah in coastal South Carolina and Georgia, Cajun in southwest Louisiana).[46] In other words, there is more than one way of speaking southern.

The South Today: What's Changed?

One of W. J. Cash's main theses about the region in *The Mind of the South* was that of continuity with the past, or as his critic, C. Vann Woodward, paraphrased with the French proverb *"Plus ça change, plus c'est la même chose."*[47] Mississippian Gavin Stevens put it another way in William Faulkner's play *Requiem for a Nun*: "The past is never dead. It's not even past."[48] So, how much of the Old South pattern just described still applies, given the modernization that has occurred in the nearly seventy years since Cash's book appeared?

Beginning with the economy, the post–Civil War rise of industries such as coal mining in Appalachia and textile manufacture in the Piedmont certainly altered the agrarian way of life for those involved—while creating new occupational subcultures and types of peonage alongside tenant farming and sharecropping.[49] Since then, farming itself has undergone dramatic changes. In Georgia, cotton production fell from two million bales in 1918 to one-fourth of that by 1923 as the boll-weevil invasion destroyed much of the crop. Fiddlin' John Carson expressed the small farmer's plight in his 1925 recording of an agricultural protest song, "The Honest Farmer":

Goodbye, boll weevil,
For you know you've ruint my home.
You know you've got my cotton,
And the merchant's got my corn.[50]

Surviving farmers diversified with the "four p's"—peaches, peanuts, pecans, poultry—and, more recently, cotton has made a comeback. Agriculture is still the most important sector of the state's economy, much of it now conducted as an agribusiness with mechanization and migrant labor.

Fiddlin' John Carson's eviction from company housing in Cabbagetown during Fulton Bag and Cotton Mills Strike, Atlanta, Georgia, 1914. He and five others of his family had been working in the mill; radio and recording success was to follow in the 1920s. Photo by Duane A. Russell; courtesy, Southern Labor Archives, Special Collections Department, Georgia State University Library.

History still ripples in the state flags of Mississippi, Alabama, Florida, and Georgia, which incorporate elements of the Confederate battle flag; former Georgia governor Zell Miller lost a bitter battle to change the old flag whose design more prominently featured the "Southern Cross."[51] The civil rights movement and desegregation certainly have had their impact on racial attitudes, especially among the younger generation; my students stare in disbelief when they hear about public facilities marked WHITE ONLY and COLORED ONLY. But every now and again, the old racial attitudes bob to the surface of our regional—and national—consciousness.[52] In politics, the "Solid South" began to break up with President Harry Truman's appointment of the Civil Rights Commission in 1946; when fellow southern Democrats saw their interests being "sold out" they created their own "Dixiecrat" platform, and have since come to realize that the Republican Party better represents their conservative agenda. In 2003 Sonny Perdue was elected as Georgia's first Republican governor in 130 years.

Since the 1960s, immigrant groups have introduced greater religious diversity to the urban South, but the region can still be described as the Bible Belt, as shown by recent disputes over public display of the Ten Commandments and the teaching of "intelligent design" versus Darwinian evolution (shades of Tennessee's 1925 Scopes "Monkey Trial"). Finally, is southern speech disappearing? Linguists have documented some recent changes, but many of the old patterns are alive and well, especially outside metropolitan centers.[53] And even there, some of the heaviest southern "accents" can be heard among second- and third-generation descendants of Greek, Asian, and Latin American immigrants. The more things change . . . ?

2. Goobers, Grits, and Greasy Greens

What's *Southern* about Southern Folk Culture?

True grits,
More grits,
Fish, grits and collards,
Life is good where grits are swallered.
 —Roy Blount Jr., "Song to Grits"[1]

Coming from the Mid-Atlantic and having spent some time in New England as well, I found the South an exotic place forty years ago, and I must confess that to a lesser degree I still view my adopted home in this way; the sense of "differentness" hasn't completely worn off. But *exotic* is not the same as *alien*; my training and perspective as a folklorist have helped me appreciate the positive values and complexity of the region. With my knowledge of northern folklore as a basis for comparison, I soon came to realize that some of the traditions I was observing were unique to, or at least concentrated in, this part of the country, and that a catalog of folk-cultural traits that distinguish the South from the North and West could add an important dimension to the historical, sociological, and linguistic approaches already used to understand the region. My catalog, then, begins with the genres of material folk culture, wherein basic survival needs are addressed through culturally preferred patterns.

Food

Arising from locally available resources and the combined culinary tastes of the early population, no realm of folklife is more evocative of a region than its foodways.[2] Greens—turnip, collard, mustard, wild pokeweed—loom large as a southern vegetable (in the North, the leaves of turnips are normally discarded as unfit to eat), boiled with fatty pork and the residual liquid ("pot likker") eaten like soup.[3] Along with black-eyed peas and hog jowls, greens are said to promote good fortune as a customary meal on New Year's Day,[4] and are linked with two other staples of southern cuisine in the chorus of an Ozark Mountain folk song:

> Turnip greens, turnip greens,
> Good old turnip greens,
> Cornbread and buttermilk
> And good old turnip greens.[5]

A family hog butchering, Winston County, Alabama, fall 1973. The bristles, loosened with hot water, are scraped from the skin prior to the actual butchering; virtually every part will be used.

In 1860 Dr. John S. Wilson of Georgia referred to the South as "the Great Hog-eating Confederacy" and suggested that the region be dubbed the "Republic of Porkdom."[6] Pork was the everyday meat of southerners until the rise of the poultry industry, reaching its pinnacle of preparation in the fine arts of barbequing and ham curing.[7] Hog butchering was a major fall activity involving the whole family; pigs were less wasteful than cattle because "everything but the squeal" could be utilized.[8] In pre–cholesterol-conscious times their rendered fat (lard) was the chief shortening and frying medium, while their small intestines, carefully cleaned before cooking, were celebrated in the following song:

> There's a quiet and peaceful county in the state of Tennessee,
> You will find it in the book they call geography;
> Not famous for its farming, its mines, or its stills,
> But they know there's chitlins cookin' in them Cheatham County hills.

> When it's chitlin cookin' time in Cheatham County,
> I'll be courtin' in them Cheatham County hills;
> And I'll pick a Cheatham County chitlin cooker,
> I've a longing that the chitlins will fill.[9]

Formerly due to the relative costliness of wheat and now more a matter of regional taste, corn remains a staple grain, enjoyed in such bread types as skillet-cooked cornbread, griddle-cooked hoecakes, molded sticks and muffins, deep-fried hush puppies, and pudding-like spoon bread.[10] So important was cornbread in the South that it is what was meant by *bread*; to refer to wheat-based bread, the prefix *light* needed to be added. Distilled "liquid corn" or whiskey—both illicit moonshine and licensed bourbon—is a southern specialty, the former creating its own subculture and body of folklore.[11] An Appalachian song humorously promoting the benefits of this "white lightning" was ahead of its time in suggesting ethanol (grain alcohol) as an alternative to gasoline as a fuel:

Moonshining, Rabun County, Georgia, early 1900s. Courtesy, Georgia Archives, Vanishing Georgia Collection, Rab-137.

My aunt Lucille had an automobile,
It ran on a gallon or two.
It didn't need no gas and it didn't need no oil,
It just ran on that good old mountain dew.[12]

Wheat-based biscuits, while not unique to the South (they're related to British scones), are emphasized here as another major bread type and eaten in a distinctly regional way, either with gravy or cane syrup.[13] And speaking of which, the making of syrup from sugarcane in the lowlands and sweet sorghum in the uplands remains a southern tradition, again as a matter of taste now rather than necessity. But prior to the introduction of granulated sugar in the twentieth century, this liquid sweetening was the only kind affordable to many southerners.[14]

Having sampled "greasy greens," we now turn to a second item in my chapter title. The southern folk name for peanut, *goober*, is a clue to the origin of the plant now grown as a cash crop: the word comes from the Kongo and Bantu *nguba*. But peanuts (also called ground-

Syrup making, Dougherty County, Georgia, ca. 1930. Sugarcane is fed into the mule-powered mill while the resulting juice is boiled and skimmed. Nowadays, a gasoline engine usually replaces the mule. Courtesy, Georgia Archives, Vanishing Georgia Collection, Dgh-249-86.

nuts or pinders) are not native to West Africa; they were introduced there in the sixteenth century from South America by the Portuguese and Spanish, then brought by the later slave trade to Virginia in the mid-1700s. A peculiarly southern preparation is boiled peanuts, now a common roadside and festival treat; Jimmy Carter is said to have sold them at age five on the streets of his hometown, Plains, Georgia.[15] During his presidency the South Korean consulate contacted me to recommend a song that would be familiar to him when greeted by a group of schoolchildren at the airport on his visit to that country. Aware of his background as a peanut farmer, I immediately thought of a well-known Confederate folk song and sent them the lyrics and melody. It still tickles me to imagine a bunch of Korean kids singing to President Carter as he deplaned from Air Force One:

Sitting by the roadside on a summer day,
Chatting with my messmates, passing time away;
Lying in the shadow underneath the trees,
Goodness, how delicious, eating goober peas![16]

Another possible African influence on southern food (and I use that word loosely here) is the curious custom of clay eating, or geophagy.[17] The practice is concentrated among African Americans, where it is often associated with pregnancy cravings and beliefs. In the past, however, poor whites also ate clay: "The Cracker child eats dirt to satisfy the continual cravings of his stomach. . . . If they do live, they grow to be thin, wiry, strong and enduring men, with a strong appetite for loafing, fighting, courting the girls and drinking whiskey."[18] Nor was just any clay eaten; as indicated in a rather unflattering 1893 portrait, "The Clay-Eaters of Georgia," the preferred variety was white kaolin, occurring along the fall line and mined commercially as an ingredient in porcelain, paint, paper, and pharmaceuticals (e.g., Kaopectate):

> . . . these people make a regular practice of eating at all times, dainty
> morsels of kaolin. . . . Whole families are afflicted with the habit,
> from the grandfather to the father, down to the skinny little tot who
> cries for his share. . . . Of course heredity has much to do with it, and
> the people dwelling in [Scotsborough, five miles south of Milledge-
> ville] transmit the habit from generation to generation. . . . There
> is no mistaking a clay-eating "cracker." Their countenances have a
> distinctly original, and most unearthly cast, resembling more
> a "death's head with a bone in its mouth" than anything else.[19]

Once home-dug from the consumer's favorite local earthen bank, the substance is now supplied commercially, a favored brand being Down Home Georgia White Dirt. Marketed by Charles Maddox of Griffin, it's sold by vendors at Atlanta's Sweet Auburn Curb Market in one-pound plastic bags labeled "Not Suggested for Human Consumption." While debate continues on the effects of and reasons for (e.g., to supplement a mineral-poor diet) clay-eating, one thing is agreed upon: it's a culturally perpetuated folk tradition. Having tried a little Down Home myself, I find it rather tasteless, which may explain why some users flavor it with vinegar and salt.[20]

On a more appetizing note, there is a family of traditional southern stews that includes Dundas (Virginia) sheep stew, Kentucky burgoo, South Carolina hash and Frogmore stew (also known as Beaufort or lowcountry boil), Outer Banks fish muddle, and the famed Brunswick stew of Virginia, North Carolina, and Georgia. The latter is defined as a mixture of meat (originally small game, now pork, beef, or chicken or a combination thereof), corn, and tomatoes; other ingredients (e.g., lima beans, onions, potatoes) are optional (plate 1). This stew is said to have gotten its name from Brunswick County, Virginia, where Jimmy Matthews, a black hunting-camp cook, prepared a memorable squirrel stew for his master, Creed Haskins, in 1828. But the coastal Georgia town of Brunswick also claims the one-pot meal, leading to recent good-natured "stew wars" between the two states. Whatever the origin of the name, there are Native American, as well as British, precedents (the latter known as pottage) for combining meat and grain in this way.[21]

Besides the previously mentioned corn whiskey, beverages emphasized in the South are water (critical for outdoor work in the heat of summer; as we'll see in chapter four, folk potters made two different types of water jugs for field use) and buttermilk (a by-product of churning and once a favorite cool drink, as in Ireland). Tea is understood here as iced and presweetened; Dolly Parton's character in the film *Steel Magnolias* calls it the "house wine of the South," and cultural geographers have dubbed the Ohio River the Sweet Tea Line to represent a culinary boundary between the North and South.[22]

The hot drink of choice was coffee, regarded as a necessary stimulant for farm work; it was not unusual for youngsters to drink it. Imported green coffee beans were bought at the general store, roasted in a skillet, ground in a mill that was a key kitchen utensil, and boiled in a coffeepot (Georgia folk potters made "coffee boilers" as early as 1820).[23] The Union blockade during the Civil War forced southerners to come up with not-very-convincing coffee substitutes, such as parched corn, acorns, and chicory roots (which remain a preferred additive in New Orleans).

Architecture

Architecture is not only essential as shelter for people, livestock, and crops but is the most public of all folklife expressions, revealing, to those able to "read" the cultural landscape, clues about the background of the builders and how they responded to a locale's physical environment.[24] A folk building's tradition is expressed in its design and construction, the design resulting not from plans by a school-trained architect but from the builder's knowledge of an area's architectural repertoire as evolved over many generations. Many older structures of the rural South were literally built by the community (with supervision by an experienced carpenter) in acts of reciprocal neighborliness known as house and barn "raisings."[25]

Southern folk architecture capitalizes on the region's rich timber resources by emphasizing wood construction, with walls of corner-notched horizontal logs or a framework covered by sawn weatherboards, and roofs of wooden shingles.[26] This is in contrast to my Mid-Atlantic home area, where masonry (stone and brick) construction was far more prevalent. The Deep South's pier-and-sill foundation is less labor intensive and drier (especially on a floodplain) than the northern approach of erecting a house on an excavated-cellar wall. The piers were made of locally available materials—for Georgia, bricks on the coast, wedges of heart pine (impervious to termites) farther inland, and fieldstone in the uplands, with granite, marble, or limestone where quarried (Elbert, Pickens, and Walker counties, respectively); nowadays, cinder blocks are used in the same way. The height of each pier was adjusted to provide a level platform for the two main support beams, or sills, running the length of the building; with the space between the piers left open, air could circulate under the floor to help cool the interior.[27]

Cypress-block piers elevating La Maison Mouton, an 1810 Acadian house with detached kitchen restored at Vermilionville Heritage and Folklife Park, Lafayette, Louisiana.

Chimney placement also was, in part, a response to the warm climate. External gable-end chimneys are the norm, a carryover from southern England (the origin of many Tidewater settlers) but also useful in restricting the heat from open-hearth cooking to just one end of the house before dedicated kitchens became common (early New England dwellings, by contrast, feature a central chimney capable of heating all rooms in the harsh winters but also a carryover from the home area of many settlers there, East Anglia). Kitchens of the antebellum period frequently were detached from the house (if sometimes connected by a covered walkway); this, too, kept the living quarters from overheating in summer, leaving only the cook to suffer from heat prostration! This separate kitchen also lowered the risk of accidental fire spreading to the house. A final feature of southern architecture reflecting the climate is the gallery, or sitting porch, a shaded warm-weather living space. Also known as a veranda or piazza, it first appears in the late 1700s (George Washington's Mount Vernon incorporating an early example), with the idea spreading north in the nineteenth century.[28]

This is not the place for a catalog of all of the South's traditional building types; such surveys can be found in the publications of American folk-architecture researchers.[29] Instead, I'll mention only three widespread, distinctive examples that to me embody the

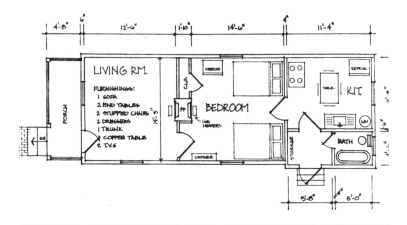

Shotgun house plan showing arrangement of furnishings, Cabbagetown mill village, Atlanta, Georgia, 1986. Overall dimensions 40' x 15'. Illustration by Katherine Pringle for Georgia Folklore Archives.

Shotgun house on Ninth Street, Columbus, Georgia, 1993. Photo by Beth Agnew for Georgia Folklore Archives, Georgia State University.

region's character, just as the saltbox house can serve as an architectural emblem for New England or the great Pennsylvania barn the Mid-Atlantic. The shotgun house is associated with the black population, both rural and urban, and was also adopted for mill-village housing as an efficient use of narrow lots. Its gable-front design, with two to four rooms one behind the other, was borrowed from Caribbean Indians for slave housing in Haiti, and from there brought by free people of color to New Orleans in the early nineteenth century. The perpendicular arrangement allows little privacy for family members but maintains spacial preferences harking back to Africa.[30] Georgian Willie Mae Workman offered this explanation of the name: "Folks used to say you could stand in front of a house like that and shoot clear through it."[31] The shotgun house, normally built of wooden-sided frame, was carried northward to Chicago's South Side and westward to California with later migration.[32]

A second typically southern folk-dwelling type is the dogtrot house. J. L. Herring of south Georgia recalled the building of such a structure from his late-nineteenth-century boyhood: "If John [the builder] was unusually ambitious, or wealthy, and essayed a 'double-pen,' there were two sets of 'pens' going up, connected by full-length sills and plates, later to have one roof and a common floor, forming a long house with two large rooms of logs [and] a wide, cool hallway between. . . ."[33] The dogtrot, then, was built as two individual pens with a chimney at each gable end, separated by an open breezeway but covered by the same continuous roof. The entrance doors face one another across the breezeway, rather than being located in the

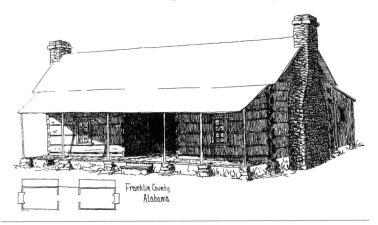

Log dogtrot house, Franklin County, Alabama. The pier-and-sill foundation, sitting porch, and external gable-end chimneys are typical southern features. Illustration by Henry Glassie, in *Mountain Life & Work*, 1963.

long side facing the road; practically speaking, this arrangement required residents to bundle up in winter to go from one room to the other!

As Herring suggests, dogtrot houses were not the homes of the poorest class; Mark Twain recalled childhood visits to the small Missouri plantation of his uncle, John Quarles (one of whose "fifteen or twenty Negroes," Uncle Dan'l, was the model for Nigger Jim of *Huckleberry Finn*), where, in the summer, the shady breezeway of the log house was wide enough to set a table with sumptuous meals.[34] While the shotgun house can be traced to Haiti, the origin of the dogtrot house is less certain. Spread through both the lowland and upland South, the earliest examples date to about 1800. The fact that some later had their breezeway converted to an enclosed hall by the addition of doorways seems to support the notion that the house type arose as a log interpretation of the late-eighteenth-century central-hallway house.[35] Whatever its origin, the dogtrot was carried westward from the Southeast; one example, the Taylor log house, was built in 1869 in Oakhurst, California, and is preserved at Fresno Flats Historical Park (plate 2).[36]

My third type of common southern folk building is not a house but an outbuilding. In an 1882 issue of *Century Magazine*, Georgian David Barrow declared that "we have no barns—at least, very few—in Georgia."[37] By that he meant few large barns of the sort he may have seen up North; many barns of the Deep South were, indeed, little more than glorified corncribs. An exception, though, is the large, rectangular structure known to researchers as a transverse-crib barn. It has six cribs, or stalls, three on each side of an open passageway that runs in the direction of the longer side and roof ridge and opens up the gable-end walls. Scholars have suggested an evolutionary sequence for this southern outbuilding type, beginning with the double-crib barn that was carried south from Pennsylvania. Farmers in the Tennessee Valley, needing a larger structure, combined two double-crib barns to create a four-crib barn, with two passageways crossing at the center; the sequence was completed when the passage in the longer side was enclosed to form two additional stalls.[38] The transverse-crib barn may then have migrated northward to

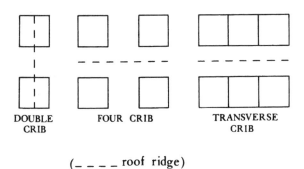

DOUBLE
CRIB

FOUR CRIB

TRANSVERSE
CRIB

(_ _ _ _ roof ridge)

Plans showing evolution of transverse-crib barn. Adapted from Fred Kniffin, in *Annals of the Association of American Geographers*, 1965.

Transverse-crib barn with V-notched log walls (later covered with siding) near Lawrence-ville, Georgia, 1967. It was built in 1932 by R. M. Davis (shown) when he couldn't afford milled lumber; the gambrel roof provided more headroom in the loft than the more typi-cal gable roof.

develop into the Midwest three-portal barn, if so another southern folk-cultural influence on other parts of the country.

I close this discussion of architecture with a feature of the related subject of landscaping, the swept yard. As the name suggests, this is a tradition—nearly displaced now by the suburban-style grassy lawn—of sweeping the yard bare of vegetation. This normally was done with a brush broom homemade of twigs bound with twine. The practice was concentrated among, but not exclusive to, the African American population; landscape historian Richard Westmacott believes this to be another African-derived folk-cultural trait.[39]

Practical explanations include preventing dry-weather brush fires from igniting a farm's wooden buildings, and discouraging unwanted "critters"—especially snakes—from getting near the house, or at least allowing people to be better able to see them coming! There are aesthetic reasons as well: white creek sand sometimes was strewn over the yard and brushed into intricate patterns, reminiscent of a Japanese zen garden. Sweeping the yard thus was a civilizing act that transformed uncontrolled nature into habitable space, as ex-

A swept yard in the African American neighborhood of Lynwood Park, Atlanta, Georgia, 2006. Photo by Janet Barrickman.

plained by Georgia literary artist Alice Walker in the opening of her famous story "Everyday Use": "A yard like this is more comfortable than most people know. It is not just a yard. It is like an extended living room. When the hard clay is swept clean as a floor and the fine sand around the edges lined with tiny, irregular grooves, anyone can come and sit and look up into the elm tree and wait for the breezes that never come inside the house."[40]

Textiles

It would be no exaggeration to say that most southern women before the twentieth century practiced traditional textile arts, the most important (and complex) of which was the weaving of cloth, supported by the skills of dyeing and spinning. Tench Coxe's 1810 *Statement of the Arts and Manufactures* reported 20,058 spinning wheels and 13,290 looms in Georgia alone. In the North, male professional weavers were common,[41] but in the South handweaving was a domestic craft practiced primarily by women. Many plantations had a loom house where slave women were trained to produce fabric for clothing, and during the Civil War even members of planter families wore homespun dresses and marched into battle with homespun Confederate uniforms.

Mountain women such as Ethel Collins Clement of north Georgia continued traditional handweaving into the twentieth century, with eye-dazzling bed coverlets among their highest artistic achievements. These southern coverlets typically are of the overshot type, lighter than their all-wool northern counterparts; their geometric patterns were built up by "floating" blocks of dyed woolen weft over an undyed cotton ground.[42] This weaving tradition was a major resource for the Appalachian handcraft revival, entering the curriculum at Berea College in Kentucky, Pi Beta Phi Settlement School in Tennessee, Crossnore School in North Carolina, and Berry Schools and Rabun Gap and Tallulah Falls Industrial schools in Georgia.[43]

Of all the South's tangible traditions, quilting remains the most vital, now recognized as an art form in museum exhibits and

Mountain weaver Ethel Collins (right, with sisters), sixteen, in front of her newly woven overshot coverlet in "Habersham Burr" pattern, Choestoe, Georgia, 1920. Ethel did her last weaving in 1949. Courtesy, Mr. and Mrs. Blueford Dyer.

learned through publications and classes as well as from family and neighbors. Collectively stitching together the three layers of material that constitute a warm and decorative "cloth sandwich" was an important social activity in the past and remains so in club settings. Distinguishing what's regional about southern quilts, however, is a task that has yet to be undertaken. One generalization can be made: the batting, or filling, material (before the recent availability of polyester) was cotton, an obvious result of its availability as a crop. Laurel Horton, a leading authority on southern quilts, has this to say about the designs: "I can think of a couple of patterns that seem to be found particularly in the South. These include 'Pineapple' and 'Rocky Mountain Road' (renamed 'New York Beauty' in the twentieth century). Looking at the earlier chintz applique quilts, southern examples tend to be more open, less jumbled, than a lot of northern examples."[44] As more state quilt surveys appear and the data base expands, any regional characteristics of American quilts should become more apparent.

There is a type of quilt concentrated in the South, however, that has been labeled as distinctly racial: African American strip quilts. Improvised during construction, their designs asymmetrically combine cloth strips of varying widths and lengths (plate 3). Such quilts seem to pulsate with a "syncopated rhythm" reminiscent of jazz, in contrast to many Anglo-American quilts that are preplanned according to the design principle of repeated blocks like the regular rhythm of a waltz. It has been suggested that African American strip quilts derive from the West African practice of weaving cloth in narrow bands that are sewn together into a larger textile (e.g., the *kente* cloth of Ghana), but antebellum examples are lacking, and "strippy" quilts were made in the British Isles as well as by white southerners, just as some creations of black quilters conform to the "Anglo-American" aesthetic of symmetry and fine stitching. The idea that certain designs in African American quilts had coded meanings meant to direct runaway slaves to sanctuary on the Underground Railroad has provoked recent debate among quilt scholars.[45]

There is no clothing style, in the past or present, that characterizes the South as a whole, but there are traditions of dress specific to certain ethnic groups in the region. From slavery times to the present, some black women have worn a headwrap, or cloth bandana. In 1786, a law was passed in New Orleans requiring Creole women of color to cover their hair with a *tignon*, or kerchief, as a sign of their racial status; complying with the law while expressing their stylistic freedom, they adopted colorful headdresses. In Louisiana today, homemade Mardi Gras costumes include the elaborate feathered creations of New Orleans's "Black Indians," and the pajama-like, fringed suits and conical masks worn by Cajuns (plate 8). Among south Florida's Seminole Indians, a distinctive style of patchwork clothing, combining southern quilting techniques with a Native American aesthetic, now serves as an important emblem of group identity.[46]

Marie Laveau (1794?–1881), voodoo queen of New Orleans and free woman of color, wearing a *tignon*, a type of cloth headwrap. Illustration by Charles Massicot Gandolfo; courtesy, New Orleans Historic Voodoo Museum.

Seminole chief Billy Bowlegs, 1852. His "long coat" is a precursor of the patchwork clothing tradition practiced today in south Florida, a southern Indian adaptation of a frontier-era European style. Courtesy, Manatee County Historical Society; in John A. Burrison, *Shaping Traditions*, University of Georgia Press, 2000.

Pottery

If material folk culture addresses basic survival needs, how does this apply to pottery, now often regarded as a leisure-time hobby? I can think of no better response than that of north Georgia folk potter Lanier Meaders: "People now think of pottery as an art form, but for us it was a way of life, our livelihood; it put food on the table."[47] Not only was this folk craft a source of income for the makers (many of whom were also farmers), but their jars and jugs were essential for processing and storing food and drink in the warm climate before factory-made containers became widely available.[48] The potter's wares, then, were linked to the southern foodways discussed earlier, supporting the agrarian lifestyle represented by buttermilk, corn whiskey, and cane syrup. And, as with the other forms of folk-cultural expression covered here, this craft has a number of regional features, both in its products and production technology.

Large jugs for cane syrup and whiskey jugs with sculpted faces will be treated in chapter four. A very different use of clay, also concentrated in the South, was for grave markers. Based on the years of death seen on inscribed examples, the tradition of ceramic markers seems to have arisen as a response to economic conditions following the Civil War, when stone markers would not have been affordable to many southerners. Usually they were made for a potter's deceased

Wheel-thrown grave markers in Laney Family Cemetery, Union County, North Carolina, 1885–1890, attributed to a potter of the Gay family. Salt-glazed stoneware. *Left*: H. 16". In Burrison, *Shaping Traditions*.

kin; however, the Loyds and Davidsons of Alabama and Mississippi marketed an elaborate design that combined a thrown base with a flat tablet, the Loyds patenting their slot-and-tab joint in 1879. Clay grave markers are distributed from Virginia's Shenandoah Valley through the Deep South to east Texas (many examples having disappeared from cemeteries due to breakage or theft).[49]

People made these ceramic grave markers by throwing on the potter's wheel (resulting in a round, hollow marker or open-top planter), or by molding or cutting out a solid slab (more closely resembling a tombstone). The slab kind was inscribed with the deceased's name and dates, often impressed with printer's type; inscriptions for the round kind, when present, normally were hand-incised. Some markers were glazed and/or decorated, others were not; this was one of the most flexible items in the repertoire of American folk potters, allowing greater creative freedom than wares restricted by a container function. The tradition was in decline by the 1920s, but Gerald Stewart of Louisville, Mississippi, made them as late as the 1970s, and a few southern potters active today, including Sid Luck and Mark Hewitt of North Carolina and Clint Alderman of Georgia, have revived the idea.

Stoneware, made of fine-grained, relatively pure clay that fires to the hardness of stone, was introduced to America from Europe in the early 1700s, and a century later was displacing the more fragile lead-glazed earthenware, or redware, that was becoming recognized as a health hazard. As in Germany and England, this stoneware was salt-glazed, resulting in a nontoxic, clear coating that reveals the gray or tan clay beneath. But by 1820, a new type of stoneware glaze had emerged in the South that was unknown elsewhere in the country. Referred to as alkaline glaze because a base (high pH) substance—slaked wood ashes or lime—is added to the dipping solution to help melt the other ingredients, this distinctly southern glaze fires green or brown and is strikingly similar to glazes used on stoneware of the Far East since the time of Christ (plates 4 and 5). The resemblance is probably no coincidence: some researchers believe that Dr. Abner Landrum of Edgefield District, South

Carolina, developed the southern alkaline glaze after reading Jesuit missionary Père D'Entrecolles's account of Chinese ash- and lime-based glazes first published in 1735. The new glaze was then carried westward by Edgefield-trained potters, reaching Texas by the 1850s and becoming the characteristic glaze for folk pottery of the lower South.[50]

The most distinctly regional piece of equipment used by southern folk potters is the rectangular crossdraft kiln, with its firebox at one end and chimney at the other, very different from the round updraft kilns of the North. Potters who still use these wood-burning ovens call them groundhog kilns when enclosed by earth, tunnel kilns when not (plate 6). Similar to stoneware and delft kilns of seventeenth-century Germany and England, they first appeared in Virginia before spreading through the South.[51]

Baskets

Lightweight containers made from plant materials were useful on southern farms for harvesting, carrying, and storing dry goods. Widespread in the region and produced by both blacks and whites are utilitarian flat-bottomed baskets woven of white oak "splits," such as the large "hamper" collecting baskets once used on every cotton-growing farm.

Other types reflect the South's ethnic diversity. Native American rivercane baskets woven in elaborate colored patterns, a thousand-year-old southern tradition, are still made by Louisiana Chitimachas, Mississippi Choctaws, and North Carolina Cherokees. Coiled sweetgrass baskets by South Carolina and Georgia Gullah speakers hark back to coastal rice plantations and, before that, Africa. Handled, curved-bottom rib (bow, egg, "buttocks," or "granny's fanny") baskets of white oak, made by Appalachian whites but adopted by some Cherokee and black makers, can be traced to Pennsylvania and, before that, perhaps to the spale baskets of England.[52]

Baskets (Gullah, Cherokee, Anglo) illustrating the South's ethnic diversity. *Back:* coiled "fanner" (for rice winnowing), Mary Jane Bennett, Mt. Pleasant, South Carolina, 1979. Sweetgrass, longleaf pine needles, palmetto binder. Diam. 23¼". *Front left:* lidded doubleweave, Rowena Bradley, Painttown, North Carolina, 1992. Rivercane with bloodroot and butternut dyes. H. 6¼". *Front right:* "nest" of four graduated rib baskets, Joan Todd, Woodbury, Tennessee, 1994. White oak. H. 8¼". Author's collection.

Furniture

While furniture is clearly not as essential for survival as food and shelter, it's hard to imagine even the rudest hut completely devoid of it. The pioneers who settled on the southern frontier would have brought with them a few, more portable, items from back East, and many men would have had at least rudimentary carpentry skills with which to fashion from the virgin forests whatever else they required for a minimum of comfort. Such a situation is described, based on the recollections of its oldest living citizens, in an early published history of Coweta County, Georgia, about twenty-five miles southwest of Atlanta, created and opened for settlement in 1826 following the Creek Indian land cession:

The pioneers lived in tents at first, many of them, and in one-roomed log-cabins, with dirt, or split puncheon [wooden slab] floors, one door; the cooking, eating and sleeping all done in the one room. . . . Children were rocked in hollow-log cradles. Built-in bedsteads—that is, holes were bored in the logs on the two walls of one corner, poles stuck in these holes met in others bored in a corner post, a side rail was tacked to the wall . . . benches made of a slab, with legs stuck in the rounding-side in auger holes; maybe a chair or two; a table; a chest—often called "chist"—if they were well-to-do . . . these summed up the maximum rather than the minimum possessions of furniture.[53]

In 1839, a decade after that part of backcountry Georgia was being settled, English actress Fanny Kemble described a somewhat different situation for the small coastal plantation of her husband, Pierce Butler, on Butler Island near Darien, Georgia:

> . . . the slaves on this plantation are divided into field hands and mechanics or artisans. . . . [The latter] are regularly taught their trades [and are] exceedingly expert at them. . . . [The carpenters] constructed the washhand stands, clothespresses, sofas, tables, etc., with which our house is furnished, and they are very neat pieces of workmanship—neither veneered or polished indeed, nor of very costly materials, but of the . . . pinewood planed as smooth as marble—a species of furniture not very luxurious perhaps, but all the better adapted therefore to the house itself. . . .[54]

It is these "neat pieces" of vernacular furniture, sometimes called "plain style," that concern us here, not the "high style" produced in the South's urban workshops that imitated more formal furniture of the North and overseas. While not elaborately decorated or in keeping with the latest fashion, this furniture was designed to serve the lifestyle of southern "plain folk," and, at its best, is elegant in its simplicity.

The carpenters who built furniture were of two types: cabinet-makers, who created case furniture assembled with sawn boards, and chair makers, whose work required fewer tools. A common wood seen in southern cabinetry is yellow pine, harder than northern white pine, with a distinctive grain pattern and, as the name suggests, a golden hue. Makers could disguise this inexpensive wood by painting a solid color (buttermilk often serving as a durable base for the pigment) or grain-painting to have it resemble a costlier wood such as mahogany.

The cabinetmaker's repertoire included several furniture types that are distinctly southern, perhaps the best known of which is the so-called huntboard, a tall-legged, shallow-cased version of the English-derived sideboard or buffet. According to folk etymology, it was light enough to be readily moved outside for serving refreshments following the hunt and tall enough so the mounted hunters could reach the food but the hounds couldn't! Nineteenth-century

Tall-legged huntboard (left: Elbert County, Georgia, early 1800s, H. 50") and pie safe (right: Laurens County, Georgia, 1850s, H. 70") in Atlanta History Museum's *Shaping Traditions* exhibition. Both are painted yellow pine, with ash-glazed stoneware ant traps by C. J. Meaders, 1997. Photo by William F. Hull, courtesy, Atlanta History Center; in Burrison, *Shaping Traditions*.

Georgia inventories listed such pieces as "slabs"; *huntboard* entered the vocabulary with the twentieth-century antiques trade.[55] They normally resided in the dining room, sometimes with locked compartments for storing silver and linen. A more logical explanation for their verticality was to discourage vermin from reaching the food. This was driven home to me when folk potter C. J. Meaders (Lanier's cousin) came to the opening of my *Shaping Traditions* exhibit at the Atlanta History Museum and declared that something was missing from the dining tableau; the next time I saw him, he presented me with two sets of saucer-like ant traps he made for the huntboard and equally tall-legged pie safe on view, the cups in the center meant to receive the feet and the surrounding trough for water or turpentine to drown any insects tempted to climb the legs, accessories he had known in his north Georgia childhood.

While pie safes—a type of food cupboard with tin panels decoratively pierced to admit air but not flies—are not unique to the South, they seem to have been concentrated here, reaching their height of development in Virginia and Tennessee.[56] Another type of cabinet that *is* specific to the South (although related to the more widespread cellarette or liquor box) is the sugar chest, a lockable box with legs or a separate stand, designed to keep sugar in the form of solid cones, a precious commodity in the nineteenth century and a luxury mainly for the upper class.[57]

A further food-related furniture item is the lazy Susan, or turn-top, table, a round dining table with a smaller turntable mounted in the center. This was a clever way of passing food to avoid awkward reaching, facilitating the custom of serving several courses of a meal at once. Lazy Susans were made in the Midwest as well as the South; the earliest Georgia examples date to the mid-1800s.[58] Here I resort to speculation, as historical evidence is scant. This is a common way of eating in China, and if it is an old one there, there may be descriptions in such publications as *Du Halde's History of China* (1736) that, like the alkaline stoneware glaze, inspired southerners to first try their hand at making them.

My last example of the cabinetmaker's craft is not food-related (except possibly as a way to lose your lunch) nor as widespread in

Joggling board at Laing School, Mt. Pleasant, South Carolina, ca. 1900. Photo by Arthur L. Macbeth; Abby D. Munro Papers, courtesy, South Caroliniana Library, University of South Carolina, Columbia.

the South: the joggling board, a springy horizontal plank mounted between two stands. A pre-trampoline delight for children, it functions something like a porch swing; also known as a courting board, a couple sitting and bouncing on it would naturally move closer together. According to tradition, it originated in the early 1800s when Mrs. Benjamin Kinloch-Huger of Scotland visited her brother at Acton Plantation near Statesburg, South Carolina. Writing home to her family in East Lothian, she complained of severe rheumatism, and they responded with a model of a springy seat that she had the plantation carpenter make full-size, allowing her gentle exercise. The idea spread through South Carolina's low country, becoming a fixture on piazzas and an emblem of local identity. The Old Charleston Joggling Board Company, founded in 1970, now makes them painted "Charleston Green."[59]

The most prevalent item of southern folk furniture, and one of the last to be made in a continuous tradition, is the mule-ear chair, so called because the rear posts curve backward with flattened fronts to resemble a mule's ears. It first made its appearance in the 1830s,

Chair maker Walter Shelnut with mule-ear "settin'" and rocking chairs, their posts turned on his medieval-style pole lathe, White Creek, Georgia, 1972.

perhaps inspired by northern, factory-made Hitchcock-style chairs with similarly shaped backs.[60] Known as a "settin'" chair, the mule-ear's shape facilitates leaning back against the porch wall, which is how it normally was used. The seats of southern folk chairs vary by topography: upland makers wove theirs basketlike of white-oak or hickory-bark "splits," while the cowhide "bottoms" of the lowlands reflect the importance of cattle herding there. The workshop of Walter Shelnut in the north Georgia foothills was typical of those once dotting the southern landscape. Primarily a small farmer, Shelnut made a dozen or so chairs a year for neighbors until his death in 1978. The most remarkable of his handmade tools was a pole lathe, powered by a springy sapling and foot treadle; of medieval design, it was one of the last such lathes in traditional use in America.[61]

Music and Song

We now shift from material folk culture to oral, musical, and customary traditions, normally associated with the word *folklore*, that have enriched southerners' leisure time and spiritual life. Folk music

Coastal Georgia's McIntosh County Shouters performing a ring-shout spiritual at the National Folk Festival, Wolf Trap Farm, Vienna, Virginia, 1981 (Andrew "Bo" Palmer beating time with broom). Photo by Margo Newmark Rosenbaum, in Art and Margo Rosenbaum, *Shout Because You're Free*, University of Georgia Press, 1998.

and song have always been major vehicles of aesthetic expression here, with the region contributing several of America's most significant musical gifts to the world. Negro spirituals, blues, jazz, and bluegrass all began as southern folk idioms, the African American presence accounting for the first three and influencing the fourth.

Black spirituals and white spirituals, consisting of biblically inspired stanzas loosely connected by a repeated refrain, arose together in the emotional fervor of early 1800s camp-meeting revivals. The two races share some lyrics and melody lines, but black spirituals developed their own repertoire and performance style, with an early type known as the ring-shout surviving today on the Georgia coast as an echo of that peculiar mix of Christianity and slavery.[62] The blues—frequently laments on lost love—emerged a century later, in the context of sharecropping and Jim Crow segregation, out of earlier song types such as the field holler. Most typically consisting of three-line stanzas (the second line a repeat of the first) sung to a twelve-bar chord progression on guitar, the blues crystallized into subregional styles. The Mississippi Delta sound is dark and intense, both vocally and instrumentally (often with slide-guitar accompaniment), as exemplified by Robert Johnson, Son House, and Muddy Waters (who urbanized the style after moving to Chicago in 1943), while the Southeastern or Piedmont sound is lighter and more restrained, with syncopated fingerpicking on guitar, as exemplified by Blind Arthur Blake, Blind Willie McTell, and Elizabeth Cotten.[63]

While there are vocal traditions associated with jazz and bluegrass (e.g., the vocables of "scat" singing and the white-gospel harmonies of bluegrass), I think of these idioms as essentially instrumental. Jazz began in New Orleans brothels and dance halls as a blend of African rhythmic and ensemble patterns and European instruments; this hybrid musical form, pioneered around 1900 by the likes of Charles "Buddy" Bolden and Ferdinand "Jelly Roll" Morton, embodies an African American genius for improvisation. Bluegrass was pioneered in the mid-1940s by Bill Monroe and brothers Ralph and Carter Stanley, who refined the old-time string-band sound while injecting a bluesy sensibility. Both idioms have since evolved from their folk roots, with some bands taking, for example, a "progressive" route influenced by classical music, others remaining closer to their origins. Jazz can now be heard in nightclubs all over the world; it may come as more of a surprise to learn that there are bluegrass bands in Bulgaria (Lilly of the West) and Japan (The Bluegrass 45)![64]

Commercial broadcasting and recording of American folk music was concentrated in the South, with record companies issuing blues and old-time performances in the 1920s and 1930s that paved the way for the popular sounds of rock and roll and country and western.[65] Recordings of early blues, and later rhythm and blues, inspired rock musicians as far away as England (e.g., the Beatles, Eric Clapton, the Rolling Stones), not to mention American pop icons like Elvis Presley.[66] In the South, musical ideas often have been exchanged across the color line even in the time of official racial segregation, with white performers such as the Carter Family, Jimmie Rodgers, and Bill Monroe borrowing material from their black neighbors.[67]

As "America's instrument," the banjo had its origins in the South; writing of the slaves on his Piedmont Virginia plantation, Monticello, Thomas Jefferson noted, "The instrument proper to them is the Banjer, which they brought hither from Africa."[68] Its early form had a gourd body with a taut animal skin covering a hole cut in front. In the early 1800s it was adopted for the blackface-minstrel stage, with white Virginian Joel Sweeney popularizing a five-string version, the "thumb" string tuned halfway up the neck as a high-pitched drone. A larger skin head, metal brackets for tightening it spaced around a wooden-hoop body, and metal frets like those of a guitar inset in the fingerboard were improvements added by commercial manufacturers. By the Civil War the five-string banjo was a mainstay of white mountain music, played either two-finger or downstroking (clawhammer, frailing) style. North Carolinian Earl Scruggs perfected a sparkling three-finger technique, adding it to the bluegrass sound when he joined Bill Monroe's Blue Grass Boys in 1945. But some banjo pickers have stayed with, or returned to, the old-time (pre-bluegrass) style, and a few folk craftsmen make fretless banjos to accommodate its chunky, more intimate sound.[69]

An instrument once found just in the southern mountains, the Appalachian dulcimer is also referred to as a plucked dulcimer to distinguish it from its distant cousin in the zither family, the hammered dulcimer. It is played horizontally on the lap or a table, its three or four strings being strummed near the tail end of the fretted fingerboard, those closest to the player noted for the melody and the others left open as drones. Beginning in Pennsylvania as a tapering, straight-sided instrument, the Appalachian dulcimer evolved into several shapes, including the wasp-waisted one popularized in the 1960s by Kentucky mountain folk singer Jean Ritchie. Her promotion of the dulcimer sparked a new interest in its making and playing.[70]

The main instrument here has always been the fiddle (what a violin is called when used to play folk or country, as opposed to classical or popular, music). The southern fiddler's preference for a three-dimensional sound, produced by bowing multiple strings while leaving one or two open or fingering a chord, may help ex-

Balis W. Ritchie and daughter Jean Ritchie playing dulcimers together at their home in Viper, Kentucky, 1950. © George Pickow.

plain why the African American banjo and Pennsylvania-German zither, both structured to create a drone sound, were adopted by mountaineers.

The South is home to some of America's most active centers of traditional music making. One is located in that part of Appalachia where southwest Virginia, western North Carolina, and east Tennessee come together. A "hotbed" of old-time and bluegrass musicians who perform and compete in public events (the largest being the Old Fiddler's Convention held annually at Galax, Virginia, since 1935), this area is also a stronghold of traditional instrument making.[71] When I asked a contestant in the 1992 Grayson County Old-Time and Bluegrass Fiddlers' Convention at Elk Creek, Virginia, to explain his community's intense involvement in folk music, he replied that until the recent arrival of satellite dishes the mountain terrain had hampered television reception, causing locals to maintain, and pass on to the next generation, their traditions of self-entertainment. While that is undoubtedly true as a partial explanation, a deep appreciation for their home-grown musical heritage is also very much in evidence.

Another especially fertile folk-music area is south Louisiana, where the accordion anchors the pulsating sound of Cajun music and its black Creole counterpart, zydeco.[72] The plethora of active bands, festivals, and radio stations featuring this music attests to its vitality; the good-time sound, with its melancholy undercurrent reflecting a harsh history, adds spice to any meal of boiled crawfish or jambalaya in a local café or dance hall. A renewed appreciation of this area's musical, culinary, and architectural heritage (the latter represented in folk museums such as Vermilionville in Lafayette and Louisiana State University's Rural Life Museum at Baton Rouge) contributes to the local economy as well as to a sense of pride in a marginalized people.

Southerners love to hear a good story, whether spoken (as with the prose narratives of the next topic) or sung. Ballads are stories told in song; generally longer and more complex than other types of English-language folk song, they have plots that can be summarized and characters who are often named. The singing of folk ballads is hardly unique to the South, but more old imported ballads have been found here (especially in the mountains) than in any other region, and the South also leads in the number of ballads created in the United States.[73] The oldest ballads, dating from the late Middle Ages to the 1600s, were brought by settlers from the British Isles in the seventeenth and eighteenth centuries. Known to folklorists as Child ballads after the American scholar who compiled them, they feature high-born characters, supernatural beliefs, and a distinctive poetic style as hallmarks of their antiquity.[74] Later ballads that entered singing tradition from broadside presses of urban Britain and Ireland in the late 1700s and early 1800s also made their way to the South.[75]

Explaining the continuing appeal to her Kentucky mountain family of these oral antiques, Jean Ritchie wrote, "These old story songs, now. We sang and listened to them, for themselves. For the excitement of the tale, or the beauty and strength of the language or of the graceful tunes, for the romantic tingle we got from a glimpse of life in the long-ago past, for the uncanny way the old, old situations still fit the present. Heads nodding over 'Lord Thomas and Fair Ellender' [Child no. 73]: 'Ain't that right, now? That's just what he *ort* to a-done to her!'"[76] This universality of situation and character that manages to transcend the passage of four centuries and transatlantic relocation was elaborated by another great Appalachian singer, Frank Proffitt of North Carolina, in describing his identification with the titular stonemason of "Lamkin" (Child no. 93) who took revenge on his aristocratic patrons after they refused payment for building a fine castle: "I never gave much thought to Bo Lamkin's feelings until I too got to building. It seemed he got angry because 'pay he got none.' I have had a occasion or two of this kind. . . . I don't claim that I had murderous intent [like Lamkin], but how I would have liked to take a big stone hammer and undone the work that pay I got none for."[77]

The South was the last stand of American folk-ballad composition, with ballads now sung traditionally that were created as late as the 1920s, recently enough for the circumstances of their authorship to be known. For example, "Little Mary Phagan," inspired by the 1913 murder trial of Leo Frank mentioned in chapter one, was composed by Atlanta's Fiddlin' John Carson, sung by him at the courthouse on the day of Frank's lynching in nearby Marietta, printed as a broadside, and recorded in 1925 on the Okeh label by his daughter, Rosa Lee ("Moonshine Kate"), developing variation as it circulated orally:

> Little Mary Phagan, she went to town one day;
> She went to the pencil factory to get her little pay.
> She left her home at eleven, she kissed her mother goodbye;
> Not one time did that poor girl think she's going thar to die.[78]

An even more prolific Atlanta folk bard was the Reverend Andrew Jenkins, said to have composed or rewritten more than eight hundred songs. His best-known, "The Death of Floyd Collins," describes the death of a young spelunker trapped in a Kentucky cave. National radio coverage of the 1925 rescue efforts prompted local record salesman Polk Brockman to commission an appropriate "tragedy ballad" from "Blind Andy," who dictated it to his daughter and received twenty-five dollars for his effort. Brockman then sold it to the Victor Record Company, which produced a hit sung by Vernon Dalhart that entered oral tradition.[79]

A few ballads have overtly southern themes, such as "The Boll Weevil," which humanizes the little black bug that migrated with his family from Texas, destroying the cotton crop while "just looking for a home," despite the farmer's efforts to eradicate it.[80] Death by murder or accident is a more frequent subject of southern ballads, and the railroad is the setting for many of the accidents. I can think of no more pervasive image in southern folk songs than the train, both as a symbol of escape and possibly a warning against modernization (Arkansas singer Johnny Cash performed a different southern railroad song on each of his network television shows in 1969–71, most of them ballads about train wrecks). When I'm teaching ballads and have time for only one American example, I choose "John Henry," a portrayal of the archetypal American occupational hero who dies on, and for, the job, in this case in a contest with a new machine:

> Well now, John Henry went to the tunnel to drive,
> The steam drill was by his side.
> Well now, John drove steel to the end of the tunnel,
> He lay down that hammer and he died.
> Lord, Lord, lay down that hammer, Lord he died.[81]

Oral Literature

What I call an oratorical aesthetic—emphasis on skill with the spoken word—permeates southern life and can be heard in religious, legal, and political oratory, while reverberating in much of the region's written literature.[82] Central to this love of speech artistry is a strong narrative impulse, channeled, as we've just seen, in ballad singing, but also in the telling of traditional prose stories and embroidered personal experiences. The thirst for a well-told tale may be rooted in influential source areas for the South's population such as Ireland and Africa, with their institutions of community storyteller (the *shanachie* and *griot*). Southerners' insularity also put a premium on storytelling; for many, oral literature in the form of folktales and legends took the place of novels and history books un-

Appalachian storyteller Ray Hicks, Beech Mountain, North Carolina, 2000. Hicks was best known for Jack tales descended through the Harmon-Ward-Hicks families. Photo by David Holt, www.davidholt.com.

til public schools and libraries brought better access to the written word in the twentieth century.

Characteristically southern folktale types include mountain Jack tales (popularized by Richard Chase) featuring a clever young hero, African American animal tales (popularized by Joel Chandler Harris) featuring tricky Brer Rabbit, and Old Master and John tales presenting a black perspective on plantation life.[83] That the latter, however humorous in tone, are revealing of racial power relationships is seen in the following, told by Cassie Mae Copeland of Atlanta:

> My mother had a joke that she told about Marse and Mistress. On Saturday nights was the only time that they could have a little recreation, because that they worked so hard during the week (I'm talking about the slaves that Marse and Mistress had). They would invite the other marse and mistress over [from a neighboring plantation]

and they would get the slaves together and learn 'em how to box and wrassle and see which one could pick up the heaviest load. And so old Marse had bragged on John; he said that John could do anything: he could beat anybody, he could tell the biggest lies. And he bragged so until it made the other old marse mad; he said, "Well, my slaves can do just as good as yours."

So he said, "All right, you bring 'em over and we'll prove it."

So he went and found a raccoon, and slipped the coon under the big black washpot.

And he come on in and said, "Well," said, "everybody's all here. All set?"

And he said, "Yeah." Said, "I want you to bring your John out here and just let him tell—being he's so smart—I want him to tell me what's under that pot."

And so John he kinda slowed up and he walked around and looked, and after awhile he scratched his head. So old Marse got uneasy about John, because it was taking John a little bit too long to tell what was under there. And he'd whisper and tell John, say, "John, now don't let me down, don't let me down!" John hated to let old Marse down; he looked around at everybody pitiful-looking and he scratched his head and said, "Well suh, I been running a long time but you caught the old coon at last!"

And the people looked with excitement and say, "Oh, John! You are just wonderful. How on earth did you know that coon was under the pot?" And old Mistress just like to fell out, because even she didn't know what was under the pot. But John just said that because he thought he had really been caught.[84]

Another form of oral literature, especially popular in the uplands, was riddling. In modern America, riddles are told as absurd jokes.[85] But not so long ago in the South, as in earlier societies, puzzling questions were posed (often to children) to be thoughtfully answered as an entertaining intellectual exercise. Such "true" riddles describe familiar features of the riddling community's environment in a misleading way, with southern farm life the subject in those recalled by Georgia mountaineer Ab Jones:

What was green and a-growing, now dead in the middle but alive at each end? [pause] It's a plow stock! It was a tree once; a tree growed, and they sawed it, made a plow out of it, and it's got a mule at one end of it and a man at the other.

What was green and a-growing, now dead, red, and a-singing? [pause] That's a fiddle! See, it's painted red.

Now I'll tell you another one, and this might sound like it's vulgar, but you can't tell till you get through. What's black without, red within, lift up your leg and stick it in? [pause] It's a boot! You see, it's black, the inside is lined with red, and you hist up your leg and stick it in.

The old woman patted it and patted it; the old man off with his britches and had at it. That don't sound right, does it? [laughs] Well, it's a bed! Yeah, a feather bed.

What runs all over the farm, has a tongue, but can't talk? [pause] A wagon!

Goes all over the pastures and woods, and every single night it sits on the shelf? [pause] Milk from a cow! Goes all over the fields when it's inside the cow, then comes in and sits on the shelf after you milk the cow.[86]

Belief and Custom

Witchcraft once was prevalent in the mountains and among African Americans, who call it hoodoo or conjure and gained from it a semblance of control as an oppressed minority.[87] Both hoodoo and voodoo combine African and European ideas, but the latter is a folk religion emphasizing spirit possession. Established in New Orleans in the 1700s, voodoo then was brought to Miami from Haiti in a somewhat different form in the 1970s (a decade after its Cuban counterpart, *Santería*, arrived in that city).[88] Another southern folk religion involving spirit possession—in this case, by the Holy Ghost—is the serpent-handling sect known as the Church of God with Signs Following, mentioned in chapter one. Concentrated in Appalachia, it was founded independently by George Hensley of Tennessee and James Miller of Alabama in about 1910, taking its inspiration from Mark 16:17–18: "In my name . . . they shall take up serpents, and if they drink any deadly thing, it shall not hurt them."[89]

A southern upland custom illustrating the centrality of the family is Decoration Day (not to be confused with Confederate Decoration Day or the national holiday now called Memorial Day). Taking place in spring or early summer depending on the community, it's both a homecoming and communion with the dead in which families clean their local cemetery and decorate ancestral graves with flowers.[90] When I visited the Central Cemetery Decoration on a beautiful hilltop in Grayson County, Virginia, in June of 1992, two long tables under an open-sided shelter adjoining the church were spread with "dinner on the grounds" brought by attendees, and white gospel music was provided by the local Flat Ridge Boys (plate 7).

A different occasion for family reunions is the African American holiday known as Juneteenth. The most enduring of emancipation celebrations, it began in Texas to commemorate the date (June 19, 1865) when Union Army Major General Gordon Granger arrived in Galveston to officially announce freedom for that state's slaves, two and a half years after President Lincoln's Emancipation Proclamation. Now spread beyond Texas, Juneteenth includes the wearing of clothes and eating of foods customarily red in color.[91]

A more localized festival is the Cajun and Creole Mardi Gras of rural southwest Louisiana, very different from that of New Orleans. As a participant explained on my 2004 visit, "We don't throw beads, we throw chickens!" In the week leading up to Fat Tuesday (preceding Lent), teams of costumed revelers from about two dozen communities make *courirs* (runs) on horseback or flatbed truck to neighbors, singing a French begging song, dancing with their hosts to music by an accompanying band, and catching a live chicken thrown from the farmhouse roof which originally went into the gumbo pot for that night's concluding dance (plate 8).[92]

A Region of Retentions

Another distinction as important as any of the foregoing is that the South has held onto certain folk traditions that have died out elsewhere in America. Isolation of the dispersed farming population from centers of change, poverty following the Civil War, and the value placed on tradition may help to explain these survivals. Rather than supporting the stereotype of the South as backward, a look at specific retentions reveals a logic and savvy that is more to be admired than maligned.

My first example is from the realm of clothing: the sunbonnet, which passed out of fashion in less sunny climes (except for "plain" sects such as the Amish) but remained a common item of women's apparel in the rural South—especially the uplands—until recently. With its wide brim in front and cape in back, this holdover from the eighteenth and nineteenth centuries protected the face and neck from sunburn, which modern science confirms is hazardous. Southern white women liked to keep their skin as light as possible;

Mrs. George Maney hoeing her garden wearing a new sunbonnet she made, Homer, Georgia, 1970. In Burrison, *Shaping Traditions*.

for them, a tan was a sign that they'd been working in the fields and were of low social status. The anti-redneck sunbonnet was one solution; another was bleaching the face with buttermilk or, more extremely, fresh cow manure![93] Since the mid-1900s the sunbonnet has been giving way to other types of women's headgear, but, where still found, may now be the only traditionally handcrafted article of southern everyday clothing, since it's not the sort of thing one can shop for in department stores.

From the food domain comes the remaining item of this chapter's heading, grits. A further illustration of the continuing importance of maize as a staple grain here, grits (for the uninitiated, a porridge of coarsely ground corn) are still routinely served—even by fast-food chains—as part of a southern breakfast, while their northern equivalents, hasty pudding and mush (made the same way from more finely ground cornmeal), are all but extinct. Grits in themselves, then, are not uniquely southern; it's their continuing viability as a food and the way they're normally eaten (like mashed potatoes, with butter or gravy with ham and eggs, in contrast to their northern counterparts that were eaten as a hot cereal with milk and sweetening) that's regional. Moving to Georgia, I was not quite so naive as the apocryphal Yankee visitor who cautiously asked if he could try "just one grit" with his first southern breakfast (no matter how small the portion, grits, like the blues, are always plural). My experience with this food ranges from the sublime (e.g., Anson Mills stone-ground grits with shrimp, grits soufflé) to the . . . well, instant. But the fact that southerners prefer the latter to no grits at all is a testament to their durability.[94]

In my earlier discussion of folk music and song I mentioned white spirituals, along with the more familiar Negro ones. Although some are true spirituals arising from camp-meeting revivals of the early 1800s, the term was applied by George Pullen Jackson to all of Anglo-American religious folk song, the domain of which once extended as far north as New England but had shrunk, by the early 1900s, to the South.[95] This can be attributed to the importance of religion in the Bible Belt as well as to the social fellowship provided by singing gatherings.

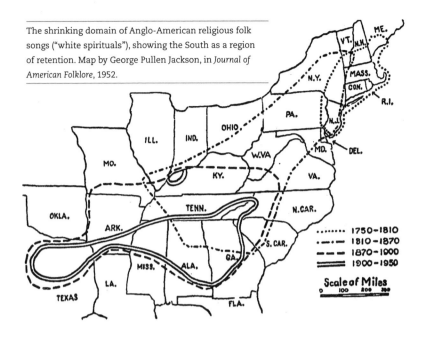

The shrinking domain of Anglo-American religious folk songs ("white spirituals"), showing the South as a region of retention. Map by George Pullen Jackson, in *Journal of American Folklore*, 1952.

.... 1750-1810
.—.—. 1810-1870
— — — 1870-1900
════ 1900-1950

Scale of Miles
0   100   200   300

Today's "white spiritual" tradition is based on shape-note hymnals such as *The Sacred Harp*, compiled in 1844 by west Georgians B. F. White and E. J. King and still in print after several revisions, with songs arranged in four-part harmony and notes in four shapes for easier recognition.[96] Sacred Harp singers constitute a part-time subculture concentrated in west and south Georgia and north Alabama, but in recent years the tradition has been spread elsewhere by such advocates as Georgian Hugh McGraw, one of America's first National Heritage Fellows.[97]

A final example of a retention, and one dear to my heart as my research specialty, is folk pottery. The South (specifically Georgia, North Carolina, and Alabama) is the only region where Euro-American folk pottery is still made, often by multigenerational families like the Meaderses, Hewells, and Browns.[98] Up North, small pottery workshops were nearly extinct by 1900, replaced by factories with their mass-production technology. At that same time in the South, scores of folk operations continued to serve the food-storage needs of a semi–self-sufficient agrarian society. Few

National Heritage Fellow Hugh McGraw leading a Sacred Harp singing, Holly Springs Primitive Baptist Church, Bremen, Georgia, 2006. Photo by Matt Hinton.

Right: Grace Nell Hewell handing on the pottery tradition (nearly extinct in the North by 1900) to three-year-old great-grandson and seventh-generation folk potter Eli Hewell, Gillsville, Georgia, 2001.

southerners still use folk pottery for churning or pickling beans; collectors are the main supporters of the tradition today, making a good living for some of its practitioners in the context of a twentieth-century handcraft revival, folk-art market, and "country" look in home decor.

In this chapter I've assembled a portrait of the South from many individual puzzle pieces, each making a contribution that, when fitted with its neighbors, creates a totality different from previous efforts to characterize the region, an image illustrating the pervasiveness of folk traditions in all walks of life here. As we've seen, some of these pieces came about as responses to climate and history; others, as I've begun to suggest, began outside the region. To make this folk-cultural portrait of the South more three-dimensional, we now turn to the origins of some of the oldest pieces of the regional puzzle.

3. An Early International Crossroads

The Diverse Roots of Southern Folk Culture[1]

Here is not merely a nation but a teeming nation of nations.
—Walt Whitman, *Leaves of Grass*[2]

Introduction: From Melting Pot to Gumbo Pot

As John F. Kennedy declared in his 1959 book title, the United States is a nation of immigrants.[3] How then, with their deep and diverse Old World roots, did our immigrant ancestors cross the cultural divide to become Americans? The prevailing view through the mid-twentieth century was that of assimilation, taking as its model the metallurgical melting pot, an image popularized by Israel Zangwill's 1908 play of that title whose protagonist proclaims, "America is God's Crucible, the great Melting-Pot where all the races of Europe are melting and re-forming."[4] The Anglo-Jewish son of eastern European immigrants, Zangwill set his play in New York, and it is to that turn-of-the-century urban population that his metaphor was most often applied.

By the 1970s this model was losing favor as ethnicity became desirable and *multicultural* entered our vocabulary. We came to realize that it is not necessary—indeed, not possible—for newcomers to fully jettison their Old World ways, and that selective continuance of those ways serves as a cultural shock absorber to facilitate accommodation. An alternative acculturation model—the "salad bowl"—was offered: despite homogenizing pressures, most ethnic groups have retained discrete cultural identities, with each component of the larger entity still distinguishable from the others. This food imagery was more palatable to our new ethnic consciousness, and seemed to approach more closely the realities of Americanization.[5]

While the salad-bowl paradigm may be useful in describing America's ethnic diversity, it doesn't go far to explain the country's regional diversity—geocultural differences so significant as to have ignited a civil war. A suitably complex model here may be the human personality. Just as an individual's personality is shaped by a combination of nature and nurture (no need to go into the debate as to which is dominant), so too does a region's "personality" arise from the encounter of heredity (cultural rather than genetic, of course) with environment, the latter being both physical (e.g., climate, natural resources) and social (contact among the region's various population groups). Since cultural heredity consists of group-shared ideas and behavior—including folklore—often brought from elsewhere, knowledge of the early influential settlers' backgrounds is crucial, and is the subject of this chapter.

At the intersection of settlement history and social environment, and key to understanding how regional cultures develop, is a process known to social scientists as creolization: the blending of ideas from different groups occupying the same area to create something new. The term is most often used in linguistics (e.g., to explain the emergence of the Gullah dialect among African Americans of coastal South Carolina and Georgia, with its mix of African and English vocabulary and grammar), but is applicable to other fields.[6]

In keeping with the southern locus of this book, and continuing the food imagery of the salad bowl, an appropriate metaphor for creolization is the gumbo pot. The hearty soup known as gumbo is a hybrid created by south Louisiana's various population groups. The cooking process begins with the French technique of *roux* (flour slowly browned in oil); the soup gets its name from *ngombo*, the Bantu word for okra, a mucilaginous vegetable transplanted from

Gumbo and its multicultural ingredients, as prepared in south Louisiana: flour and oil for *roux* (French), okra (*ngombo*, African), and filé (Native American). Photo by William F. Hull, courtesy, Atlanta History Center; in John A. Burrison, *Shaping Traditions*, University of Georgia Press, 2000.

Africa and often added to the pot; while the alternative thickening and flavoring agent, *filé* (powdered sassafras leaves), is a Choctaw Indian contribution. (Aromatic vegetables, spices, and fish and/or meat complete the dish, which is served with rice.) The gumbo pot thus creates a distinct regional flavor by combining African, European, and Native American elements.[7]

Gullah and gumbo are examples drawn from southern folk culture in the genres of speech and food. With their grassroots expression of largely local concerns, such forms of interperson-ally-learned, group-shared tradition are central to a region's cultural identity, and when linked to settlement history reveal the role of continuity and adaptation in shaping that identity.

Here First: The Native American Base Culture

"Native" Americans began as immigrants from eastern Asia more than ten millennia ago; in their movements through the Americas they developed very different cultures with discrete languages.[8] Some regional American patterns thus were already in place before the first European settlement. Contrast, for example, the Plains Indians' tipi, a conical, hide-covered mobile home designed to follow the migrations of their chief source of subsistence, the buffalo, in the upper Midwest, with the Pueblo Indians' low-rise apartment complexes of adobe, or sun-dried brick (the country's oldest continuously inhabited buildings), in the Southwest. The Indians of the South were settled agriculturalists whose villages and towns consisted of square houses with vertical framing posts and wattle-and-daub walls.[9] Southern Indians then adopted aspects of the European settlers' lifestyle, including their typical frontier dwelling, the log cabin. Some, such as north Georgia Cherokees Joseph Vann, Major Ridge, and John Ross, owned plantations and black slaves.[10]

By 1840, many southeastern Indians had been relocated to Oklahoma. Some groups remain, though, in North Carolina (Eastern Cherokees and Lumbees), South Carolina (Catawbas), Alabama (Poarch Creeks), Florida (Seminoles and Miccosukees), Mississippi (Choctaws), and Louisiana (Houmas, Coushattas, and Chitimachas).[11] Even in Georgia, which lost its indigenous peoples through treaty cessions and forced removal, Native American influence remains in the form of place names. These include original words such as *Chattahoochee* and *Okefenokee* from the languages of Creeks, Cherokees, and other groups, as well as English translations such as Ball Ground and Ball Play Creek, locations associated with the Cherokee stickball game related to northern lacrosse.[12]

Key Native American gifts to southern culture are maize (such an important staple among colonists that it was given the British generic name for cereal grain, corn) and tobacco (sacred to southern Indians and the region's first plantation crop). Southerners still have a taste for corn in a variety of bread types as well as in their whiskey (both illicit moonshine and licensed bourbon) and breakfast grits,

A Cherokee Indian cabin of frontier log construction, Qualla, North Carolina, 1888. Cultural blending is further suggested by the European-style clothing and southern Indian mortar and pestle for milling corn. Photo by James Mooney; courtesy, National Anthropological Archives, Smithsonian Institution, neg. 1000A.

Hominy, a Native American contribution to southern foodways. These cooked corn kernels that have swollen and slipped their hulls after soaking in lye were served at a Hewell family meal, Gillsville, Georgia, 1998.

as we saw in chapter two. Although southern folk medicine has a strong European heritage, settlers must have learned about native plants from Indian contact.[13]

Such traits first entered the frontier culture complex in the Delaware Valley and Virginia, but borrowing continued after this initial contact. In discussing his family's "good for what ails you" five-plants recipe in 1968, north Georgian Bennie Caudell declared, "That's an old Indian remedy—my grandmother's side; she was three-quarter Cherokee."[14] And the traditional Seminole *chickee*, an open-sided, palmetto-thatched dwelling, recently was adopted as an outdoor shelter by the general population of south Florida.[15]

Southern culture also absorbed aboriginal influences from the West Indies. In chapter two I discussed the shotgun house, which began in Haiti as the Arawak Indian *bohio*, then was adopted for slave housing on French colonial plantations, finally arriving in New Orleans and spreading through the region as housing for black and mill communities. Barbeque, the South's quintessential cooking technique, takes its name from the Caribbean Indian word *barbacoa*, a wooden framework on which meat was slow-cooked over coals.[16] And the pirogue, a log boat still being built in Cajun Louisiana, has Caribbean origins for its name as well; such dugout canoes, the chief form of water transport among southern Indians, were adopted by white and black boatbuilders of the region.[17]

Making Transatlantic Connections: Four Cornerstones

Tracing some threads of an American region's folk culture back to their Old World sources is a useful way of revealing the diversity of early settlement and the contributions of those populations to the formation of a distinctly regional culture. But by no means was this a one-way street; folk-cultural influences flowed across the Atlantic *from* the United States as well. As this story is far less recognized than the export of American popular or mass culture, two illustrations specific to Britain and the genre of folk song are in order. "The Texas Rangers," a mid-nineteenth-century American ballad, was recorded from singers in Aberdeenshire, Scotland, in 1954 and 1960,

Pokeweed, a native plant probably introduced to settlers by Indians, is used both for food and medicine in southern folk culture. The leaves are cooked (poke "sallet"), while the roots and berries (the latter made into wine and taken only in small doses) are said to relieve rheumatism.

most likely brought years earlier by a returning emigrant; while Pennsylvanian Ed Foley's 1892 satirical take on coal miners' barroom boasting, "The Celebrated Workingman," was spread to colliers of County Durham, England, by "Yankee Jim" Roberts about the time of World War I.[18]

Cross-fertilization from both sides of the Atlantic has occurred in scholarship as well as in the lore itself. Again, two examples from the realm of song should suffice. That monumental study of old British ballads that now generically bear their compiler's name was the work of Bostonian and Harvard professor Francis James Child; while that great salvager and promoter of English folk songs, Londoner Cecil Sharp, also was responsible for some of the earliest "song-catching" (1916–18) in the Southern Appalachian Mountains.[19]

Exploring the Old World background of the South's folk culture is facilitated by research on American settlement history. Especially noteworthy are three nearly simultaneous publications that establish broad cultural links between Old and New World regions. David

Hackett Fischer's *Albion's Seed* (1989) describes regional cultural patterns ("folkways") transplanted to the colonies by settlement waves from different areas of Britain. Since Fischer excludes the contributions of immigrants from Ireland (especially Ulster) to the southern backcountry, Grady McWhiney's *Cracker Culture* (1988) partially compensates for that omission, but by relying on ethnocentrically biased travelers' accounts for the South and the "Celtic fringe" of the British Isles his findings tend toward negative stereotyping. Finally, *The American Backwoods Frontier* (1989), by Terry Jordan and Matti Kaups, focuses on the Delaware Valley's role in shaping southern backcountry culture.

Now we're ready to follow those early immigrants who joined Native Americans to build the foundations of southern folklife. My comparisons are based on similarities (as diagnostically specific as possible) between Old World and southern traditions, using knowledge of settlers' origins to eliminate all but the most likely candidates for influence.[20] More complex than that of New England, the South's early settlement history includes migration from the Mid-Atlantic as well as direct travel from the Old World. These influences can be organized into four foundation groups.

British

Southern England supplied a large number of colonists to the coasts of Virginia, the Carolinas, and Georgia, while northern England, Wales, and lowland Scotland influenced the backcountry less directly via the Mid-Atlantic. In addition, Cape Fear, North Carolina, and Darien, Georgia, became eighteenth-century Highland Scots strongholds.[21] These British groups contributed a wide range of traditions in oral literature, custom, play, and material culture to the core of southern folklife.

The oldest ballads sung in the South, such as the romantic tragedies of "Barbara Allen" (Child no. 84) and "Lord Thomas and Fair Eleanor" (Child no. 73), are British imports, and, as we saw in chapter two, more of these Tudor-era story-songs are found in the region—especially the uplands—than in other parts of the country.[22] Likewise, some of the oldest folktales told in the South are English;

for example, the following, recorded from Georgian Emily Ellis in 1970, dates to the fifteenth century:

> One night two tramps were walkin', and they had to pass a cemetery. And they heard voices, so they stopped and listened. And they heard this voice saying, "You take this one an' I'll take that one, you take this one an' I'll take that one." And what they didn't know was that two men had come along earlier and shook a walnut tree, and they were dividin' up the walnuts. And they set there listenin' to "You take this one, I'll take that one."
>
> And they said, "What is that?" And one of them said, "Well, I think it's the Devil and the Lord dividin' up the people in the cemetery."
>
> And just as they had reached this conclusion one of the men said [loudly]: "And I'll take the two on the outside." An' nobody saw the tramps anymore![23]

In the southern Christmas custom known as "riding fantastic" or "sernatin'" (serenading), disguised young people visited neighbors on horseback or foot and received treats; homemade masks called "dough faces," cross-dressing, and prank playing were variables. This practice, active in north Georgia as late as 1950, was a survival

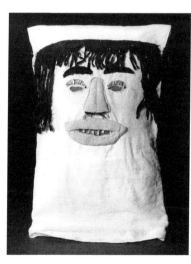

A "dough face," or homemade mask, by Maebelle White, Banks County, Georgia, 1975, based on childhood memories of Christmas "sernatin'," a southern survival of British "mumming." Photo by William F. Hull, courtesy of Atlanta History Center; in Burrison, *Shaping Traditions*.

of British mumming, or guising, traceable to the Middle Ages.[24] The southern superstition that a household will be blessed with good luck if a man is the first to enter on New Year's Day appears to derive from the "first foot" tradition of Scotland and northern England.[25] Even the slave marriage ritual of "jumping the broom," now revived among African Americans and thought to be of African origin, is actually British; in Wales it was known as a besom wedding.[26]

In the frontier custom of the "turn-out," pupils barricaded themselves in the schoolhouse to prevent their teacher from entering and force from him a holiday; this curious practice dates to the 1500s in northern England and lowland Scotland, where it was known as "barring out."[27] The southern folk game of "town ball" (also played in the North, where it was formalized into baseball) originated as "bittle-battle" in England, where the game evolved into cricket.[28]

To gain an Easter holiday, children of Columbia County, Georgia, defend their barricade of the log "academy" against schoolmaster Michael St. John's efforts to enter, a southern frontier custom derived from the British "barring out." Illustration from "The Turn Out," in A. B. Longstreet, *Georgia Scenes. . .*, 2nd ed., Harper & Brothers, 1859.

Single-bay cottages in England and the South, with British continuity seen in the latter's form, typically about sixteen feet square. *Top*: Much Wenlock, Shropshire, 1600s, stone walls. *Bottom*: Walker County, Georgia, ca. 1850, hewn log walls with half-dovetail corner notching.

British storage jar and southern counterpart, both with four lug handles and trailed slip (liquid clay) decoration. *Left:* probably Newcastle upon Tyne, England, early/mid-1800s, lead-glazed earthenware. *Right:* by Thomas Chandler, Edgefield District, South Carolina, ca. 1850, alkaline-glazed stoneware.

Antique British children's games and associated rhymes, such as "Green Gravel" and "Three Dukes a-Riding," have survived more or less intact in the South, especially Appalachia.[29]

In southern folk architecture, the square one-room cabin harks back to lower-class cottages of medieval England, while the hall-and-parlor house is a middle-class Renaissance form.[30] For folk pottery, antecedents of our antebellum cane-syrup jugs and lug-handled food-storage jars can be found in northern England.[31] The southern (and general Anglo-American) quilting tradition received its eighteenth-century impetus from England with solid-color, whole-cloth quilts textured by ornate stitching, and appliqué quilts in which printed chintz was cut and stitched onto a white top in a bordered central design. It was with pieced quilts—their tops assembled from colored pieces—that American quilts diverged from English models with the innovation of repeated blocks (recurring colored-pattern squares), which then crossed the Atlantic in the other direction (e.g., the 1860s "Log Cabin" type) to influence British Isles quilting.[32]

African

As America's only large body of involuntary immigrants, enslaved Africans representing a variety of tribal and language groups were brought from a crescent of west-central Africa marked by Senegal at its north and Angola at its south.[33] To counter the notion that African Americans have no Old World culture other than a borrowed and perverted European one, scholars searched for, and found, kinship between the cultures of West Africa and black America.[34] At times, however, this search for "Africanisms" has overshadowed analysis of creative adaptation and creolization.

Southern speech incorporates such African vocabulary as *chigger* (the Wolof word for small flea) and *juke* (also Wolof, meaning disorderly); Africanisms are especially prevalent in the Gullah dialect of coastal South Carolina and Georgia.[35] Many of the African

Brer Fox sets his Tar-Baby to trap Brer Rabbit, in a literary adaptation of a southern folktale with probable African origins. Illustration by A. B. Frost, in Joel Chandler Harris, *Uncle Remus, His Songs and His Sayings*, D. Appleton-Century, 1933.

Detail from *The Old Plantation*, a late-1700s South Carolina watercolor of a slave quarters showing a gourd-bodied, skin-headed banjo prototype derived from West Africa. Courtesy, Abby Aldrich Rockefeller Folk Art Museum, Colonial Williamsburg Foundation, Williamsburg, Virginia.

African American grave in Mt. Zion Cemetery, Marion County, Georgia, 1970, with halves of a carefully broken ceramic bowl serving as head and foot markers. Other durable objects, including alarm clocks, medicine bottles, and a child's tricycle frame, were nearby, a grave-decoration custom similar to that of West Africa. Photo by Cathy Fussell for Georgia Folklore Archives, Georgia State University.

Winnowing rice with a coiled "fanner" basket (rice-hulling mortar and pestle at right), Sapelo Island, Georgia, 1920s. This technology was introduced to coastal plantations by slaves from rice-growing areas of West Africa. Courtesy, Georgia Archives, Vanishing Georgia Collection, Sap-94; in Burrison, *Shaping Traditions*.

American animal folktales popularized by Joel Chandler Harris in his Uncle Remus books, and featuring the trickster Brer Rabbit, are now accepted as having African origins, as Harris himself suspected.[36]

The banjo, later adopted for upland white folk music, began as a slave instrument based on West African prototypes such as the *bania*, *molo*, and *halam*.[37] From antebellum spirituals and work songs to later jazz and black gospel, musical traits such as antiphony (call-and-response) and syncopated rhythm are rooted in West African style. A case also has been made for the blues tradition echoing the song compositions of African *griots*.[38]

The African American burial custom of grave decoration, in which durable objects owned by the deceased are placed on the grave, has West African antecedents, while log mortars and pestles for hulling rice, coiled-grass baskets, and circular cast-nets for fishing are coastal folk artifacts with probable African origins.[39] Of broader import is "the Africanization of the New World palate," as food historian Jessica Harris put it; plants now integral to the southern diet, such as the aforementioned okra, black-eyed peas, watermelons, and *benne* (sesame) seeds, were introduced from Africa.[40]

Irish

When it comes to southern folk culture, the Emerald Isle's most influential immigrants were the Scotch-Irish, whose forebears—mainly Presbyterian lowland Scots and English borderers—had settled in Ireland's northern province when James I established the Ulster Plantation in 1609. A century later they began an exodus across the Atlantic to escape economic and religious restrictions imposed by England, moving into the backcountry from Pennsylvania and several South Atlantic states to transplant northern Irish traditions in the Appalachian and Piedmont frontier.[41]

The Scotch-Irish adapted their Ulster distilling technology to the New World grain for their most mythologized gift to southern folk culture, the illicit corn whiskey known as moonshine.[42] They also brought an old rectangular cabin type, with front and rear opposing doors in the larger, fireplace room, grafting that design to the log construction of the backcountry.[43] Many upland cabins were equipped with an item of furniture also common in Ireland, a lidded meal bin having two compartments, one for cornmeal (oatmeal back in Ireland) and the other for wheat flour.[44] The making of stave-built wooden containers called *piggins* and *noggins* was most likely an Appalachian continuation of an ancient Irish coopering tradition.[45]

The characteristic style of southern fiddling, with its simultaneous bowing of multiple strings, owes a debt to the fiddling of Ireland and Scotland, which in turn echoes the droning sound of the bagpipes; many older southern fiddle tunes, such as "Soldier's Joy," "Leather Britches," "Bonaparte's Retreat," and "The Devil's Dream," can be traced to those countries as well.[46] The southern mountain and bluegrass singer's "high, lonesome" sound, with its ornamentation and nasality (e.g., Jean Ritchie, Bill Monroe, Ralph Stanley), is very likely rooted in Ireland's *sean nós* ("old style").[47]

An English-language tradition of European *Märchen*, or fairy

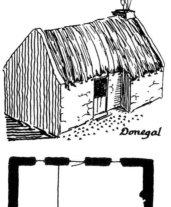

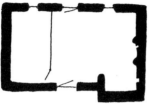

Two-room cabin of northern and western Ireland, an ancient design with front and rear opposing doors in the main room. The walls would have been of stone, mud, or turf, the roof thatched with straw. From E. E. Evans, *Irish Heritage*, Dundalgan Press, 1942.

Scotch-Irish cabin of the McClure family near Helen, Georgia, 1967. The floor plan is much the same as in Ireland, but the log walls (here with half-dovetail corner notching), half-storey loft, external chimney, sitting porch, and pier-and-sill foundation are southern adaptations.

tales, is concentrated in the upland South. The best known of these are the Jack tales featuring an adolescent hero named Jack, whose positive character traits (cleverness, helpfulness, teachability) allow him, in the course of his adventures, to overcome obstacles. There is evidence for Jack tales in Appalachia as early as the 1760s, and they've remained an active part of the story repertoire in western North Carolina. Some scholars believe these mountain *Märchen* to be of mainly English background, but such tales have been stronger

Meal bin by W. Harvey Welborn, Banks County, Georgia, 1908. Painted poplar. H. 30½". This upland furniture type likely came from Ireland; the smaller compartment was for wheat flour, the larger for less costly meal (corn in the South, oats in Ireland). Welborn, a skilled carpenter said to be of Irish ancestry, cut the front legs in an elegant cabriole shape. Photo by T. J. Smith for Georgia Folklore Archives; collection of Sandra and Chester Hewell.

Rick Stewart learning coopering from grandfather Alex Stewart, Sneedville, Tennessee, 1980. Alex's great-grandfather, Jim Stewart, is thought to have brought the tradition from Ireland before the Revolutionary War. Photo by Dan Yearout, courtesy, Tennessee Valley Authority; in Burrison, *Shaping Traditions*.

in the oral storytelling of Scotland and Ireland, including Ulster, pointing to the need to reevaluate the role of the Scotch-Irish in introducing this tradition.[48]

Continental European

Continental influences on southern folk culture tend to be localized to sections of particular states and vary widely within the region. A major exception, however, are Finno-Swedish and Germanic contributions to backcountry folk culture that were carried south from the Mid-Atlantic. One of these is horizontal log construction. While acknowledging that Finno-Swedes in the Delaware Valley were the first to employ the building technique (mid-1600s), some scholars felt this group was too small and insular to have so significantly impacted frontier culture, shifting their attention to later immigrants from Switzerland and east-central Europe who were part of the Pennsylvania "Dutch" (German) population. The debate recently was revisited with fresh fieldwork and archival evidence to make a case for Finno-Swedish diffusion of horizontal log walls as well as the "snake" or "worm" fence of split rails stacked zigzag fashion, once so common in the upland South.[49] And the widespread use of wood (typically white oak) shingles for roofing (rather than the thatch, clay tiles, or stone of the British Isles) also may owe a debt to that woodland group.

Central Europeans certainly reinforced the American log-building tradition, however, and made other contributions as well. The stringed instrument known as the Appalachian dulcimer most likely developed from the *Scheitholt*, a type of German zither made in Pennsylvania.[50] The making of sauerkraut (salt-pickled cabbage) also carried over from the Pennsylvania Germans to the southern uplands,[51] while the "Dutch" folk arts of *Fraktur-Schriften* (illuminated manuscripts), painted dower chests, and inlaid hunting rifles migrated into Virginia and the Carolinas.[52] More direct Central European influence is seen in the material culture of Missouri's German settlements and in the Moravian pottery of North Carolina, with examples of Continental building types and *fachwerk* (half-timbering) still standing in both states.[53] Finally, the German

An old split-rail worm fence separating two farms near Summerville, Georgia, 1967. This fence type is believed to have migrated south and west from Finno-Swedish settlement in the Delaware Valley.

custom of Christmas and New Year "shooting rounds" brought to the Carolinas and Missouri paralleled the more widespread southern practice, derived from Britain, of shooting firecrackers and guns.[54]

Other Continental influences can be seen in south Louisiana, home to two distinct groups of French ancestry. Creoles (white and black) claim descent from the original French settlers, while Cajuns came to the bayous and prairies as refugees from Acadia, Canada. French folklore correspondences include the celebration of Mardi Gras and the numskull folktale character Jean Sot.[55] As suggested by our gumbo-pot metaphor, though, interaction with Native Americans, African Americans, and other groups in the area has created a truly creolized culture best described as south Louisianan with a French accent.[56]

A different Mediterranean influence in another part of the South is the building tradition of *tabby*, a concrete mix of lime, sand, water, and an abundant coastal resource, oyster shells, tamped into wooden

Ernest Hodges playing an old Appalachian dulcimer, Murrayville, Georgia, 1968. Unlike more typical bulge-sided dulcimers, its straight-sided, tapered form closely resembles its Pennsylvania-German forerunner, the *Scheitholt*. In Burrison, *Shaping Traditions*.

Six-gallon kraut jar by Cheever Meaders, Mossy Creek, Georgia, 1950s, with cabbage chopper. Alkaline-glazed stoneware. H. 16½". North Georgia potters made such large, cylindrical jars for salt-pickling sauerkraut, a Pennsylvania-German food tradition brought to the upland South. Collection of Folk Pottery Museum of Northeast Georgia; in John A. Burrison, *Brothers in Clay*, University of Georgia Press, 1983.

Single Brothers House, a Moravian communal dwelling with Germanic roots, restored in Old Salem, North Carolina. The *fachwerk* (half-timber) main section dates to 1769, the brick addition to 1786. Illustration courtesy, Old Salem, Winston-Salem, North Carolina.

Saddlebag-type slave cabin with tabby walls, Ossabaw Island, Georgia, ca. 1845. This coastal concrete, with oyster-shell lime and aggregate, may have developed from a Spanish building technique brought to Florida in the 1500s. Photo by Laura Drummond, 2004; courtesy, Heritage Preservation Program, Georgia State University.

forms to create the thick walls of plantation mansions, slave quarters, and rice mills. The basic technique was introduced by Spanish settlers to St. Augustine, Florida, in the 1580s (the name comes from the Spanish *tapia*, or "mud wall"), then, with its shell aggregate, was adopted in the 1700s in British-settled communities of coastal South Carolina and Georgia.[57] Like adobe in the Southwest, tabby is now such a marker of local identity that some low-country contractors apply a faux-tabby stucco to new construction.

Journeys of Yearning

It is one thing for me, a nonnative of the region, to write dispassionately about these vital arterial connections to other countries. But what of the practitioners of the transplanted traditions: are they aware of their centuries-old folk-cultural roots, and if so, do they feel an emotional tie to the source areas? Recent research by folklorists, anthropologists, and historians and a growing interest in genealogy, along with access to libraries and the Internet, now make it possible for traditional craftspeople, musicians, and storytellers to explore the origins of their heritage beyond what may have been learned as oral history. For some there is indeed a curiosity, akin to the yearning of fosterlings to fill the void of their unknown biological parentage, to discover those missing links.

One such case, and a relatively early one, is that of Appalachian folk singer Jean Ritchie. Growing up in Viper, Kentucky, in what she describes as a "singing family," she moved to New York in 1947 after graduating in social work from the University of Kentucky. Using her inherited songs to entertain the children in her care at Henry Street Settlement School, she soon became part of the early folksong revival, giving her first formal concert in 1948. As Kenneth Goldstein wrote in his liner notes for one of her albums, "As she became aware of the immense treasure that was hers, she took greater interest in her songs, and on frequent trips back to the mountains she began to set down the words and tunes of the many songs known by her kinfolk and neighbors. In doing this she learned more about the history of the Ritchie family and the

Kentucky mountain folk singer Jean Ritchie recording Irish *uilleann* piper and singer Seamus Ennis in London, England, on her 1952 British Isles field trip. © George Pickow.

source of their tremendous song repertoire. And so, she started to dream of going to the British Isles in the hope of tracing down her own family strains there, and of finding the wellspring of her own songs."[58] In 1952, at age thirty, Jean realized that dream when she was granted a Fulbright Fellowship for a year's visit to Britain and Ireland with photographer-husband George Pickow to record traditional singing and music.

Jean traces her ancestry to five Ritchie brothers who sailed "from an unknown port in England" before the Revolutionary War. One brother went to Virginia, and his family later settled in the Kentucky mountains. Ritchie is a common British Isles name, making a search for specific family folklore connections problematic. Jean contacted known performers and collectors for her trip, including those associated with the English Folk Dance and Song Society (whose director, Douglas Kennedy, was one of the singers she recorded). Given the two centuries of divergence in Old and New World traditions, I wondered about the correspondences Jean found between her Appalachian song heritage and that of the British Isles, and this question offered an opportunity to renew contact with one of those responsible for my early interest in folklore. Jean's reply to my query bears quoting:

> As to my feelings about making musical connection with the Old Countries, yes—very strong, very moving ones at the time. When I would sing for someone, say, "False Sir John" [Child ballad no. 4], and have that person repay me by singing his/her own version—and not much different a version—well! I'd get such a powerful sense of family, of cousinship, of almost being at home—certainly in my own Kentucky community, visiting a neighbor. The feelings? Excited interest from a collector's viewpoint; sudden stabs of sentiment (laughter, tears, etc.) as though finding new family members; wonder at the distance the song had traveled, the time it had endured, the realization of its being a belonging—as loved tools and cooking pots are belongings.[59]

My other cases involve African American singers whose curiosity about their ancestry was likely stimulated by the popularity of Alex Haley's 1976 novel, *Roots*. As a result of American anthropologist Joseph Opala's research into links between Sierra Leone, West Africa, and the Gullah culture of coastal South Carolina and Georgia, a delegation of Gullah community leaders, including Frankie and Doug Quimby of the Georgia Sea Island Singers, was invited to that country for a week in 1989. The film documenting the "homecoming" shows a number of folk-cultural similarities between those two rice-growing areas of the world. A second, more focused, visit was arranged and filmed in 1997 to trace a Mende-language song survival on the Georgia coast, recorded in the 1930s by linguist Lorenzo Dow Turner and still known by the Moran family there, to its origins in Sierra Leone.[60]

My final example involves the African American choir from Mt. Zion Church of Killin, Alabama, paired with Gaelic psalm singers of Back Free Church from the Scottish Isle of Lewis in a 2005 Celtic Connections concert at Glasgow Cathedral. This seemingly incongruous pairing resulted from the conviction of jazz musician Willie Ruff, on Yale University's music faculty, that antiphonal black gospel singing, and the earlier "lining out" style (found also in Appalachia), arose not out of African musical impulses but from the influence of Presbyterian Highland Scots who came to the South in the mid-1700s and taught their slaves to sing in their "precenting" way (i.e., the group repeating each line sung by the leader). Needless to say, this theory has provoked some controversy in the African American musical world, but it does raise the profile of an early group not usually credited with lasting influence in the region.[61]

Conclusion (But Not the End of the Story)

Only the clearest and most supportable examples of Old World influence on southern folk culture have been selected for this essay. Some southern traditions, such as field sleds, querns for milling corn, and chair makers' pole lathes, have Old World roots but cannot be traced to a single source area; others, such as basketry fish traps, corn cribs, and gourd containers, probably resulted from the merging of similar Native American and Old World ideas.[62] To illustrate the difficulties of such comparative research, I return to the overshot coverlets discussed in chapter two to briefly explore the source of this distinctive four-harness weaving technique, so prevalent in the South and surviving in Appalachia into the twentieth century.[63] I've found no evidence of overshot weaving in England or Ireland; bedcovers of Wales (*carthenni*) and Germany seem to have been produced with other weaving methods (double-cloth and Jacquard). A number of overshot ("monk's belt") patterns are known for Sweden; but most promising so far is the tradition of overshot blankets in Highland Scotland that apparently harks back to the eighteenth century.[64]

Equally difficult to document as such uncertain cases of diffusion, but no less significant, are the processes of recontextualization and synthesis as these disparate influences came together and adapted to New World conditions.[65] Behind what may appear to be a mechanistic approach to cultural history are flesh-and-blood people who introduced, spread, and creatively expanded these traditions, although their names and lives are seldom recoverable from the mists of time.[66] And these foundation groups are just the beginning of the story. As we'll see in chapter six, the gumbo that is southern folk culture continues to cook and develop an even more complex flavor as new ingredients are added with the arrival of later immigrants.

In the next chapter I pursue a ceramic form—the jug—back to its Old World origins while demonstrating how its history in the United States distills something of the southern spirit. But I'll close this chapter with thoughts by two distinguished southern scholars on the subject of diversity. Even the extremes of racial strife this region has seen couldn't prevent members of clashing groups from exchanging traditions with one another. As sociologist and Tennessean John Shelton Reed expressed it, "From the start the South has been the home of peoples whose intertwined cultures have set them off from other Americans. And where the economic and political story has been largely one of conflict, division, and separation, the tale of the cultural South is one of blending, sharing, mutual influence—and of continuing unity and distinctiveness." South Carolina folklorist and historian Charles Joyner adds, "Every southerner, regardless of race, shares both African and European traditions. . . . The central theme of southern folk history might well be described as the achievement of cultural integration."[67]

4. Journey of the Jug

An Artifact-Based Case Study[1]

> His two jugs were part of his dress. They hung across his shoulders, before and behind, suspended to a wide black greasy leather strap.
> —Harden E. Taliaferro, "Ham Rachel, of Alabama"[2]

On a sunny fall Saturday in 1997, Hewell's Pottery in the north Georgia countryside was in the midst of its annual Turning and Burning festival, a homegrown celebration of traditional pottery making. The guest of honor was Lanier Meaders, arguably America's most famous folk potter, who had made it to the age of eighty. This was his birthday party, with hundreds on hand to wish him well. Lanier had kept alive Georgia's old alkaline-glazed stoneware tradition virtually single-handedly until others, inspired by his success, picked it up and carried it on; our meeting in 1968 had inspired me to research and write the first in-depth survey of a southern state's ceramic heritage.[3]

The Hewell and Meaders "clay clans" of northeast Georgia (the country's last stronghold, along with North Carolina and Alabama, of Euro-American folk pottery) have maintained ties for nearly a century. William J. Hewell of Gillsville in Hall County did much of his potting at Mossy Creek, fifteen miles to the north in the Appalachian foothills of White County, introducing the concept of the face jug there to Lanier's father, Cheever Meaders, in about 1920. Hewell, in turn, probably had acquired the concept from his in-laws, the Fergusons, north Georgia's first known makers of jugs with modeled faces, who likely brought the idea from antebellum South

Ham Rachel of Alabama and his "sperrit" jugs. Illustration by John McLenan, in Harden E. Taliaferro, *Fisher's River*, Harper & Brothers, 1859.

Below: Hewell's Pottery annual Turning and Burning festival, Gillsville, Georgia, October 2005.

Carolina. When face jugs became Lanier's specialty in the 1970s, earning him a national reputation and prompting him to adopt the citizens-band radio "handle" of "Jughead," his young friend Chester Hewell revived his own family's making of them, bringing the local tradition full circle.

The county-fair atmosphere of Lanier's birthday bash was tinged with sadness, for he was gravely ill (and would die four months later). Under the big tent the Hewells had set up for the occasion, I was asked to say a few words over the public address system about Lanier and his importance in American ceramics history, after which I fed him a slice of his birthday cake. When he clutched my sleeve from his wheelchair as a sign that he had something to tell me, I leaned down to catch his barely audible whisper: "John, you're Jughead now." In what otherwise might have been taken as an insult, he was conferring on me the honor of his nickname, knowing that soon he would have no need for it.

Belying the stereotype of the isolated country craftsman who's never ventured from home, Lanier served as a U.S. Army paratrooper in World War II, returning to Mossy Creek from his air base in Britain and combat in Germany some three centuries after the jug, with which his career as a potter was to become inextricably bound, took much the same routes in its journey to America. I've written about jugs in the context of Georgia ceramics history, but that Turning and Burning festival has caused me, as the newly anointed Jughead, to more broadly ponder a clay artifact type that became the quintessential American pot form (even giving rise to an American musical idiom, the jug band),[4] and to attempt to trace its life history much as I'd written about Lanier's.

Semantic Juggling: What's Pot-Bellied, Skinny-Necked, One-Armed, Yet Full of Spirit?

In tracing the travels of this seemingly ubiquitous ceramic item, the first order of business is to clarify just what a jug is.[5] This is complicated, however, by different meanings for the term in American and British English; as George Bernard Shaw wryly put it, "England

A classic southern meal at Harold's Barbeque, Kennesaw, Georgia, 2002, consisting of Brunswick stew, barbequed pork ribs, crackling cornbread, coleslaw, and sweet tea. Photo by Andy Sharp; courtesy, *Atlanta Journal-Constitution*.

Southern dogtrot house built by William and Margaret Taylor at Oakhurst, California, in 1869, restored at Fresno Flats Historical Park. Photo by Laura Maish and Bill Storage.

African American pieced quilt in strip and "Brick Work" patterns by Annie Howard, Madison, Georgia, 1957. Author's collection; photo by William F. Hull, courtesy, Atlanta History Center; in John A. Burrison, *Shaping Traditions*, University of Georgia Press, 2000.

Jar, China, Han dynasty (ca. first century B.C.). Stoneware with wood-ash glaze on upper half, very similar to that later used in the South. H. 12½". Private collection.

Jar attributed to Clemons Chandler (the initials said to be for his brother-in-law), Mossy Creek, Georgia, 1843. Stoneware with wood-ash version of alkaline glaze, locally known as "Shanghai" glaze. H. 12". Private collection.

"Blasting off" the rectangular, wood-fueled "groundhog" kiln of Catawba Valley folk potter Burlon Craig in the last hours of firing, Vale, North Carolina, 1977.

Decoration Day at Central Cemetery, Flatridge, Virginia, June 1992.

The spirit of Cajun Mardi Gras: LeJeune Cove *courir* (run), southwest Louisiana, February 2005. Photo by T. J. Smith.

Reproductions of seventeenth-century English lead-glazed earthenware jugs, John Hudson, Mirfield, West Yorkshire. *Left*: Claret jug, 1991, after a London delftware example. H. 6¾". *Right*: Slip-trailed owl jug, 2004, after one attributed to Thomas Toft of Staffordshire, with its cup-top beside it. H. 8¾". Author's collection.

American lead-glazed earthenware jugs with typical regional handle placements. *Left*: New England (Massachusetts provenance), ca. 1800, copper-green glaze accent and shoulder tooling. H. 7¾". *Right*: Pennsylvania, early/mid-1800s, iron or manganese glaze coloring and extruded handle. H. 6½". Author's collection.

Typical northern stoneware jugs in the Germanic tradition, both from Manhattan. Salt glaze with cobalt-blue highlighting. *Left:* Thomas Commereau, ca. 1815. H. 11¾". *Right:* Clarkson Crolius Jr., ca. 1840. H. 11". Author's collection.

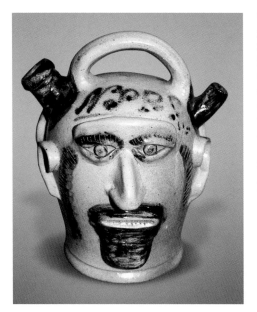

Two-face, monkey-form jug attributed to Henry Remmey Jr. or his son Richard, Philadelphia, Pennsylvania, dated 1858. Salt-glazed stoneware highlighted with cobalt blue. H. 11". Remmey face vessels are likely an Americanization of German "graybeards" and may have influenced the southern face-jug tradition. Ex-collection of Tony and Marie Shank.

Recent jugs from Seagrove, North Carolina, a community of one hundred pottery shops, several of which are rooted in local tradition. Salt-glazed stoneware. H. 11½". *Left:* David Stuempfle, 2001. *Right:* Ben Owen III, 2004. The streaks on both were caused by the dumping of glazing salt directly over the pots through holes in the kiln arch; Stuempfle's also has a partial ash glaze. Author's collection.

Rooster, Charlie West, White County, Georgia, 2001, illustrating some of today's folk potters' decorative work geared to collectors. Earthenware with commercial glazes. H. 20¾". A great-grandson of ballad singer Lillie West (featured in chapter five), Charlie was trained in the garden pottery tradition. Collection of Folk Pottery Museum of Northeast Georgia, Sautee Nacoochee Center.

Urban folk art in Atlanta, Georgia: wall graffiti by several different "writers," Krog Street and Edgewood Avenue, 2006.

Embroidered story cloth by May Tong Moua, Lilburn, Georgia, 1991, depicting the Hmong exodus from Laos with village under Communist attack. This refugee folk art recently was introduced to the South. Author's collection; photo by William F. Hull, courtesy Atlanta History Center; in John A. Burrison, *Shaping Traditions*, University of Georgia Press, 2000.

Folk potter Dwayne Crocker shaping a jug's narrow neck on his electric wheel, Gillsville, Georgia, 2001. The vertical loop handle that also defines the form will be added once the clay dries a bit. Photo by Chris Swanson.

and America are two countries separated by the same language."[6] In Britain, the word can mean either a small pitcher (as in a cream jug for tea) or a drinking vessel which, in reference to medieval wares, is tall and often baluster-shaped (really an early tankard).[7] In the United States, however, the term has come to mean a narrow-necked (so it can be stoppered), flat-bottomed (free-standing) vessel for keeping and transporting liquids (although it certainly can be drunk from), with one or two vertical loop handles for grasping and pouring. In Britain, such a vessel is called a flagon or bottle; what we Americans call a bottle normally lacks a handle. So the subject of the eighteenth-century English poem, "The Brown Jug," was an ale mug, while the American song of a century later, "The Little Brown Jug," refers to a narrow-necked container for distilled spirits.[8] It is the American meaning that this essay addresses.

Peregrinating Pots: Old-World Origins and Diffusion

As defined above, the jug form evidently arose in the ancient world as a response to technological advances. By 2500 B.C. in the Near East, the fermentation into wine of date and grape juice and the extraction of oil from olives and aromatic and medicinal plants, along with a growing trade in these liquids, required inexpensive containers for storing and transporting them. The potter's wheel, beginning as a low turntable in Mesopotamia at about the same time and later improved in Greece and Egypt as a kickwheel with added flywheel and raised headblock, offered the speed to support large-scale pro-

Wheel-thrown jug, Gaza, Palestine, ca. 1500 B.C. Unglazed earthenware. H. 11¼". Courtesy, Palestine Archaeological Museum, Israel Antiquities Authority, Jerusalem.

duction and facilitated the continuous drawing in and up of the jug neck.[9] The Far East experienced similar advances, but the loop handle that helps to define the jug never caught on as an addition to the bottle form favored there.

The jug first appeared in Palestine during the second phase of the Early Bronze Age, about 2800 B.C., then was adopted in Greece (where it was called a *lekythos*), Egypt, and Persia by 1500 B.C.,[10] migrating west, with Phoenician trade, to the Etruscans and Romans. The Roman Empire helped to spread the form beyond the Mediterranean into Germany and Britain, where it became part of the Romano-Celtic ceramic repertoire.[11]

In Germany, earthenware jugs continued to be made into (and after) the Middle Ages.[12] The form came into its own there, however, with the emergence of stoneware in the fourteenth century, perhaps to support the expanding trade in Rhenish wine.[13] German stoneware jugs were most notably manifested as the *Bartmann-krug*, or graybeard, with a sprig-molded face mask on the neck and medallion on the belly, thousands of which were shipped to Britain in the sixteenth and seventeenth centuries.[14] German salt-glazed

Bartmannkrug (graybeard jug), Frechen, Germany, late 1500s. Brown salt-glazed stoneware with sprig-molded mask and armorial medallions. H. 12". Courtesy, Potteries Museum, Hanley, Stoke-on-Trent, England.

stoneware jug production remained robust through the nineteenth century, and continues in some areas today.[15]

The jug form's linkage to the potter's wheel is especially evident in the ceramic history of England. When Roman withdrawal and Anglo-Saxon invasion ushered in the Dark Ages, the wheel fell out of use and shaping technology reverted to hand-building, with open-mouthed forms such as cooking pots and cremation urns dominating as in the prehistoric period.[16] Reintroduction of the wheel in the seventh to twelfth centuries by later Saxons and Normans set the stage for the jug's revival in the Middle Ages, although the form was less common than the baluster-shaped drinking vessel known to British ceramics historians as a jug.[17] The chief alcoholic beverage for ordinary medieval folk was beer, brewed locally and drunk as fresh as possible, hence little need to store and transport it. The upper class drank wine, but England's climate was not conducive to viticulture and most wine was imported in containers also made on the Continent.

Some British earthenware jugs of the Early Modern period were a domestic answer to imported German stoneware, with London

Two-tone Scots jug made in Glasgow for an Inverness hotel, late 1800s. Stoneware, Bristol glaze with partial iron wash. H. 12". Bristol glaze contains feldspar, whiting as a flux, and zinc oxide a whitener and opacifier; it was developed in 1835 and adopted in the United States, including parts of the South, in the late 1800s. Photographed at a restaurant in Scotland.

delftware potters of the 1620s–1670s producing tin-glazed examples inscribed "sack," "claret," and "Renish [*sic*] wine," potables now affordable to a growing middle class (plate 9).[18] Country potters continued to make lead-glazed earthenware jugs through the nineteenth century along with other "coarsewares" still needed for storing and processing food and drink.[19] The earliest British stoneware (1640s–1670s), by German immigrants and then John Dwight in the London area, included Rhenish-style jugs, while salt- and later Bristol-glazed stoneware jugs continued to be made in England and Scotland through the nineteenth century, finally mass-produced in urban factories.[20]

The Jug Comes to America

Documentation for the colonial period, especially the first century of settlement, is too sparse for us to know what role jugs played in early American life. Again, semantics contribute to the problem, for early written references to jugs would have carried over the English meaning as a wide-mouthed drinking vessel. By the early nineteenth century, however, the American meaning of the word was established.[21]

The chief Old World influences on Euro-American ceramics were England and Germany, whose immigrant potters transplanted earthenware and stoneware traditions in the seventeenth and eighteenth centuries. England provided precedents for the colonial redware (earthenware) of New England and the Tidewater South, while that of the Mid-Atlantic exhibits a mix of British and German ideas.[22] Pioneer scholar of New England ceramics Lura Woodside Watkins declared, "Jugs of redware were, I believe, not so common in the eighteenth century as in the years that followed."[23] Surviving American earthenware jugs of the eighteenth to early nineteenth centuries are ovoid or turnip-shaped. Decoration normally was limited to incised circumferal lines (tooling) and use of a metallic oxide (copper or manganese) to color the lead glaze green or brown-black. As for regional distinctions, handle placement often is lower on Mid-Atlantic and southern examples, with the upper

STONE WARE,

FOR SALE BY

CLARKSON CROLIUS,

At his Manufactory, No. 4, Cross-street, back of the City Goal and New City Hall,
and opposite the Manhattan Wells, at the following prices:

				Wholesale Per Dozen.			Retail Per Piece	
				L.	*s.*	*d.*	*s.*	*d.*
Pots,	Jugs,	Strait and bellied Jars of 4 galls.	-	3	4	0	7	0
Do	do	do 3 1-2 do	-	2	16	0	6	0
Do	do	do 3 do	-	2	10	0	5	6
Do	do	do 2 1-2 do	-	1	18	0	4	0
Do	do	do 2 do	-	1	12	0	3	6
Do	do	do 1 1-2 do	-	1	6	0	3	0
Do	do	do 1 do	-	1	2	0	2	6
Do	do	do 1-2 do	-	0	14	0	1	6
Do	do	do 1-4 do	-	0	9	0	1	0
Do	do	do 1-8 do	-	0	5	0	0	9

			L.	*s.*	*d.*	*s.*	*d.*
PITCHERS of 3	gallons	-	2	16	0	6	6
Do	2 1-2 do	-	2	4	0	5	0
Do	2 do	-	1	18	0	4	0
Do	1 1-2 do	-	1	12	0	3	6
Do	1 do	-	1	6	0	2	9
Do	1-2 do	-	0	16	0	1	9
Do	1-4 do	-	0	9	0	1	0
Quart mugs	- -	-	0	9	0	1	0
Pint do	- -	-	0	5	0	0	8
Oyster pots	- -		0	8	0	1	0
Spout do	- -	-	0	18	0	1	9
Chamber do	-	-	0	16	0	1	9

Kegs from 1 pint to 10 gallons
Churns from 1 to 10 do
Fountain and common Ink Stands equal to glass.

New-York, March 28, 1809.

Price list of Manhattan stoneware potter Clarkson Crolius, 1809. Such early illustrations of jugs, associated with the word, help establish when the American meaning came about. Courtesy, American Antiquarian Society.

Jug attributed to Abner Landrum's Pottersville Stoneware Manufactory, Edgefield District, South Carolina, 1821. Alkaline-glazed stoneware with incised date. H. 14¼". The double-collared neck of this earliest dated Edgefield jug became the norm there. Ex-collection of Tony and Marie Shank; courtesy, McKissick Museum, University of South Carolina.

end applied to the jug's shoulder or shoulder-neck juncture, while the upper handle terminal on New England examples typically was attached to the neck at or near the mouth (plate 10).[24] This regional handle placement also applies (with exceptions, of course) to American stoneware jugs.

Salt-glazed stoneware technology was introduced to the East Coast in the early eighteenth century from both Germany and England.[25] Many of the oldest surviving American stoneware jugs have a reeded or cordoned (tooled) neck, a feature carried over from Germany and England; those in the Germanic tradition have cobalt blue (less commonly, manganese purple) brushed within an incised design, around handle terminals, and highlighting a stamped maker's mark (plate 11), while a partial iron-oxide dip created a two-tone effect for those in the English tradition.[26] Stoneware jugs of the antebellum South, both salt- and alkaline-glazed, often have a pronounced lip; in Edgefield District, South Carolina, a collar was thrown around the middle of the neck as well.[27] These early neck and lip treatments apparently served both as a design element and an aid in securing a stopper with a cord or wire.

Historians of American ceramics have noted a general shift in

Jugs illustrating the general shift from curved to straight sides. Salt-glazed stoneware. *Left*: Nicholas Fox, Chatham County, North Carolina, ca. 1840. Approx. H. 8". *Center*: Luther Funkhouser (retailer), Strasburg, Virginia, 1890s. *Right*: Peter Hermann, Baltimore, Maryland, 1890s. Ex-collection of Charles G. Zug III.

Continuity in jug shape over time at Mossy Creek, Georgia. Alkaline-glazed stoneware. Left: David Dorsey, ca. 1850. "Flint" subtype of lime glaze. H. 9¼". Private collection. Center: Cheever Meaders, ca. 1950. Flint glaze. H. 9¾". Right: Lanier Meaders, 1972. Ash glaze. H. 9¾". The ovoid Meaders jugs (author's collection) could be mistaken for antebellum ones except for lack of a lip.

Lanier Meaders unloading ash-glazed "shoulder" jugs from his "tunnel" kiln, Mossy Creek, Georgia, 1974. Both he and his father, Cheever, made such cylindrical jugs alongside the earlier ovoid shape.

the shape of stoneware jugs from sensuous to severe that began in the 1860s.[28] Bulbous and ovoid jugs tended to give way to those with straighter sides, culminating in the development of a distinctly American type, the cylindrical "shouldered" or "stacker" jug with a shoulder ledge to support a production collar so that jugs could be stacked in a column to make efficient use of kiln height.[29] This shift to less curvaceous sides sacrificed graceful proportions for greater volume, making the clay jug more competitive with factory-made glass and metal containers. The change also may reflect a decline in throwing skills as pottery manufacture became more industrialized. However, in conservative, family-run shops like those of the rural South, earlier styles sometimes were maintained alongside later ones; for example, Cheever and Lanier Meaders made both ovoid and cylindrical jugs in the mid- and late twentieth century.

Eddie Averett's Crawford County, Georgia, "groundhog" kiln, 1890s, with unloaded whiskey jugs (ranging in shape from squatty "beehive" to ovoid and cylindrical) ready for sale to local moonshiners or licensed distillers in nearby Macon. Courtesy, Georgia Geologic Survey; in John A. Burrison, *Brothers in Clay*, University of Georgia Press, 1983.

Focus on the South: Form Follows Functions

The generic jugs described so far might have been used to hold any liquid, depending on the owners' needs. Since the form's origins, however, the emphasis has been on fermented or distilled drink. In the United States especially, jugs with a capacity of a quart to two gallons normally were meant for rum or whiskey, sometimes being made to order for distillers. In the eighteenth century, the medieval technology for converting grain to whiskey was brought from Ireland and Scotland to Appalachia (via Pennsylvania) and was adapted to the New World grain, maize, for moonshine and bourbon, eventually spreading to the lowland South.[30] As Annie Becham Long, who was born into one middle Georgia "clay clan" and married into another, put it, "Half the people in our part of Crawford County were making jugs and the other half were making liquor to put in 'em."[31]

The form's importance in the South is underscored by the frequent identification of potters as "jug makers" in the federal censuses, the nickname "Jug" for several potters,[32] and the place-name "Jugtown" for at least six pottery-making communities.[33] Southern potters specializing in whiskey jugs saw their trade decline in the early 1900s with Prohibition and the availability of affordable glass and metal containers. Long before that, though, the basic jug had been modified to serve a number of other, more specialized, needs.

Building on the Form: Big Jugs, Squatty Jugs, Multineck Jugs, Water Jugs

It required no great leap of imagination for American potters to increase jug size to accommodate other uses, just the skill and strength to throw such "bigwares." A capacity of five gallons was the upper limit of most potters' normal range, but jugs as large as twenty gallons are known.[34] Those of four and more gallons often had a second loop handle on the other side of the neck, creating a graceful, amphora-like symmetry while making them easier for two people to lift and carry when full. There were northern English precedents for such large, two-handled jugs,[35] but the idea could have arisen independently in response to New World circumstances.

Four-gallon, two-handled jug from vicinity of Liverpool, England, ca. 1830, suggesting possible prototypes for southern syrup jugs. Brown salt-glazed stoneware. H. 16½". Photographed at an antiques shop in England.

Four-gallon syrup jug attributed to Pottersville Stoneware Manufactory, Edgefield District, South Carolina, late 1830s. Alkaline-glazed stoneware. H. 16½". Author's collection.

One use for big jugs in the United States was as a water cooler or cistern before indoor plumbing; these typically had a spigot hole in the lower wall. Decorated examples may also have been used in taverns as beer, wine, or punch dispensers; nonporous stoneware would have been more sanitary (easier to clean) than wooden kegs.[36] As explained in chapter two, until the early 1900s sugar was an expensive commodity in the South; for ordinary folk cane syrup was the chief sweetening, making syrup jugs of three or more gallons a mainstay of the southern stoneware repertoire.[37] Kept in the kitchen or nearby smokehouse, the syrup would be handy for cooking or table use. Some potters widened the mouth to facilitate pouring the thick liquid, but this required the owner to fabricate a wooden plug, as the usual corncob stopper would not have made a tight fit.

Besides increasing its size, another approach to adapting the basic form to specialized uses was to compress it, which created a jug with a low center of gravity. Southern potters made squatty "buggy jugs" (proportionately, the top half or third of a regular jug), designed to keep that special stock of "antifreeze" from tipping over on a bumpy buggy or wagon ride. Localized to north Georgia and North Carolina's Catawba Valley, alkaline-glazed "flower jugs" for displaying cut blossoms elaborated the basic jug form with the addition of necks (usually four, separately thrown "off the hump") around the central one.[38] Made as presentation pieces—an inscribed Georgia mountain

Buggy jug attributed to Billy Bryant, Crawford County, Georgia, late 1800s, stamped "BB" on handle top, inscribed "J. E. Bryant." Alkaline-glazed stoneware. H. 5¼". Collection of Museum of Southern Stoneware at River Market Antique Mall, Columbus, Georgia.

Flower jug, James A. Jones, Young Cane, Georgia, 1870s, signed by maker, inscribed "Miss L. A. Wilborn." Alkaline-glazed stoneware. H. 9". A previous owner's oral history claims that the five spouts of this mountain "wedding jug" were meant for the minister, bride, groom, best man, and maid of honor to drink from at the ceremony. Author's collection; in Burrison, *Brothers in Clay.*

example has an oral history as a "wedding jug"—in the mid-to-late 1800s and revived by folk potters a century later, they are related to English and Dutch quintals that were, in turn, based on a vase type introduced to Europe from Persia along with the tulip in the 1600s. The Old World examples, however, lack the loop handle that helps to define a jug.

Two types of water, or "harvest," jugs are known in the United

Ring jug, William J. Gordy, Cartersville, Georgia, 1991. Stoneware with "Mountain Gold" glaze. H. 12¾" (with stopper). Gordy's early training was rooted in Georgia's Jugtown, where ring jugs are said to have been used as canteens by Confederate troops in the Civil War. Author's collection.

States, each with different Old World roots. Although occasionally made in the North, their concentration in the South can be attributed to the region's agrarian economy and warm climate; hours of field work in the heat of the day could produce a powerful thirst. Unlike the jug variations discussed above, these designs involve major alteration of the basic form. The ring jug is a European type known in ancient Greece, but its inspiration in America most likely was the German stoneware tradition.[39] Its wheel-thrown production is something of a potter's "secret": starting with a clay disk, the potter scoops out the center with a flat tool called a rib, leaving a solid ring. A trough is created by pulling up the outer and inner edges, which are then curved toward each other and joined.[40] After this hollow ring has been cut off the wheel and has dried to leather hard, the flat side that lay on the wheel's surface is trimmed to the round and a separately thrown neck is attached over a hole cut in the arch. It is at this stage that the potter has the option of creating a jug or a bottle; if the former, one or two loop handles and a thrown or solid-block base are added.

The ring jug's donut shape allowed it to lie flat for easier transport, with the center hole placed on a saddle horn, the hame knob of a plow animal's collar, or the lower branch of a tree; in some cases this opening is large enough to insert an arm for carrying on the shoulder. Marie Rogers of Jugtown, Georgia, calls them "Confederate" jugs, having heard from her husband, Horace (from whom she learned to make them), and his father, Rufus, that they were used as canteens by Rebel soldiers in the Civil War.[41] Georgia-born Javan Brown glazed his "old-time" ring jugs on one side only; that side faced out so that the sun bounced off the shiny glaze, the porous unglazed side allowing limited evaporation of the water to keep it cool.

A second type of water jug is the "monkey" jug, perhaps getting its name from an Afro-Caribbean term for thirst. It is distinguished by a stirrup handle across the top and two tubular, canted (off-center and angled) spouts. The separately thrown spouts are located

Monkey jug, central North Carolina, ca. 1860. Salt-glazed stoneware with melted-glass decoration and corncob stoppers. H. 12". Oral history claims that a slave drank from one spout and his master from the other. Private collection.

either below the handle terminals in the plane of the handle or on opposite sides of it. This form, also traceable to ancient Greece,[42] is concentrated in Africa and Mediterranean Europe; called a *botijo* in Spain, it is almost a national symbol there, with three museums devoted to its seemingly infinite variety in shape, glaze, and ornamentation.[43] Imports from Europe may have inspired nineteenth-century monkey jugs made in the northern United States; in the South, where the form was made by slave potters, a West African origin is more likely.[44]

Craft into Art: Making Faces on Jugs

Since they work in such a malleable medium day in and day out, it is not surprising that potters the world over have seen their clay as a kind of mirror and accepted its challenge to model a human likeness on a pot, pushing utilitarian craft into plastic art. This anthropomorphizing impulse is stronger in some clay-working societies than others; in England, for example, it surfaced several times, first with Romano-British burial urns, then medieval "face-on-front jugs," and finally Toby "jugs" of late-eighteenth-century Staffordshire that initiated an industrial tradition of slip-cast character mugs continuing to this day.[45] It is my belief, though, that England was not the source for the South's face-jug traditions.

In reviewing what is known of those traditions, three points should be made by way of introduction. First, although many humanoid vessels made in the United States are indeed jugs, some take the form of pitchers, cups, jars, and bottles. Second, not all depict just faces or heads; some are full figures. Third, Native Americans of the South made humanoid effigy pots during the Mississippian era (A.D. 800–1540), too early to have influenced the southern face jugs discussed here.[46]

As with other adaptations of the jug form in the United States, face vessels—as both a historical and living tradition—have been concentrated in the South. However, the oldest known Euro-American examples are from the early-nineteenth-century Philadelphia workshop of Henry Remmey Jr., whose great-grandfather, stoneware potter John Remmey, immigrated to Manhattan from the Rhineland in the 1730s. John would have been familiar with the gray-beard jugs still being made in Germany, and if he made them in New York and passed the concept to his descendants, then Remmey face vessels are Americanizations of the German tradition (plate 12).[47]

A substantial group of early southern face vessels was made between 1863 and 1865 by enslaved African American potters at Colonel Thomas Davies's Palmetto Fire Brick Works at Bath, in the old Edgefield District of South Carolina.[48] The pieces are distinguished by bulging eyes and bared teeth of kaolin inset into the stoneware clay body, and the iron-rich mineral that darkened the alkaline glaze on some, along with the wax resist used to keep the glaze off the white eyes and teeth to maximize contrast, leave little doubt that they were meant to represent their makers' race. Pioneer ceramics historian Edwin AtLee Barber, after corresponding with Davies, was the first to discuss them in print in 1909: "These curious objects . . . possess considerable interest as representing an art of the Southern negroes. . . . The modeling reveals a trace of aboriginal art as formerly practiced by their ancestors in the Dark Continent."[49] Nothing was said, however, of the makers' motivations. Sixty years later, Yale University art historian Robert Farris Thompson

Face jugs attributed to slave potters at Thomas Davies's Palmetto Fire Brick Works, Bath, South Carolina, early 1860s. Alkaline-glazed stoneware with kaolin eyes and teeth. Ex-collection of Tony and Marie Shank.

An Aesthetic Darkey, in a series of stereoscopic cards by photographer J. A. Palmer of Aiken, South Carolina, 1882. This earliest known image of a southern face jug has a "monkey" form and was likely made by a local (Edgefield District) African American potter. Courtesy, J. Garrison Stradling.

advanced Barber's suggestion of African origins, arguing that later white face-jug makers such as Cheever Meaders appropriated the "Afro-Carolinian" tradition.[50]

If American face jugs were not invented independently and had Old World roots, then I see Africa and Germany as the two most likely possibilities. Anthropomorphic clay vessels were indeed made in West Africa, perhaps early enough for the slave era. The Yungur of Nigeria, for example, made portrait pots called *wiiso* to honor ancestral spirits at shrines,[51] and the Mambila of Cameroon made similar figural vessels. The angry expressions of some Afro-Carolinian face vessels, which could be interpreted as a nonverbal protest against enslavement, and a few tantalizing hints that these vessels may have been used in magico-religious or mortuary practices, at least suggest that they had a meaning distinct from the face jugs made by whites. This begs the question of whether white potters in the South made face vessels as early as the slave-made ones.

Monkey-form face jug, Thomas Chandler (stamped "CHANDLER/MAKER"), Edgefield District, South Carolina, ca. 1850. Alkaline-glazed stoneware. H. 11½". Its happy countenance is in contrast to angry ones of a decade later by slave potters in the same area. Private collection; courtesy, McKissick Museum, University of South Carolina.

Face jugs and wheel-thrown "wig stand," Lanier Meaders, Mossy Creek, Georgia, 1969–1978, displaying the maker's sculptural skill and creativity. Alkaline-glazed stoneware. The devil jack-o'-lantern jug is 9¾" H. Author's collection; in Burrison, *Brothers in Clay*.

Fifth-generation potter Bobby Ferguson of Gillsville, Georgia, with one of his face jugs in 2004, a year before his death. An ancestor may have introduced face jugs to north Georgia from antebellum Edgefield District, South Carolina.

In 1995, a piece in a private collection surfaced that answers that question. An ash-glazed, happy-faced jug with the monkey form, it is stamped "CHANDLER MAKER," the mark of Thomas Chandler, a white potter who worked in Edgefield District from 1838 to 1852.[52] Dating to about 1850, it preceded the slave-made face vessels from the Davies workshop by a decade. Before moving to South Carolina, Virginia-born Chandler is thought to have worked as a potter in New York State; it is remotely possible that in his northern sojourn he learned of face vessels from one of the Remmeys.[53] Did Chandler then introduce the concept to Edgefield slave potters, or were they working in a separate, perhaps African-based, tradition? At any rate, we now know that the face jugs of Cheever and Lanier Meaders were part of a continuous Anglo-southern tradition, but whether ultimately inspired by slave-made examples, as Thompson suggests, may never be learned.

Conclusion: The Jug Today

Jugs are still indispensable for keeping liquids, from bleach to milk and larger volumes of wine. Now, though, they rarely are made of clay, as glass and plastic containers are less expensive to produce, the latter having the further advantage of being less breakable. In recent years, a few whiskey companies have used mold-made clay jugs to reinforce the old-fashioned image of their product, and school-trained potters may occasionally throw a jug to show that they are not embarrassed to make a useful form despite the current trend of studio pottery as Art.[54]

In the 1980s and 1990s, it seemed as though every potter in the South, folk and otherwise, was trying his or her hand at face jugs, by then a regional art icon for which Lanier Meaders deserves much of the credit.[55] Today, however, the handcrafting of jugs, with or without faces, is largely the prerogative of a small number of traditionally trained potters, and the domain of a form that once dominated utilitarian American ceramics has shrunk to North Carolina, Alabama, and Georgia (plate 13). The market has become one of collectors and home decorators, and the everyday uses of these fluid vessels have all but dried up.

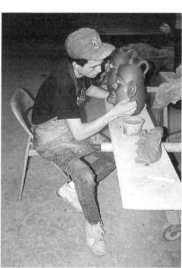

Sixth-generation potter Matthew Hewell sculpting face jugs, Gillsville, Georgia, 1992. Lanier Meaders's success influenced Matthew's father, Chester, to revive the Hewell face-jug tradition.

5. Georgia on My Mind

A Place-Based Case Study[1]

An' hell's broke loose,
Hell's broke loose,
Hell's broke loose in Georgia!
—Stephen Vincent Benét, "The Mountain Whippoorwill"[2]

Mention *Georgia folklore* to the oldest living generation of Georgians, and the first thing likely to come to their minds is the African American Brer Rabbit folktales popularized by author Joel Chandler Harris through his storytelling character, Uncle Remus. To later generations the phrase may conjure up images of mountain life from the Foxfire publications, or even exotic festivals and ethnic foods introduced by recent immigrants. Georgia folklore is, in fact, all these things, and much more. In this chapter I focus on the southern state I know best and examine how Georgia (and by implication, any particular state) is characteristic of the region as a whole while at the same time producing its own unique traditions.

What's Special about Georgia Folklife?

Located in the center of the lower Southeast, Georgia is surrounded by the five other states of this subregion. Since folklore is culture-based and seldom respects artificial political boundaries, we would expect Georgians to practice many of the same traditions as residents of adjoining states; for example, folklife on the Alabama side of the lower Chattahoochee River is no different from that of the

A Sacred Harp all-day singing (Terry Wootten, leading) at Holly Springs Primitive Baptist Church, Bremen, Georgia, 2006. In this musical tradition of Georgia origin, singers of the four harmony parts arrange themselves in a "hollow square." Photo by Matt Hinton.

Georgia side.[3] At the same time, Georgia's particular geographic situation and economic, political, and settlement history could not fail to have influenced its folk culture.

The answer to the question posed above, then, is not a simple one. There are uniquely Georgian traditions, but much of our folk culture shares in a larger regional heritage. The Sacred Harp shape-note singing mentioned in chapter two, for example, was created by Georgians, but belongs to the larger tradition of white spirituals and has spread beyond Georgia. Georgia folk pottery participates in a larger regional complex (alkaline stoneware glazes, rectangular crossdraft kilns), yet differs from the pottery of adjoining states. In what way is it different? There were nine pottery centers here, each having developed its own stylistic features; when these local "schools" are seen together, they make up a picture different from that of neighboring states. In other words, there is no statewide, recognizably Georgian ceramic tradition, no "typical" piece of Georgia folk pottery; but in the sum of its parts, at least, Georgia's ceramic heritage is special.[4]

Georgia's Frontier Folklife

The last of America's thirteen colonies, Georgia saw substantial settlement directly from the Old World only in its first three decades, mainly along the coast and lower Savannah River corridor. To a large extent, then, the state's early folk culture arose within the agrarian society of Virginia and the Carolinas and was carried into Georgia's backcountry by westward migration in the late 1700s and early 1800s. Many of these new Georgians were therefore seasoned southerners two or three generations removed from their Old World ancestors. This partially explains why a strong—largely Germanic—decorative impulse in the folk arts of Virginia and the Carolinas is absent for Georgia, yielding to a more utilitarian, frontier-generated, aesthetic in our material culture.

Many Georgia folk traditions tied to the frontier lifestyle became extinct by the twentieth century and can only be reconstructed through historical documents and semifictional accounts in nineteenth-century literature. For example, humorists Augustus Baldwin Longstreet (in *Georgia Scenes*, published in 1835 but describing the town of Augusta in 1798) and Charles H. Smith (creator of Bill Arp, a rustic character so popular among readers that a town in Douglas County was named for him) both portrayed a folk sport embodying the rough-and-tumble spirit of the southern frontier, the gander pulling. A vague echo of medieval jousting tournaments, contestants galloped their horses along a track while trying to yank the greased head off a live male goose suspended by the feet from above; the victor was awarded the collected entrance fees. In 1847, Smith witnessed one such event in northwest Georgia won by the real-life model for his character:

As Bill's turn came again the crowd ejaculated: "Now, watch him boys." "Can't he ride, though?" "See how he sots on his critter." "Blamed if he ain't tarred to his nag." . . . "He's a-gwine to carry that gander's head a half a mile before he stops." "Farewell, goose, I'll preach your funeral."

And sure enough, Bill got the right grip this time and in a trice had given the neck a double and something had to break as the pole and the line swiftly followed his motion. For a moment it seemed uncertain what would break . . . as Bill's nag went on at full speed. For a little while the quivering, headless body swung backwards and forwards and was then at rest. Then came the shouts and wild hurrah. . . .

These rough, rude people were the original Georgia crackers. . . . Their class is fast disappearing from our midst. Civilization has encroached upon them, and now their children and their children's children have assimilated with a higher grade of humanity.[5]

A *Gander-Pull*. Frederic Remington's oil painting of 1894 depicts this region-wide, fron-tier-era folk sport in West Virginia; the sport is documented for Georgia as early as 1798. Private collection.

Bloodthirsty though they were, gander pullings (which apparently last occurred in Georgia in the late 1860s) were no more cruel than the present-day southern traditions of cock and dog fighting.

Rural Georgia's dispersed settlement made community "workings" especially welcome. Neighbors reciprocally helped each other with agricultural chores that could overwhelm a single family. Especially popular were log rollings, in which teams of men carried away felled trees to clear new ground for planting, and corn shuckings, in which the shucks (*husks* to Yankees) were stripped from a large pile of harvested corn; African Americans elaborated the latter into an art form with competition between two teams led by "generals," call-and-response work songs, and wrestling matches.[6] Such gatherings often included a square dance and feast prepared by the women (who also participated in a "quiltin'" at the host house), and thus had a social as well as practical function.

A corn shucking on the London farm near Dahlonega, Georgia, ca. 1890. Courtesy, Georgia Archives, Vanishing Georgia Collection, Lum-142; in John A. Burrison, *Shaping Traditions*, University of Georgia Press, 2000.

In some cases these customary, frontier-generated get-togethers continued into the early twentieth century, as recalled by Georgia mountain ballad singer Mrs. Lillie West:

They'd have corn shuckings. Enough women would stay at the [host] house to cook dinner, and everybody else shucked corn, you know. And to make them work harder, they'd have a little race or contest. Mixed in with the white corn were some red ears—just solid red—and some was streaked, they called that strawberry. Well, the strawberry counted so many points, and the solid red was double, you know. We'd keep count of how many we found before the day was over; some little old something was the prize.

Then at night, we'd have a candy pulling for pastime, make molasses taffy. They'd be about fifteen or twenty of the neighbors come in, young folks. Two of us usually went out to the kitchen to get ready; but before, we'd get Mother's consent, promise her the kitchen would be cleaned up just like we found it. We'd just boil a big pot full of surp [sorghum syrup], enough for every couple: if there was six, we'd make enough for six couples to have a handful to pull. Well, you'd be on one side and me on the other, and to get it started you catch here and I catch over there and we'd pull it in strings. Keep doing that and it'd get harder and turn white. Sometimes we got to cutting-up and acting crazy; they'd take a string of that candy and wrap it around one of 'em's neck [laughs]. But now, Dad and Mother didn't have to know about that!

My uncle liked to got his house burned at a log rolling. They wanted to have a party that night, something unusual that he didn't agree with. So he told them they could—if they quilted so many quilts. He thought it was impossible, they couldn't do it. But they was going to try, anyhow. The boys was in there helping the girls. When you card that cotton up, fluff it up into batting [the middle layer, or stuffing], it burns almost like powder when it's dry. Well, they was putting that cotton on [the lining], and one of them turned a kerosene lamp over on it, set it afire. And boy, the house liked to went with it. But the men was coming in from the log rolling and they managed to put it out. But they didn't get that extra quilt quilted, so they didn't have the party that night. Oh, those quilting bees were something when boys would get to helping the girls quilt. There was some of the messiest quilting you ever heard tell of![7]

Georgia's Last Old-Time Ballad Singer?

Lillie Etta Mulkey West (1888–1980) was a classic Appalachian ballad singer of the sort I'd studied in my college folklore classes and hoped to find in Georgia. As a singer, quilter, and family herbal doctor (that lore inherited from her grandfather), she was a true traditionalist, but something in her genes or upbringing (perhaps that independent spirit said to be a trait of mountain folk) made her unconventional, too: she read the *New York Times* under a huge magnifying glass, didn't share many of her neighbors' and kinfolks' superstitions (but enjoyed talking about them), and reared some very progressive offspring. Like potter Lanier Meaders and other exemplary practitioners of folklore I've known, she had one foot in the past but the other firmly planted in the modern world.

The eighth of twelve siblings, Lillie grew up on a 160-acre farm in the mountains of Gilmer County, in a way of life little changed from the days of her pioneer ancestors. Her father, Asberry Kimsey ("Kim") Mulkey, operated a sorghum syrup mill and made the family's furniture, while her mother, Talitha Prudence Sparks, made the clothes and the soap to wash them. Drying, pickling, or smoking their homegrown food meant that there was little need to shop in town; Lillie was sixteen before she saw the county seat, Ellijay. In 1905 she married James Oliver West, and they raised a family of nine in Devil's Hollow at the foot of Burnt Mountain. One of those children, Don, later recalled that hardscrabble life: "Earliest memories are woven around the struggles of my Dad and Mother to dig a living from our little mountain farm."

Around 1920, the family moved to the lowlands of Cobb County to sharecrop cotton and work in the textile mills for a "better living." But the depression years took their toll, and Lillie's husband died in 1939. As their son Don wrote, "Dad died young—toil and hunger, too much work, and too little of the right kind of food. . . ." In 1948,

Ballad singer Lillie West at her general store in Union County, Georgia, 1968.

with her six surviving children grown, Lillie moved to Lower Young Cane outside Blairsville (her mother's hometown) in Union County and opened a tiny general store, where neighbors and fishermen on nearby Nottely Lake would stop by to chat and buy soft drinks, canned goods, or tobacco. She occupied herself there with the songs learned from her family back in Gilmer County. When a customer commented that she "must be mighty happy to sing so much," her response was, "I sing to keep from crying."

Lillie's granddaughter Hedy West (daughter of Don, himself a "red clay poet," labor activist, and founder of the Appalachian South Folklife Center at Pipestem, West Virginia) was a prominent figure in the 1960s folksong revival after learning many songs from Lillie and Lillie's brother Gus. Lillie could play the banjo and guitar, but was at her best singing unaccompanied in the "high, lonesome" mountain way. On my visits to her store in Union County, her singing voice was well past its prime (she was eighty), yet never failed to send a shiver up my spine.

What follows is a small sample of Lillie's active repertoire, ballads she remembered and continued to sing later in life. Since they represent just a portion of her former storehouse, any analysis of what they might reveal about her can only be tentative. Almost a third of her recorded songs are of British Isles origin, one of them a Child ballad ("The Little Old Man That Lived Out West"), the others derived from later broadside tradition. That three of her ballads are from the American West should come as no surprise, as some singing southerners brought them home after leaving to seek work or follow their wanderlust. Viewed as a group, the texts of Lillie's songs show an interesting tension between a jaundiced view of romance/ marriage on the one hand and Victorian sentimentality/conventional morality on the other. What makes this collection especially valuable is her comments about the function and meaning of the songs and music in her life.[8]

Memories of Music Making

Well, on Saturday nights, people used to visit each other, you know, and have a lot of fun. We'd gather maybe ten, twelve, fifteen, there at my father's house, sit around and sing sacred songs. Father loved them dearly; he'd ask us to sing some old [religious] songs he loved. Well, it didn't take but about one to get him to sleep; then we carried on and sing just anything we happened to think of! We had music with it too; I had one brother, he was tops on the violin, and I played the guitar, and my other brother played the banjer.

But my father [had been] bitterly opposed to a violin in the home. He thought it was the most sinful something; he was raised that way, you know. Well, my oldest brother [Charlie] brought [a fiddle] in there; but he couldn't carry a tune on it far enough to bury it! So he left it, and my second brother [Gus], he got to fool around with it, and he learned to play it. Why, he was good; but he had to dodge and hide it. My oldest brother kept it locked up when Dad was around. He had him a little desk that he'd built, a nice little thing, and he put a lock on it and kept the fiddle there. Dad was a kind-hearted man, always let us have our way in things that was all right; but he was very strict, and in that case we was afraid to tell him.

But Dad was on the grand jury once and he had to go to Ellijay, and it'd usually take the biggest part of a week when he'd go down there, you know. He'd go on Monday and stay 'til usually Friday. Well, we always had a ball when he was gone. My brother played that old fiddle for a fare-you-well! Mother—she was a very sweet person, she just had different ideas from what he [Lillie's father] did—didn't see any harm in it. It was just fun to us, and she never did mention it to Dad.

And one night—it was a Tuesday night, I believe—we was just a-having a grand time, we was a-singing. Oh, we'd been on some of the awfullest songs you ever heard, and [Gus]'d play one [on the fiddle], and we'd each get us a song and sing like that, you know. And so, we was having a time. But it just so happened, he started on "The Uncloudy Day." He was playing that [sings]:

O they tell me of a home far beyond the skies,
O they tell me of a land far away;
O they tell me of a home where no storm clouds rise,
O, they tell me of an uncloudy day.

Well, just as we finished that up, Dad cleared his throat out at the gate. And of all the skedaddling you ever saw, it was done! [Gus] got that fiddle, slid it under the bed or somewhere, and we was just a-setting there just as meek as mice. But [Dad] was out far enough, we didn't think he'd caught anything. Well, he come in. He said, "You boys feed the horses?"

And they said, "Yeah, we fed them."

And Mother said, "What in the world you come home this time of the week?" Said, "I wasn't looking for you 'til Friday."

He said, "The judge got sick, had to adjourn court." And said, "You got anything cooked?"

And of course, we jumped up just as smart as you ever saw and fixed him something to eat. We wasn't sure what he knew. So we got his supper, and he eat and eat. It was pretty cool, and he warmed his feet a little while, setting there by the fire. Finally he said, "When I got up to the gate a while ago," said, "I heard some kind of music;

sound like I heard somebody singing. Does anybody know anything about it?"

Well, of course Mother felt guilty, and she knew she was going to have to tell him. She said, "Oh, it was the children."

Well, he said, "What was that you was singing?"

And I said, "Hit was 'The Uncloudy Day.'"

He said, "Where was that music coming from?" Well, we had to tell him! He said, "Get that thing, let me see it!"

Well, they brought the fiddle in, you know; so Dad looked at it, turned it around a little while (he never could play anything). He said, "That was the prettiest music I ever heard. I'm going to bed; sing a few of them songs and I believe I can go to sleep."

Well, you know, we didn't get through with "The Uncloudy Day" 'til he was snoring and making a bigger noise than we was!

From then on, it made no difference what kind of foolish songs we sang; every night we had that pleasure of singing him to sleep, then we'd carry on anything we wanted to afterward. Oh, you don't know how we enjoyed it. Dad told us he'd always thought it was bad business to have a fiddle around, and he just had the mistaken idea that nothing but dance music could be carried on on it, but he learned better. He never would object to it anymore when they'd play a little old jig like "Black-Eyed Susie" and things like that. Why, it was kinda amusing to him; he thought my brother could make the fiddle do anything he wanted to. On Saturday nights, when the neighbors would come in, we'd have that, and finally my older brother bought me a guitar, and I had to learn on it, and one of them learned the banjer. Lord, we had a string band, almost![9]

A Woman's Confession (Frankie Silver)

I had an uncle—my dad's youngest brother—he could sing; used to enjoy singing more than anything. And I can remember a song that he sung. I'd just give anything if you could hear him sing that; he had the purtiest voice I ever heard. I was about five years old first time I heard him sing this, and I wasn't satisfied 'til I learned it—it'd just give me the creeps, but I did love to hear it. He worked in

North Carolina once (I don't remember what kind of work he was doing) and he learned this song and he also heard this story there. I read later that she [Frankie Silver] was the only woman ever hanged in the state of North Carolina.

This happened on Toe River. This girl, she was from the lowlands, and she went up there [to the mountains] and fell in love with this John Silvers. They got married. She was a teacher, and she tried to teach him to read and write, and she read a lot to him. Well, they had one child, and when this child was about two years old she went back to the lowlands to visit her folks, and some of them talked to her about how she'd married beneath herself, you know: she'd injured herself by marrying this poor mountain man. And the more she studied about it, the worse she hated the deed she had done. And she couldn't find no remedy for it, only just to get rid of him.

Well, just before Christmas, he was going hunting for a bear, getting the Christmas meat (that was the habit of that section in North Carolina, everyone did that). He was going with a friend that lived over the mountain. So he worked all day chopping down a big hickory tree and splitting it up for wood to last her and keep her and the baby warm while he was gone on the hunting trip. Well, that night when bedtime came, he lay down on the floor in front of the fire, put his coonskin cap on a cedar block for a pillow. He was lying there with the baby on his chest, told her to go ahead to bed. He said, "I won't go to bed; I'll just lie here and rest awhile, so when I go on the hunt I won't have to disturb you."

Well, she had everything ready. She went to bed and listened 'til she knew he was asleep. She had the ax hidden in the house, and she got up and bashed him in the head with it. When she hit him he rared up, and she jumped back in the bed and covered up her head and ears. When she was sure he was dead, she started cutting that body up, burning it piece by piece, used all of that pile of wood. Daylight was a-coming too quick for her, so she pried up a board in the cabin floor and put part of it—some of the bones—under there, and the other she carried out on the river and hid in the rock crevices. Then she went back and cleaned out the fireplace and mopped the floor, tried to get all the evidence that she could out of sight.

And as soon as daylight come, she took the baby and went over to his father's and told them that she was worried about him, felt like something was going to happen to him. His mother said, "Now, you know John, he's sure-footed, he's very careful." And said, "I'll guarantee he don't come back until he gets meat; you got nothing to worry about."

Well, she just kept on and on until she got his father worried. He said, "You're so worried, you got me stirred up." And says, "I'll just walk over the mountain and see about him." Going over to Young's, the man he was going hunting with. And she [Frankie] said she'd go along. Well, they got over there, and this fellow Young hadn't seen John. And right off she started accusing him of doing him some bodily harm. She liked to give herself away there. But Young said, "Come on, I know John as well as any of you"; said, "I dare say we'll find him when we get back to your home."

They were circling around and got back to the cabin where she'd killed him, and there was no sign of him there. They hadn't been there but a little while 'til his old dog come up—she'd forgot about the dog—and Young said, "I told you, now John's not far behind"; said, "that dog knows what he's doing." When the dog came on up, he had John's cap with blood on it in his mouth. And the old man took him back and they found his shoes and things in the river.

Well, then the old man went clear up into Kentucky and got an old nigra man had one of these, what they call a conjure ball, you know, a crystal ball; he'd hold it on a string and wave it around. When they was gone after this man, everybody scattered off and left the sheriff there. Well, he prowled around 'til he found parts of burned flesh where she'd dumped the ashes. When the old nigra man came with that crystal ball, he went inside and come to that plank in the floor where the bones were. He told somebody to get an ax and prize it up, and the sheriff said, "No use in it; I know what's under there."

Well, she denied it bitterly. Her daddy come and told her not to tell a thing. He said, "Let them guess at it and they'll never know whether they're right or not." So, she wouldn't tell anything. But they got close enough on to her [that] they put her in jail, where she wrote this song. She never did confess to anything, only in this song, so the people up there told my uncle. So they took her up on the gallows to hang her. They asked her if she had anything to say, and she sung this song:

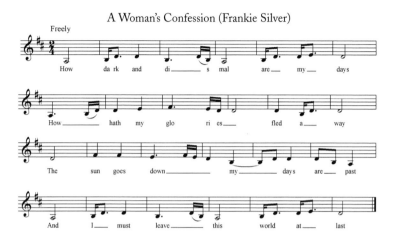

A Woman's Confession (Frankie Silver)

How dark and dismal are my days,
How hath my glories fled away.
The sun goes down, my days are past,
And I must leave this world at last.

Judge Daniel has my sentence passed,
These prison walls I leave at last.
Nothing to cheer my drooping head,
'Til I am numbered with the dead.

For weeks and days I spent my time
In planning out the awful crime.
And on one dark and dismal night,
I put his body out of sight.

His feeble hands fell slowly down,
His clattering tongue had lost its sound.
To see his soul and body part,
It strikes a terror to my heart.

I took his blooming days away,
Left him no time to God to pray.
And if his sins fall on his head,
Must I not bear them in his stead?

How can I stand to see the face,
Whose blood I spilled upon this earth?
With pleading eyes, he to me say,
"Why did you take my life away?"

A falling deed to think of death,
In perfect health to lose your breath.
With little time to God to pray,
Before I start this awful way.

Farewell, good people, you can see,
What my bad conduct brought to me.
To die in shame and sad disgrace,
Before the world of Adam's race.

All you that see and on me gaze,
Be careful how you spend your days.
And try to serve your God in time,
Do not commit the awful crime.

My heart and mind and soul just roll,
My little child, God bless his soul.
All you that are of Adam's race,
Don't let this crime a child disgrace.[10]

The Little Old Man Who Lived Out West

The Little Old Man That Lived Out West
(The Wife Wrapped in Wether's Skin)

There's a little old man he lived out west,
    Dandoo, dandoo.
Little old man and he lived out west,
    Clash to my clingo.
Little old man and he lived out west,
He had a wife that was none of the best.
    Plama lama lingo.

This little old man went whistling to the plow,
    Dandoo, dandoo.
Little old man went whistling to the plow,
    Clash to my clingo.
This little old man went whistling to the plow,
He said, "Old woman, any bread baked now?"
    Plama lama lingo.

"There's a little piece of crust lying on the shelf,"
    Dandoo, dandoo.
"Little piece of crust lying on the shelf,"
    Clash to my clingo.

"There's a little piece of crust lying on the shelf,
If you want any more you can cook it yourself."
    Plama lama lingo.

He went on out to his sheep fold,
    Dandoo, dandoo.
He went on out to his sheep fold,
    Clash to my clingo.
He went on out to his sheep fold,
He caught a wether was tough and old.
    Plama lama lingo.

He hung him up on two little pins,
    Dandoo, dandoo.
He hung him up on two little pins,
    Clash to my clingo.
He hung him up on two little pins,
'Bout three jerks, divest his skin.
    Plama lama lingo.

He wrapped it 'round his old wife's back,
    Dandoo, dandoo.
He wrapped it 'round his old wife's back,
    Clash to my clingo.
He wrapped it 'round his old wife's back,
Got him a stick and made it crack.
    Plama lama lingo.

"Go tell your people and all your kin,"
    Dandoo, dandoo.
"Go tell your people and all your kin,"
    Clash to my clingo.
"Go tell your people and all your kin,
I do as I please with my own sheep skin."
    Plama lama lingo."[11]

A Fair Maid in the Garden

Pre tty fair maid out in the gar den___ A- watch ing sol___ diers pass ing by One

stepped up to___ her and ad dressed her___ Said, "Pre tty fair maid, will you marry me?" ___

A Fair Maid in the Garden

Pretty fair maid out in the garden,
A-watching soldiers passing by.
One stepped up to her and addressed her,
Said, "Pretty fair maid, will you marry me?"

"I have a lover on the ocean,
Seven long years been gone to sea.
And if he stays there seven years longer,
No man on earth can marry me."

"Oh, perhaps he's in the ocean drownded,
Or perhaps he's in the battle slain,
Or perhaps he's to some fair girl married,
And will never return to you again."

"Oh, if he's in the ocean drownded,
Or if he's in the battle slain,
Or if he's to some fair girl married,
I'll love the girl that married him."

He took his hand out from his pocket,
His fingers being very small.
Said, "Here's the ring that you once gave me,"
And straight before him she did fall.

He picked her up so very gently,
And gave her kisses one, two, three.
Said, "If I'd stayed there seven years longer,
No girl on earth could have married me."[12]

When I was Single

When I Was Single

When I was single, oh then,
When I was single, oh then.
When I was single my pockets would jingle,
And I wish I was single again.

I married a wife, oh then,
I married a wife, oh then.
I married a wife, she troubled my life,
And the world went mighty bad then.

My wife got sick, oh then,
My wife got sick, oh then.
My wife got sick, her pulse beat quick,
And the world went mighty well then.

My wife she died, oh then,
My wife she died, oh then.
My wife she died and I laughed 'til I cried,
Because I was single again.

But I married another, oh then,
I married another, oh then.
I married another, she's the devil's grandmother,
Then I wished I was single again.

She beat me, she banged me, oh then,
She beat me, she banged me, oh then.
She beat me, she banged me, and said she would hang me,
The world went mighty bad then.

She got a rope, oh then,
She got a rope, oh then.
She got a rope, my neck it did choke,
And the world went mighty bad then.

The rope did break, oh then,
The rope did break, oh then.
The rope did break and my neck did escape,
And the world went mighty well then.

Young men, take warning from this,
[Young men, take warning from this,]
Be good to the first, for the last will be worse,
And you'll wish you were single again.[13]

The Drunkard's Child

I used to know all of those [sentimental ballads]; girls used to
go around and visit each other, you know, and they'd write those
songs down. I can remember some of the neighbor girls writing
that "Rosewood Casket" for my sister when she was ten years old.
But I never did especially care for them; I wanted something with
a little more life to it. They just never seemed too real to me. Well
now, "Put My Little Shoes Away," that had some meaning for some
people: when a little fella would die, the mother couldn't stand to

hear that song, you know, it'd just upset her so. Some didn't want anything else but that; but I never did like for someone to come to me and air their troubles, I always felt like I had enough of my own.

But they's some of them that were right nice things; I used to sing "The Drunkard's Child." I like that song especially because I had a little friend, a very sweet child, oh, we was just as close as sisters; and she had the same experience [as in the song]. She'd talk to me a lot about it, 'bout her father and how much she wished that he'd change and be different. It [the song]'d go through my mind, you know, when I'd be with her. Oh, I just felt terribly sorry for her. And after her mother died, I felt worse about it. Then I'd think about that song, and think how true it was in her case. I started to sing it to her one day and then I thought, I just won't; didn't want to stir it up any more, I knew she was hurt bad enough. That's why I like that one; I was acquainted with what she was going through, and that song made it clearer.

The Drunkard's Child

My father is a drunkard, my mother now is dead.
And I am a poor orphan child, nowhere to lay my head.
As o'er this world I ramble, they turn me from their door.
Sometime I'll find a welcome on heaven's golden shore.

Oh, once we were so happy, and had a happy home,
'Til Daddy got to drinking rum and then he gambled some.
He left my darling mother, she died of a broken heart,
And as I tell my story, I see your teardrops start.

Don't weep for me and Mother, although I know 'tis sad.
But try to get someone to cheer my poor old lonely dad.
My mother's up in heaven with God where the angels smile.
And now I know she's watching her lonely orphan child.[14]

Joe Bowers

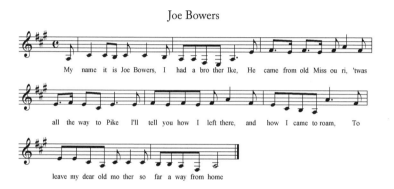

Joe Bowers

My name it is Joe Bowers, I had a brother Ike,
He came from old Missouri, 'twas all the way to Pike.
I'll tell you how I left there, and how I came to roam,
To leave my dear old mother so far away from home.

I used to court a gal there, her name was Sally Black,
I asked her if she'd marry me; she said it was a whack [laughs].
Said she to me, "Joe Bowers, before we hitch for life,
You better git a little home to take your little wife."

"Oh Sally, dear Sally, oh Sally, for your sake,
I'll go to California and try to raise a stake."

Said she to me, "Joe Bowers, you are a man to win,
Here's a kiss to bind the bargain"; she hugged a dozen in.

When I got in that country, I hadn't nary "red" [a cent],
I had such wolfish feelings, I wished myself most dead.
But the thoughts of my dear Sally soon made them feelings git,
And whispers hope to Bowers; I wish I had 'em yet.

At last I went to mining, put in my biggest lick,
Came down upon the border just like a ton of brick.
I worked both late and early, through sun and rain and snow,
I's working for my Sally, that's all the same to Joe.

At length I got a letter from my dear brother Ike,
It came from old Missouri, 'twas all the way from Pike.
Hit brought the durndest news that ever I did hear:
Said Sal had married a butcher, and the butcher had red hair
    [laughs].[15]

The Texas Ranger (from Lillie's manuscript; not recorded on tape)

This song is another of my favorites my mother sang. She had a
lovely voice and enjoyed singing. Sometimes for a change she would
tell us stories (true of course) of her experiences during the Civil
War. . . . She sang many of the songs I know at night when she
would assemble all sixteen of us children around a pile of beans to
have us take the strings off. The beans would then be made into
pickled beans, packed in huge jars or barrels. Some of them were put
on threads [and] hung up to dry for leather britches—that was snap
beans dried with the hulls on. She amused us with her songs, therefore we did more beans. Happy days.

Come all you Texas Rangers wherever you may be,
I'll tell you of the trouble that happened unto me.

My name is nothing extra and that I will not tell,
But to all you Texas Rangers I'm sure I wish you well.

When at the age of sixteen I joined the jolly band,
We marched to western Texas into the Yankee land.
My captain he gave orders, perhaps he thought it right,
"Before you reach yon mountain, my boys, you'll have to fight."

I saw the Yankees coming and heard them give a yell,
My feelings at that moment no human tongue can tell.
I saw the smoke arising, the bullets around me hailed,
My heart then sank within me, my courage almost failed.

We fought for nine long hours before the fight was o'er;
The like of dead and wounded I never saw before.

I thought of my dear mother who oft to me did say,
"To you they all are strangers, at home you better stay."
I thought she's old and childish and perhaps she did not know,
My mind was set on roving and I was bound to go.

Perhaps you have a mother, likewise a sister too,
Perhaps you have a sweetheart to weep and mourn for you.
If this be your condition, I'm sure you'll have to mourn,
I'll tell you by experience, you had better stay at home.[16]

The Honest Farmer

I got this song from my brother. During the depression, when the
farmers were all doing their best just to make a living—they's all
sharecroppers, you know—the landlord, he would come in and take
all they had. They'd work all the year, make a good crop, then at the
end of the year they'd owe the landlord more than they made; he got
it all.

The Honest Farmer

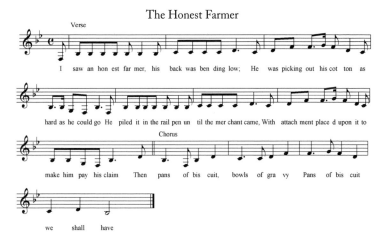

I saw an honest farmer, his back was bending low;
He was picking out his cotton as hard as he could go.
He piled it in the rail pen until the merchant came,
With an attachment placed upon it to make him pay his claim.

> Then pans of biscuit, bowls of gravy,
> Pans of biscuit we shall have.

I saw him in the evening, his back against a tree.
His poor old back was aching, he fell upon his knee.
"I'll be compelled to go home or I will surely die;
My head has started aching," I heard the farmer cry.

> Then pans of biscuit, bowls of gravy,
> Pans of biscuit we shall have.

I looked again and saw him, he'd made it up the hill,
And raised a little cabin, and sat upon the sill.
"I toiled all my lifetime but still I find I'm poor.
Without an education, my children's left my door."[17]

My heading introducing Lillie asks if she was Georgia's last old-time ballad singer. In the past, folklorists motivated by the "devolutionary premise" (the notion that folklore was dying out and that our mission was to "catch it before it went over the edge") were quick—sometimes too quick—to declare that they had discovered the "last" practitioner of a given tradition. As it happens, Lillie is not the only ballad singer represented in the Georgia Folklore Archives. In 1967, one of my students realized that her mother, Myrtle Cantrell of Fannin County (just east of Lillie's home county), was a traditional singer, and recorded thirty songs—several also known to Lillie—that Myrtle had learned from her grandmother and great-uncle, including three Child ballads.

Art and Margo Rosenbaum, who made extensive field recordings of north Georgia folk music and song in the 1970s and '80s, found another ballad singer, Maud Thacker of Tate (twenty-five miles south of where Lillie learned her songs). It may well be that their generation, now gone, was the last to carry on a community-based oral tradition of these story-songs. The prognosis for the continuation of folk-ballad singing in Georgia is not hopeful, to quote the Rosembaums: "Maud's songs do mean a lot to her, and she recognizes their rarity and value; she wishes her voice were not so cracked with age and that she could sing them as she used to. 'Lots of times I go to bed at night, sing 'em to myself, just whisper. I wrote all them off, to give to my daughter. She got 'em, but I don't guess she can sing ary one of 'em.'"[18]

Ballads, though, may not be the best way to gauge the overall health of Georgia folk culture; they had their heyday when access to other forms of entertainment was quite limited. Ballad singing is an intimate, contemplative performance mode requiring a receptive audience, in contrast to the flashy theatrics of today's pop-music idols that Georgia's younger generation has grown to expect. In chapter six we'll broaden our horizons to ask what kinds of traditions are alive and well in this and other southern states.

Study of Georgia Folklife

Although Georgia's folklore compares quite favorably with that of adjoining states, you'd never know it from the early published record. When public interest in American folk music was at its height in the 1960s, for example, there was no comprehensive folk song collection for Georgia comparable to those available for neighboring states. A partial explanation for this paucity of earlier research is that American folklore collecting has often been based in educational institutions, and folklore was not an established academic subject in Georgia until 1966, which marked the start of Georgia State University's Folklore Curriculum and Rabun County's high school–based Foxfire program (using mountain folk culture and local history to produce student publications).

By comparison, Frank C. Brown of Duke University compiled his monumental collection of North Carolina folklore (mainly songs, tales, and superstitions) between 1912 and 1943, later to be published in seven volumes.[19] Brown worked in collaboration with an active state folklore society, another research asset lacking in Georgia (a nominal Georgia Folklore Society did put on an annual folk festival in the 1970s and 1980s). Finally, Georgia simply was not fated to have a pioneering scholar like Brown in the early days of southern folklore study. Even a transient like English folklorist Cecil Sharp, who collected Appalachian folk songs in 1916–18, never made it into Georgia. Some Georgia material was recorded for the Archive of American Folk Song (now the Archive of Folk Culture) at the Library of Congress starting in 1926, but little has been issued publicly.

Georgia did, of course, have a pioneering folklorist in the person of Joel Chandler Harris, whose *Uncle Remus, His Songs and His Sayings* (1880) and *Nights with Uncle Remus* (1883) brought African American folklore into the public spotlight. Harris had heard many of the tales and other material featured in those two compilations from slaves in east-central Georgia's Putnam County. But in his dialect retelling for print years later, with a fictitious setting and characters, he was displaying the skills of a literary artist more than those of a scholar.

Harris's success encouraged another white Georgian, Charles Colcock Jones Jr., to try his hand with similar material in *Negro Myths from the Georgia Coast* (1888), this time represented in the Gullah dialect. The most significant Georgia folklore publications in

the first half of the 1900s further document black coastal traditions. *Drums and Shadows* (1940), taken from interviews with ex-slaves conducted by the Savannah Unit of the Georgia Writers' Project (a branch of President Roosevelt's depression-era Work Projects Administration), features African survivals, especially in folk belief. And *Slave Songs of the Georgia Sea Islands* (1942), by amateur folklorist Lydia Parrish, who organized a performing group that became the Georgia Sea Island Singers, features a type of danced spiritual called the ring-shout.

This emphasis on African Americans in early Georgia folklore collecting makes the rural-life reminiscence, a type of nonfiction local-color literature, an important alternative resource for traditions of white Georgians. Two valuable memoirs of this type are J. L. Herring's *Saturday Night Sketches* (1918), an account of late-1800s folklife in south-central Georgia's Wiregrass country, and Floyd C. Watkins's and Charles Hubert Watkins's *Yesterday in the Hills* (1963), an interview-based portrait of farm life in the vicinity of Ball Ground, Cherokee County, around 1900.

By the 1970s and 1980s, a greater presence of folklorists in the state was yielding more representative publications, as well as folk festivals and notable exhibits of traditional art. An index of Georgia folklore's higher profile in recent years is the awarding of eleven National Heritage Fellowships (America's equivalent of Japan's Living National Treasures honor) to Georgians since the National Endowment for the Arts began this program in 1982. Recipients include Georgia Sea Island Singer Bessie Jones of Saint Simons Island, Sacred Harp song leader Hugh McGraw of Bremen, and potter Lanier Meaders of Mossy Creek.[20]

When Bess Lomax Hawes was director of the NEA's Folk Arts Program, she did her best to see that every state had an "official" public-sector folklorist, usually based in the state arts agency; Georgia was one of the last holdouts. But Georgia Humanities Council director Ronald Benson was hearing from local organizations that they needed professional help in developing programs relating to folk culture (then an initiative of that agency), so with NEA start-up funding and guidance from an advisory committee, the Georgia Folklife Program was established in 1987, finding a home four years later at the Georgia Council for the Arts. The program's accomplishments include fieldwork surveys of previously unexplored areas of the state, a grants program to help fund projects in the state through nonprofit organizations, publication of a pictorial essay and bibliography on Georgia folklife (both no longer in print), a cassette and CD called *Georgia Folk: A Sampler of Traditional Sounds*, a public forum on folk art, and an apprenticeship program linking master traditional artists with younger members of their communities to encourage the handing-on of traditions.

Conclusion

In the final analysis, Georgia folklife is best described as a multi-patterned patchwork quilt rather than a bolt of cloth woven in one piece. From the Atlantic seaboard to the Appalachians, folklorists have found a wide range of traditions arising from locale, ethnicity, and occupation. Such diversity can even be present in a single place; in metropolitan Atlanta, for example, a strong black gospel music heritage, transplanted traditions of recent immigrants, and urban lore of office "paper pushers" coexist. From the fishing and African American Geechee ways of the coast to the swamp lore of the Okefenokee, from the pottery and blues traditions of the Piedmont to the ballad singing and banjo picking of the mountains, the folk streams of the state's culture distill a sense of place and add a rich and meaningful texture to the lives of its residents.[21]

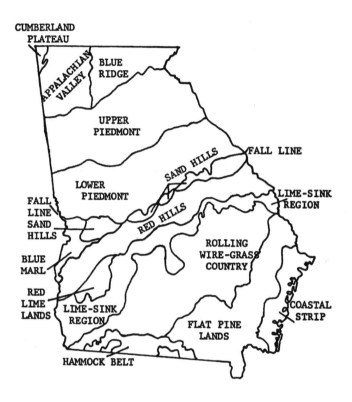

Georgia's physio-
graphic divisions.
Folk-cultural differ-
ences within the state
can result from such
environmental varia-
tions. Map by Roland
M. Harper, in *Georgia
Historical Quarterly*,
1922.

6. Branches and New Shoots

Southern Folk Culture Today and Tomorrow

> I always liked the story of the little girl whose family is moving from Albany, Georgia, to Atlanta. And she's saying her prayers the night before the move, and she says, "God bless Mommy, and God bless Daddy, and God bless the little dog," and all like that. And then she says, "And now it's goodbye, God, we're moving to Atlanta." —Henry Malone, former dean of the School of General Studies, Georgia State University[1]

This last chapter is the most difficult to write. For one thing, I don't have a crystal ball, and doubt that there's anyone with the ability to predict the future of southern folk culture. Folk traditions are slippery; they have a way of disappearing, then resurfacing when conditions are right. So one thing this chapter will not be is an obituary for southern folklore, although I have in fact witnessed the passing of certain rural-based traditions; it was that distinctly regional culture, deeply rooted in the soil, that attracted me to the region. I am less interested in the lore created by my own urban society, which is, of necessity, a big part of this chapter's story.

But perhaps I can still make a useful stab at it. It seems to me that the current state and future of southern folk culture can be broken down into three basic situations: first, the continuing practice of more durable regional traditions, either unaffected by modernization or stimulated by new circumstances; second, a body of lore reflecting the experience of modern America, following the transition from an agrarian society to an industrial and urban/suburban one; and third, traditions of recent immigrants to the South, transplanted from other countries and adapting to the American, and more specifically southern, way of life.

Old Times Not Forgotten

In chapter two I listed some still-active traditions rooted in the old agrarian society, among them southerners' unabated taste for such foods as grits, cornbread, barbeque, and sweet tea; the vitality of folk music in parts of Appalachia and Louisiana; maintenance of the pre-Christian Green Corn ceremony among southern Indians; and the celebration of Mardi Gras in Louisiana. Tracking such traditions over time reveals cycles of waning and waxing, including revivals sometimes managed or influenced by outsiders.[2] Some older traditions thrive on their own, supported by the communities that "own" them; others, especially handcrafts tied to a market economy, depend on outside support.

This leads us to new audiences for southern folklore, or to quote the title of a recent exhibit, "new ways for old jugs."[3] Once-declining traditions such as folk pottery, blues, and Sacred Harp singing have been given a new lease on life by a largely urban, and not always southern, audience. The folk potter's customer base began to shift in the 1920s from fellow farmers who needed his wares to preserve their food to collectors who proudly display his creations in their homes, causing him to become less a production potter and more of a decorative artist (plate 14). Belonging to the generation caught in that transition, Georgia's Lanier Meaders was dismayed by the demand for his face jugs: "Seems like the more useless I make something, the more they'll trample each other to get to it!"[4] Venues for blues artists have shifted out of juke joints to upscale clubs like Blind Willie's in Atlanta and concert series like Nothin' But the Blues at the Atlanta History Center, the audiences for which are largely white and well-to-do. And due to the missionary work of zealots like Hugh McGraw and the popularity of such films as *Cold Mountain*, Sacred Harp singing now has a following outside the country churches that were once its only home.

Martin-gourd sculpture in downtown Atlanta, Georgia, part of a "folk art" installation created for the 1996 Olympic Games. Such birdhouses, a traditional feature of southern farms, here seem to reference the rural roots of the city's working-class population.

The Country in the City

One thing that distinguishes a city like Atlanta as southern is that, until the influx of workers from Mexico in the 1990s, its blue-collar labor force was drawn from the surrounding countryside, in contrast to the immigrant groups (Irish, Italian, etc.) constituting the working-class core of northern cities. Atlanta's textile communities—Whittier Mill Village, Scottdale, Cabbagetown—were (until the mills closed and gentrification followed) enclaves preserving rural southern patterns of speech, worship, and foodways.[5] Another fact that may surprise some Atlantans is that, in the first three decades of the twentieth century, the "Empire City of the New South" was a mecca for traditional country musicians. The irony, and inevitable clash of musical cultures, was not lost on an *Atlanta Constitution* reporter in 1915:

When time hung heavy on the hands of Jim Shelton, Joe Brown, P. A. Ludwig and Shorty Harper, delegates to the Fiddlers' convention yesterday, they proceeded to put the [Kimball House hotel] orchestra out of business by a demonstration of the superiority of the fiddle to the violin.

The four had gathered together with their fiddles at noon on the mezzanine floor. For a time they listened in bored tolerance to the "Melody in F," "The Barcarolle" and other classics rendered by the Kimball orchestra, until finally Shorty Harper could stand it no longer, and the regular orchestra was startled to hear the strains of "Billy in the Lowground," with the accompaniment of patting feet. "The Barcarolle" began to wane, until finally it died altogether, and left the fiddlers in triumphant possession of the audience.[6]

Industrial and Urban Lore

As former farming folk flooded into the South's mining and mill towns beginning in the late 1800s, they brought with them, as just described, their love of traditional music and song. But living for the first time in proximity to their neighbors, there was greater opportunity to share complaints about working conditions, and a strain of social consciousness crept into new songs being created and sung. Industrial protest songs are not unique to the South, but southern song makers had the advantage of a rich singing heritage to draw on. Such a one was Aunt Molly Jackson, champion of miners in the coal fields of eastern Kentucky. Her "Dreadful Memories" of 1935 was inspired by a coal-company doctor's refusal to visit sick children of miners blacklisted for joining the union:

> I can't forget them coal miners' children
> That starved to death without one drop of milk,
> While the coal operators and their wives and children
> Were all dressed in jewels and silk.
>
> Dreadful memories! How they haunt me
> As the lonely moments fly;

Child laborers (two "doffers" and a sweeper) in the spinning room of a southern textile mill, early 1900s. Courtesy, Southern Labor Archives, Special Collections Department, Georgia State University Library.

Oh, how them little babies suffered!
I saw them starve to death and die.[7]

Dorsey Dixon, who worked in the textile mills of Piedmont South and North Carolina, also had children on his mind when he wrote "Babies in the Mill" in 1945:

I used to be a factory hand when things was moving slow,
When children worked in cotton mills, each morning had to go.
Every morning just at five the whistle blew on time
To call them babies out of bed at the age of eight and nine.

Come out of bed little sleepy-head
And get you a bite to eat.

The factory whistle's calling you,
There's no more time to sleep.

Those babies all grew up unlearned, they never went to school.
They never learned to read or write; they learned to spin and spool.
Every time I close my eyes I see that picture still,
When textile work was carried on by babies in the mill.[8]

Child-labor laws corrected that problem, and in any case most of the mills are now closed. But coal mining continues in Appalachia, and at least some of those songs, and newer ones, still support the struggle for better working conditions in that occupational subculture.

More widespread is the relatively recent tradition of urban legends generated by the anxieties of modern American life. While few are strictly southern (some are even known in other countries), when narrated by a good storyteller they can acquire a regional flavor and local details. Take, for example, this variant of a well-known story normally presented as the "true" experience of a "friend of a friend," but here told in the first-person vein of a tall tale by south Georgian Edgar Tillman to his granddaughter, Tammy:

Tamara, you been wanting to know about the truck. You know, there's a camper to this thing. And your grandma sure were set to have one, so we bought one. And we decided to go on a vacation. Well, she wanted to go up to South Carolina. And at that time I was in pretty bad health, but I decided I would go along with her. Well, she wanted to do the driving. You know how your grandmaw is, wants to be a big shot. And I says, "I'll do the driving my own self."

She says [affects a falsetto voice], "You can do your own driving when you're alone if you want to"; says, "you're sick now."

I says, "Well, it don't matter if I am sick, I'll do the driving!" Well, we packed our groceries and plenty of water and made up our bed in there. And up the road we went. Well, we went around Savannah; we were gonna cross the river and go on over to some good camping ground in South Carolina, you see.

Anyway, we got on up there, and I got to feeling really, really bad. I mean, I was feeling bad. I says, "Bertie, old gal, do you think that you can drive this rig?"

She says, "I shore can!"

I says, "Okay, I'm gonna get in the back and lay down, and you just go on across the toll bridge, now." I says, "It won't take you long to get over there in South Carolina." And she looked like a Philadelphia lawyer setting up there under that steering wheel, you know.

When I got back there in the camper, it was a little bit warm; hadn't got the windows open. So I pulled my shirt off. I says, well, I think I'll really strip off here and get into my underwear. And I pulled my britches and shoes off. And I rolled them [window] glasses out, and that cool air blowing in the windows made me more comfortable, and in just a few minutes I was fast asleep.

All of a sudden I hear a WHAM! And I wake up and say, Oh Lord, she done hit something and tore it up. I opened the door at the back end of the camper; when I bent over, the back of my underpants busted open. Well, the light turned green, and she hit the gas and shot on ahead. And I mean, out in the middle of the road I landed! I went to waving and hollering, "Stop that truck!" But she tore on down the road. Nothing but women and younguns coming by, and me running down that road in my underwear and barefooted.

And about that time I heard a [makes a siren sound]. Police officers drive up, say, "Get outta here, drunk. Whatcha doing out here like that?" Say, "Ain'tcha drunk?"

I says, "If I could get to where I could get me a quart, I'd do my best to get that way." Said, "See that camper that turned the curve down yonder?"

"What camper?"

Well, Bertie done turned the curve and headed across the bridge, you know, out of sight. But I sorta convinced them guys that it really did happen, you know. And they called ahead. And do you know where she was at? She was all the way over in South Carolina. And do you know where I was at? I was in that patrol car in my underwear and barefooted.

And they got her stopped. They said [assumes a gruff voice], "Where are you going, lady?"

"We're going on a camping trip."

"By yourself?"

"No; well, my husband's back there in the camper."

"You better take a look."

She got out, you know, went back and looked, and she didn't have no husband!

I came up a few minutes later and I was going for the camper for to get my britches on. People was passing me; they would snigger, you know, me a-holding the seat of my underwear to keep 'em from gaping open. Them old women would look at me and turn their noses up; it was a sight!

And to wind up, we did make up, me and her, after we had a big quarrel. And we went on up in South Carolina; we did have a pretty good time. You know what I've done from then on? I've done the driving! I don't take no chances.

Ain't you gonna laugh?[9]

The "southernizing" of this nationally distributed legend is a recent illustration of a process that has been at work for a long time; Emily Ellis's story quoted in chapter three, "Dividing the Walnuts," brought from England about three centuries ago, was absorbed into the southern folktale repertoire and is sometimes grafted to the African American Old Master and John cycle. That this adaptation process is flexible enough to accommodate traditions of modern society bodes well for the future.

There is probably no more urban American folk-art expression than wall graffiti. Arising in the 1960s with the availability of canned spray paint, the spread of this art form from the East to West Coast has been aided by the use of train cars as one type of outdoor "canvas." Superficially, this graffiti seems to display a recognizable generic style regardless of locale, but it may be that southern cities such as Atlanta are contributing to an emerging regional tradition, as suggested by a local graffiti "writer" who describes the city's style as "bubbly, real playful, bright colors; Atlanta does kinda have that down-South funky feel to it." This is in contrast to the West Coast, where "there's a lot of sharp edges, really evil-looking stuff; they get their style from, mostly, the Mexican gangs."[10] A middle-class suburban upbringing is not unusual for Atlanta's graffiti artists, some of whom associate with loosely-knit "crews," learning from, and looking out for, each other while developing individual approaches. Unless sanctioned by property owners the practice is illegal, part of its attraction to youths drawn from the similarly risky skateboarding subculture. East Atlanta, especially Krog Street Tunnel in Cabbagetown, has become a showplace for such work (plate 15).

What would a folktale created in the South but incorporating a modern sensibility look like? Here's an example of such southern urban lore in the making, arising in the social milieu of the Trackside Tavern, a neighborhood bar near Agnes Scott College in Decatur, Georgia, just east of Atlanta. It belongs to a group of humorous character anecdotes that form a site-specific, leisure-time tradition among Trackside's regular patrons, who are described by one restaurant reviewer as "a comfortable mix of alternative lifestyle types, students, blue-collar townies and middle-aged guys":

> Then there's the story—this is one of my favorites. Some guy walks in here one day, and he walks to the end of the bar—Beth, about where you're sitting—and sits down. Only problem is, he's got a big old can full of Budweiser in his hand; puts it on the bar. And I think it was David A. who owned the bar then. David comes down and says, "Sir, I'm sorry but you can't bring that in here. You're gonna have to pour it out."
>
> "Can I take it outside and drink it?"
>
> David said, "Sure."
>
> So he gets up and staggers outside. David's sitting there looking at him, thinking to himself, "Well damn, I can't serve this guy." So he comes staggering back in and sits back down. David walks up to him, says, "Sir, I'm sorry but I can't serve you." The guy gets real mad and he storms out. Goes out the back door there, gets in his car, pulls out, drives down the alley, turns to the left, comes in front of the Track-

side, stops, blows his horn, holds up a tall Bud, and shoots us a bird [gesture with extended middle finger].

Then he proceeds to drive into the intersection over there by Eva's cafe and gets into a traffic accident: we hear this CRASH! So we go running outside. The guy had pulled in front of somebody and caused a wreck. Next thing we know, he's in handcuffs. We're out there shooting him the bird![11]

Reinternationalizing Southern Folk Culture

I know it's hard to believe, but when I moved to Atlanta in the mid-1960s there weren't many more than a dozen restaurants in the city, the most "exotic" being the Chinese American Eng's Gourmet. It wasn't customary back then for Atlantans to do much eating out, except on Sundays after church at standbys like Mary Mac's and the Collonade. How things have changed since then! Now, Buford Highway on the north side of town offers the world on a plate: Thai, Vietnamese, Korean, Mexican, you name it. So how did this happen?

The answer, of course, is a wave of immigrants since the 1970s, many from the similarly warm climates of Asia, Latin America, and the Caribbean.[12] The homeland traditions of these newcomers—foods, festivals, arts—serve them well in adjusting to this new place, as had been the case with the immigrants of centuries earlier who built the South's folk foundations. As an example, the textile arts of east Atlanta's Hmong community, limited to clothing back in Laos, have been expanded to decorative wall hangings, including embroidered story cloths, that bring income to some of these families while reminding the next generation, born here, of their origins. The story cloths illustrate scenes of village life, folktales, and the exodus across the Mekong River to refugee camps in Thailand as their villages were attacked by Communist forces (plate 16).[13] These textile artists also make items geared to a non-Hmong Georgian clientele, such as Christmas tree skirts incorporating traditional *Pa Ndau* (flower cloth) designs.

Between this recent wave and the South's initial settlers there have been other immigrants, each group making its contribution. Atlanta's Greek Orthodox Cathedral of the Annunciation was established in 1905; seventy years later, as an outreach strategy to share some of its congregation's traditions—food, music, dance—with the city, it held its first annual Atlanta Greek Festival, which has since grown exponentially. Southern folk culture remains strong and distinctive enough to continue absorbing such influences, while at the same time converting newcomers to southerners, a give and take that can occur in subtle ways.

Instances of food assimilation have occurred frequently in the experience of southern Jews, who took part in the region's early settlement (Savannah's Temple Mickve Israel was founded in 1735) but also came later, especially in the late 1800s. The favorite *Shabbas* (Sabbath) meal of an Anniston, Alabama, Jewish family around 1900 was described as "oyster stew; steak, ham, or fried chicken; Mama's homemade biscuits and corn bread, too; hoppin' john . . . and sweet potato pie for dessert."[14] And one of my students, Leslie Gordon, supplied these more recent examples from her Savannah-based family:

Sissy Levy, formerly of Birmingham, Alabama, tells of her Macon, Georgia, cousin's fantastic matzoh-ball soup served at their Passover Seder meal. The recipe was not complete without the inclusion of a ham hock!

My family kept kosher until I was about nine years old. Although the separate sets of dishes were no longer kept, and foods marked with the K symbolizing kosher weren't the only ones bought, we still observed the dietary laws in general: we never had shellfish, ham, or pork chops in the home (although we did eat shrimp, crab and oysters at restaurants). However, my father was very fond of bacon. So every morning, along with breakfast, we always had bacon. This was the only pork product served at our house.

Another example of adaptation to southern ways would be my Grandma Flo's mandel bread (mandel means almond in German). Flo made the best mandel bread in Chatham County. It was, however, made with pecans!

Matzoh Ball Gumbo: Culinary Tales of the Jewish South by Marcie Cohen Ferris, an exploration of one ethnic group's adaptation to southern foodways. © 2005 by Marcie Cohen Ferris; used by permission of University of North Carolina Press, www. uncpress.unc.edu.

Finally, in all branches of my family, the Seder meal always includes a squash casserole. The squash used is the yellow summer crookneck variety, certainly not available in Vienna, Kobryn, or any of the other places my family came from.[15]

As with other groups, however, the influence has been a two-way street: for many southerners today bagels satisfy morning hunger instead of biscuits.

Conclusion

It is not immigration—past, present, or future—that poses a threat to southern folk traditions; if anything, it has served as a revitalizing hedge against cultural stagnation. But that doesn't mean that the region's older folklife isn't endangered. To distance themselves from the deprivations of former poverty, southerners' rush to modernize has accelerated since the mid-twentieth century with the growth of the Sun Belt's economy, resulting in the abandonment of rural-based traditions that were once part of their behavior and now exist only as museum relics or words and images in books such as this one. This poses questions of cultural conservation that only southerners with access to their communities' traditions can answer. Are the material comforts, electronic conveniences, and global connections now being embraced worth the price of losing a precious heritage? I'm not proposing a return to the "bad old days" (as some in the older generation refer to them), just reiterating that the practice of folklore today is a matter of choice, one that offers alternatives to the mass culture that so dominates American society.

Southerners who choose to carry on folklore may well gain personal satisfaction from becoming the newest branch of a deeply rooted tree. But for many of these traditions to thrive, there also must be an appreciative audience; folklore practice is a social act, a conversation—not a monologue. The careers of two younger traditionalists from Appalachia illustrate the benefits as well as pitfalls of choosing old ways in the modern world. Sheila Kay Adams of Mars Hill, North Carolina, is a singer and storyteller who learned ballads and tales from relatives, mainly her cousin, Cas Wallin, and great-aunt, Dellie Chandler Norton, who is quoted as saying, "[Sheila] might not always know where she's going, but she sure knows where she comes from." A recipient of the North Carolina Folklore Society's Brown-Hudson Award, she has carved out a successful career performing at festivals, colleges, and on concert tours.

Appalachian singer and storyteller Sheila Kay Adams, Mars Hill, North Carolina, 2003. Photo by Tim Barnwell; courtesy, Sheila Kay Adams.

In contrast there is Rick Stewart of Sneedville, Tennessee, a fifth-generation cooper who learned that woodcraft from his grandfather, National Heritage Fellow Alex Stewart. Rick himself was awarded a National Endowment for the Arts grant to refine his skills with coopers in Japan. But an attempt at full-time coopering made him realize that he couldn't support his family that way. As he says on his home page, "Although I expanded my career into the Automotive Industry (managing a car dealership), I still love to Cooper in my spare time. Unfortunately, due to my busy schedule, no orders can be taken at this time." For those who choose southern folklore as a profession, this balance of the old with the new can be a delicate one.[16]

Folklorist Henry Glassie quotes his Northern Irish "history teacher," Hugh Nolan, as saying, "The two things happen at the one time. Things get better. And they get worse."[17] Not all change is progress. What we've gained in technology we seem to have lost in the social cohesion for which folklore served so effectively as glue; cell phones and computers are poor substitutes for storytelling sessions and quilting bees. Ballad singer Lillie West spoke of this loss when I asked what was the greatest change she'd seen in her eighty years in the Georgia mountains. "The biggest change," she replied, "began with the coming of the automobile. Everybody's in too big a hurry now, they don't have time for their neighbors."[18]

The small family farms that kept so much of the South's older regional folklore alive are fast becoming obsolete. The future of southern folk culture, then, lies with those determined to carry on those older traditions, with the recent lore of urban America, and with the immigrants who add their diversity to the region's folk foundations. Southern folklore isn't dying, but changing in character; I'm just grateful to have known some of its finest practitioners.

NOTES

Introduction: A Pennsylvania Yankee in Governor Lester Maddox's Court

1. "Going to Georgia," as sung by Lawrence Eller of Upper Hightower, in Art Rosenbaum and Margo Newmark Rosenbaum, *Folk Visions and Voices: Traditional Music and Song in North Georgia* (Athens: University of Georgia Press, 1983), 8.

2. William Faulkner, *Absalom, Absalom!* (1936; reprint, New York: Modern Library, 1951), 174.

3. William Bartram, *Travels of William Bartram*, ed. Mark Van Doren (1928; reprint, New York: Dover Publications, 1955); John A. Burrison, *Brothers in Clay: The Story of Georgia Folk Pottery* (Athens: University of Georgia Press, 1983), 101–107; Bradford L. Rauschenberg, "Andrew Duche: A Potter 'A Little Too Much Addicted to Politicks,'" *Journal of Early Southern Decorative Arts* 17, no. 1 (1991): 1–101; Dewey F. Mosby, *Henry Ossawa Tanner* (Philadelphia, PA: Philadelphia Museum of Art, 1991), 116–20; Marcia M. Mathews, *Henry Ossawa Tanner: American Artist* (Chicago: University of Chicago Press, 1969), 33–40. Mathews speculates that Tanner's 1893 painting was based on sketches he may have made while visiting Highlands, North Carolina, while Mosby includes a photograph with models posed in Tanner's studio as the direct basis of the painting.

4. John A. Lomax and Alan Lomax, *Negro Folk Songs As Sung By Lead Belly . . .* (New York: Macmillan, 1936); Richard M. Garvin and Edmond G. Addeo, *The Midnight Special: The Legend of Leadbelly* (New York: B. Geis, 1971); Charles K. Wolfe and Kip Lornell, *The Life and Legend of Leadbelly* (New York: HarperCollins Publishers, 1992). The biopic film *Leadbelly* was directed by Gordon Parks in 1976.

5. Bruce Galphin, *The Riddle of Lester Maddox* (Atlanta: Camelot Publishing, 1968). For an African American folk perspective on the former governor see "John Meets Lester Maddox" in John A. Burrison, ed., *Storytellers: Folktales and Legends from the South* (Athens: University of Georgia Press, 1991 [paper ed.]), 241–42.

6. "Wee Midnight Hours" seems to have been a favorite of Georgia blues artists; Curley Weaver and Willie McTell recorded it on the Regal label in 1949 (Bruce Bastin, *Red River Blues: The Blues Tradition in the Southeast* [Urbana: University of Illinois Press, 1986], 119), and Buddy Moss recorded it for Biograph's *Rediscovery* album in 1966.

7. This is how I heard Mrs. Kilby's "Short Life of Trouble" and wrote it in my field notes; I later found that the narrator of this Appalachian lyric folk song normally is male ("Poor boy with a broken heart"). The song was recorded in the 1920s by Dick Burnett

and Leonard Rutherford, Buell Kazee, and G. B. Grayson and Henry Whitter; it was later popularized by the Blue Sky Boys and Lester Flatt and Earl Scruggs, and is the title song of a recent album on the Rebel label by Ralph Stanley.

1. The Core of the Culture: Folk Traditions and the Big Regional Picture

1. Charles Joyner, *Shared Traditions: Southern History and Folk Culture* (Urbana: University of Illinois Press, 1999), 222, 150.

2. The term *folklife* was coined in the 1960s to reflect the addition of material culture (art and craft, architecture, clothing, food) to the oral, musical, and customary traditions previously studied as folklore, and to suggest the integration of all these expressive forms into people's lives.

3. John A. Burrison, "Folklore," in *American History through Literature 1820–1870*, ed. Janet Gabler-Hover and Robert Sattelmeyer (Farmington Hills, MI: Charles Scribner's Sons/Thomson Gale, 2006), 427–29.

4. "Fast-Running Dog," in Harden E. Taliaferro ("Skitt"), *Fisher's River (North Carolina) Scenes and Characters* (1859; reprint, New York: Arno Press, 1977), 148–51. The tale has a European precedent in *The Surprising Adventures of Baron Munchausen* (London, 1785), in which the fast-running animal is a hare, and is first reported in the United States in 1808.

5. Bessie Jones, *For the Ancestors: Autobiographical Memories*, ed. John Stewart (1983; reprint, Athens: University of Georgia Press, 1989), 34, 177.

6. Jean Ritchie, *Singing Family of the Cumberlands* (1955; reprint, Lexington: University Press of Kentucky, 1988), 254.

7. Quoted in *Contemporary Artists and Craftsmen of the Eastern Band of Cherokee Indians* (Cherokee, NC: Qualla Arts and Crafts Mutual, 1987), 2.

8. Quoted in George P. Reynolds et al., eds., *Foxfire 10* (New York: Doubleday, 1993), 439.

9. Quoted in John Beardsley et al., *Gee's Bend: The Women and Their Quilts* (Atlanta: Tinwood Press, 2002), 384.

10. Cultural geographer Wilbur Zelinsky addressed this question in "Where the South Begins: The Northern Limit of the Cis-Appalachian South in Terms of Settlement Landscape," *Social Forces* 30, no. 2 (1951): 172–78; more recently, Richard Pillsbury took a similar approach with "Landscape, Cultural," in *Encyclopedia of Southern Culture*, ed. Charles Reagan Wilson and William Ferris (Chapel Hill: University of North Carolina Press, 1989), 533–41.

11. Charles Keil, *Urban Blues* (Chicago: University of Chicago Press, 1966); Mike Rowe, *Chicago Blues: The City and the Music* (New York: Da Capo Press, 1981); Robert Gordon, *Can't Be Satisfied: The Life and Times of Muddy Waters* (Boston: Little, Brown, 2002); Bruce A. Rosenberg, *Can These Bones Live? The Art of the American Folk Preacher*, rev. ed. (Urbana: University of Illinois Press, 1988); Gerald L. Davis, *I Got the Word in Me and I Can Sing It, You Know: A Study of the Performed African-American Sermon* (Philadelphia: University of Pennsylvania Press, 1985).

12. Reported in the "News of the Weird" column of the Atlanta weekly newspaper, *Creative Loafing* (January 30, 1999), 12.

13. Carl N. Degler, *Place over Time: The Continuity of Southern Distinctiveness* (Baton Rouge: Louisiana State University Press, 1977).

14. Carroll E. Reed, *Dialects of American English* (Cleveland: World Publishing, 1967), 90.

15. Allen Tullos, ed., *Long Journey Home: Folklife in the South* (Chapel Hill, NC: Southern Exposure, 1977); Celeste Ray, ed., *Southern Heritage on Display: Public Ritual and Ethnic Diversity within Southern Regionalism* (Tuscaloosa: University of Alabama Press, 2003).

16. Recognition of the importance of folklife in the overall picture of southern culture is seen in the eighty pages devoted to the subject in Wilson and Ferris, eds., *Encyclopedia of Southern Culture*, and its forty pages in Rebecca Mark and Rob Vaughan, eds., *The Greenwood Encyclopedia of American Regional Cultures: The South* (Westport, CT: Greenwood Press, 2004); a substantial Folklife section also is part of *The New Georgia Encyclopedia*, issued online by the Georgia Humanities Council in 2004 (http://www.georgiaencyclopedia.org/nge/Home.jsp).

17. From a speech in Washington, D.C., January 17, 1925.

18. The experience of enslavement and its later impact on African Americans are discussed in Edward D. C. Campbell Jr. and Kym S. Rice, eds., *Before Freedom Came: African-American Life in the Antebellum South* (Charlottesville: University Press of Virginia and Museum of the Confederacy, 1991); Charles Joyner, *Down By the Riverside: A South Carolina Slave Community* (Urbana: University of Illinois Press, 1984); Lawrence W. Levine, *Black Culture and Black Consciousness: Afro-American Folk Thought from Slavery to Freedom* (New York: Oxford University Press, 1977); and Leon F. Litwak, *Been in the Storm So Long: The Aftermath of Slavery* (New York: Knopf, 1979).

19. Frank Lawrence Owsley, *Plain Folk of the Old South* (1949; reprint, Baton Rouge: Louisiana State University Press, 1982); ch. 3, "Southern Folkways," emphasizes customary community gatherings for work and recreation. For a recent appraisal and expansion of Owsley's thesis, see Samuel C. Hyde Jr., ed., *Plain Folk of the South Revisited* (Baton Rouge: Louisiana State University Press, 1997).

20. "Head Us, Stacie," recorded in 1970 from Benjamin Franklin ("Frank") Reid, 80, of Loudsville, Georgia, by Charles H. Bryson for the Georgia Folklore Archives (hereafter abbreviated GFA). Unlike folk songs and tunes, folktales normally are not given titles by their tellers; this and subsequent tale titles are mine for the purpose of identification.

21. Weather omens recorded in 1968 from Frank Reid by Kyle Davis and Dawn Fitzgerald for the GFA; see also Chip Callaway's feature on Reid, "Cold—Signs Say So," Atlanta *Journal* (December 2, 1970): 22A, and Eliot Wigginton, ed., *The Foxfire Book* (Garden City, NY: Anchor/Doubleday, 1972), 208–11. Some southerners still farm by the signs of the zodiac and phases of the moon, for which see Wigginton, 212–27. The twelve Foxfire books are a good resource for the folk knowledge of Appalachian farmers; for the jack-of-all-trades skills of a single mountaineer, see John Rice Irwin, *Alex Stewart: Portrait of a Pioneer* (West Chester, PA: Schiffer Publishing, 1985); and for folk artifacts supporting life on the land, see John A. Burrison, *Shaping Traditions: Folk Arts in a Changing South* (Athens: University of Georgia Press, 2000), 37–47, 109–14.

22. "The Unreconstructed Rebel" (also known as "The Good Old Rebel") is attributed to Innes Randolph and appears in Manly Wade Wellman, *The Rebel Songster: Songs the*

Confederates Sang (Charlotte, NC: Heritage House, 1959), 51–53; Arthur Palmer Hudson, *Folksongs of Mississippi and Their Background* (1936; reprint, New York: Folklorica Press, 1981), 259–60; Vance Randolph, *Ozark Folksongs*, ed. Norm Cohen (Urbana: University of Illinois Press, 1982), 216–17; and Newman Ivey White, gen. ed., *The Frank C. Brown Collection of North Carolina Folklore* (Durham, NC: Duke University Press, 1952–64), 3: 464–66.

23. "A Rebel Trick," recorded in 1969 from Milton Coleman, 33, of College Park, Georgia, by Patricia and Larry Hester for the GFA. For serious legends told by southerners, see Elissa R. Henken, "Taming the Enemy: Georgian Narratives about the Civil War," *Journal of Folklore Research* 40, no. 3 (2003): 289–307; John A. Burrison, ed., *Storytellers: Folktales and Legends from the South* (Athens: University of Georgia Press, 1991 [paper ed.]), 342–44; Thomas E. Barden, ed., *Virginia Folk Legends* (Charlottesville: University Press of Virginia, 1991), 64–77.

24. John A. Burrison, "Handicrafts," in *Encyclopedia of the Confederacy*, ed. Richard N. Current (New York: Simon & Schuster, 1993), 2: 735.

25. John A. Burrison, *Brothers in Clay: The Story of Georgia Folk Pottery* (Athens: University of Georgia Press, 1983), 216–17, 30, 140.

26. Gail Andrews Trechsel, "Covering Alabama: Nineteenth-Century Quilts and Needlework," in *Made in Alabama: A State Legacy*, ed. E. Bryding Adams (Birmingham, AL: Birmingham Museum of Art, 1995), 116; Ruth Haislip Roberson, ed., *North Carolina Quilts* (Chapel Hill: University of North Carolina Press, 1988), 13–14; Julia Anderson Bush, "Tattered Veterans and Genteel Beauties: Survivors of the War Between the States," in *Georgia Quilts: Piecing Together a History*, ed. Anita Zaleski Weinraub (Athens: University of Georgia Press, 2006), ch. 3.

27. "The Homespun Dress," attributed to either Carrie Belle Sinclair or a Lieutenant Harrington, appears in Hudson, 265–66; White, 3: 453–56; and H. M. Belden, ed., *Ballads and Songs Collected By the Missouri Folk-Lore Society*, rev. ed. (Columbia: University of Missouri Press, 1955), 360.

28. Allen H. Eaton, *Handicrafts of the Southern Highlands* (1937; reprint, New York: Dover Publications, 1973); Garry G. Barker, *The Handcraft Revival in Southern Appalachia, 1930–1990* (Knoxville: University of Tennessee Press, 1991); Jane S. Becker, *Selling Tradition: Appalachia and the Construction of an American Folk* (Chapel Hill: University of North Carolina Press, 1998).

29. W. J. Cash, *The Mind of the South* (New York: Alfred A. Knopf, 1941); for later appraisals, see C. Vann Woodward, "W. J. Cash Reconsidered," *New York Review of Books* 13, no. 10 (1969): 28–34, and Charles W. Eagles, ed., The Mind of the South: *Fifty Years Later* (Jackson: University Press of Mississippi, 1992). Further attempts at describing a southern mindset and regional character types, with a focus on the white population, are John Shelton Reed, *Southern Folk, Plain and Fancy: Native White Social Types* (Athens: University of Georgia Press, 1986); Florence King, *Southern Ladies and Gentlemen* (New York: St. Martin's Press, 1993); and Grady McWhiney, *Cracker Culture: Celtic Ways in the Old South* (Tuscaloosa: University of Alabama Press, 1988). African American character types (not exclusively southern) are presented in John W. Roberts, *From Trickster to Badman: The Black Folk Hero in Slavery and Freedom* (Philadelphia: University of Pennsylvania Press, 1989).

30. Sometimes the positive and negative traits combine in bizarre ways, as in Alabamian day-trader Mark Barton's shooting rampage at an Atlanta investment firm after politely greeting people, then reportedly saying, "I hope I'm not upsetting your trading day" (Michael Alvear, "Atlanta's Burning," http://www.salon.com/news/fea ture/1999/08/03/atlanta/index.html, as of January 10, 2007). A whole section is devoted to violence in Wilson and Ferris, 1469–1513.

31. "In Atlanta, Georgia," *Negro Songs of Protest*, Rounder Records 4004. The song may have been a response to the 1906 Atlanta race riot, in which more than two dozen African Americans were killed (David F. Godshalk, *Veiled Visions: The 1906 Atlanta Race Riot and the Reshaping of American Race Relations* [Chapel Hill: University of North Carolina Press, 2005]; Gregory Mixon, *The Atlanta Riot: Race, Class, and Violence in a New South City* [Gainesville: University Press of Florida, 2005]; Rebecca Burns, *Rage in the Gate City: The Story of the 1906 Atlanta Race Riot* [Cincinnati, OH: Emmis Books, 2006]). For folk narratives expressing African American attitudes toward southern race relations, see the Old Master and John tales in Burrison, *Storytellers*, 6, 147–51, 232–42; B. A. Botkin, ed., *Lay My Burden Down: A Folk History of Slavery* (Chicago: University of Chicago Press, 1945); and Richard M. Dorson, *American Negro Folktales* (New York: Fawcett Premier, 1967), ch. 10.

32. "Bump, Bump," recorded in 1974 from a twenty-year-old college student in Atlanta (who was from New Orleans) by A. Irene Hosse for the GFA. While the joke's point is that southern whites harbor even more prejudice against African Americans than those from other parts of the country, it also makes fun of the black protagonists for their naivete.

33. C. Vann Woodward, *The Strange Career of Jim Crow*, 2nd rev. ed. (New York: Oxford University Press, 1966).

34. This racial code is revealed through interviews with residents of a Black Belt town exploring the impact of the civil rights movement in Bob Adelman's *Down Home: Camden, Alabama* (New York: McGraw Hill, 1972), especially 76–79; in the oral-history autobiography, *All God's Dangers: The Life of Nate Shaw*, ed. Theodore Rosengarten (New York: Alfred A. Knopf, 1974); and in the semiautobiographical first novel of Georgian Ferrol Sams, *Run with the Horsemen* (Atlanta: Peachtree Publishers, 1982), 67–70. Further complicating the picture is the South's class system, for which see John Dollard, *Caste and Class in a Southern Town*, 3rd ed. (Garden City, NY: Doubleday Anchor, 1957).

35. The classic study is V. O. Key Jr., *Southern Politics in State and Nation* (New York: Vintage Books, 1949); a southern reactionary Populist is presented in C. Vann Woodward's *Tom Watson: Agrarian Rebel* (New York: Macmillan, 1938).

36. Gene Wiggins, *Fiddlin' Georgia Crazy: Fiddlin' John Carson, His Real World, and the World of His Songs* (Urbana: University of Illinois Press, 1987), 117–22.

37. Ibid., 5–6; John A. Burrison, "Fiddlers in the Alley: Atlanta as an Early Country Music Center," *Atlanta Historical Bulletin* 21, no. 2 (1977): 67.

38. Samuel S. Hill and Charles H. Lippy, eds., *Encyclopedia of Religion in the South*, 2nd ed. (Macon, GA: Mercer University Press, 2005); Paul F. Gillespie, ed., *Foxfire 7* (Garden City, NY: Anchor Press/Doubleday, 1982).

39. Ralph C. Wood, *Flannery O'Connor and the Christ–Haunted South* (Grand Rapids, MI: William B. Eerdmans Publishing, 2004).

40. Steve Oney's *And the Dead Shall Rise: The Murder of Mary Phagan and the Lynching of Leo Frank* (New York: Pantheon, 2003) is the most recent book-length analysis; the case also inspired a 1988 TV miniseries and a 1999 musical, *Parade*, by Alfred Uhry and David Mamet. The lynching (an echo of the old blood libel/ritual murder accusation?) was motivated by more than anti-Semitism; Frank, New York–born superintendent of the National Pencil Company in downtown Atlanta, symbolized the northern exploitation of factory workers in the New South. A folklore connection is Fiddlin' John Carson's ballad, "Little Mary Phagan," which entered the repertoire of southern folk singers (Wiggins, 26–43). For a later (1958) case of anti-Semitic violence in Atlanta, see Melissa Fay Greene, *The Temple Bombing* (Reading, MA: Addison-Wesley, 1996).

41. "The Evangelical Cabby," recorded in 1974 from Lawton Sewell of Cumming, Georgia, by Rita Thompson for the GFA. For other preacher tales see Burrison, *Storytellers*, 7–8, 76–83, 264–74; J. Mason Brewer, *The Word on the Brazos: Negro Preacher Tales from the Brazos Bottoms of Texas* (Austin: University of Texas Press, 1953); Loyal Jones, *The Preacher Joke Book* (Little Rock, AR: August House, 1989); and Gary Holloway, *Saints, Demons, and Asses: Southern Preacher Anecdotes* (Bloomington: Indiana University Press, 1989).

42. Gillespie, 370–428.

43. John Witthoft, *Green Corn Ceremonialism in the Eastern Woodlands* (Ann Arbor: University of Michigan Press, 1949); William L. Ballard, *The Yuchi Green Corn Ceremonial: Form and Meaning* (Los Angeles: University of California American Indian Studies Center, 1978); Jason Baird Jackson, *Yuchi Ceremonial Life: Performance, Meaning, and Tradition in a Contemporary American Indian Community* (Lincoln: University of Nebraska Press, 2003).

44. Jan Harold Brunvand, *The Study of American Folklore*, 4th ed. (New York: W. W. Norton, 1998), chs. 4 and 23.

45. Raven I. McDavid Jr., *Varieties of American English* (Stanford, CA: Stanford University Press, 1980); Michael B. Montgomery and James B. McMillan, *Annotated Bibliography of Southern American English* (Tuscaloosa: University of Alabama Press, 1989); Lee Pederson, ed., *Linguistic Atlas of the Gulf States* (Athens: University of Georgia Press, 1986–).

46. J. L. Dillard, *Black English: Its History and Usage in the United States* (New York: Random House, 1972); Walt Wolfram, *Appalachian Speech* (Arlington, VA: Center for Applied Linguistics, 1976); Michael B. Montgomery and Joseph S. Hall, *Dictionary of Smoky Mountain English* (Knoxville: University of Tennessee Press, 2004); Vance Randolph and George P. Wilson, *Down in the Holler: A Gallery of Ozark Folk Speech* (Norman: University of Oklahoma Press, 1953).

47. Woodward, "W. J. Cash Reconsidered," 31.

48. William Faulkner, *Requiem for a Nun* (New York: Random House, 1951), 92.

49. Archie Green, *Only a Miner: Studies in Recorded Coal-Mining Songs* (Urbana: University of Illinois Press, 1972); Guy and Candie Carawan, *Voices from the Mountains* (New York: Alfred A. Knopf, 1975); Jacqueline Dowd Hall et al., *Like a Family: The Making of a Southern Cotton Mill World*, rev. ed. (Chapel Hill: University of North Carolina Press, 2000); Allen Tullos, *Habits of Industry: White Culture and the Transformation of the Carolina Piedmont* (Chapel Hill: University of North Carolina Press, 1989).

50. Carson's "The Honest Farmer" (Wiggins, 234–37) was his reworking of a song of

the same title sung by Lillie West in the present book's chapter five. He also recorded the better-known "Ballad of the Boll Weevil" (Wiggins, 233–34), sung by blacks and whites alike but thought to have originated with the former.

51. Tony Horwitz's *Confederates in the Attic: Dispatches from the Unfinished Civil War* (New York: Pantheon, 1998) documents the now-atypical hangers-on to the Lost Cause.

52. As I write this, an African American exotic dancer's accusation of rape against white members of the Duke University lacrosse team, and the racial division it has stirred up in Durham, North Carolina, is very much in the news.

53. Michael B. Montgomery and Guy Bailey, eds., *Language Variety in the South: Perspectives in Black and White* (University, AL: University of Alabama Press, 1986); Margaret Bender, ed., *Linguistic Diversity in the South: Changing Codes, Practices, and Ideology* (Athens: University of Georgia Press, 2004).

2. Goobers, Grits, and Greasy Greens: What's *Southern* about Southern Folk Culture?

1. "Song to Grits," in Roy Blount Jr., *One Fell Soup, or, I'm Just a Bug on the Windshield of Life* (Boston: Little, Brown, 1981), 56–57.

2. The term *foodways* describes the entire culture complex, including sourcing, preparation, presentation, consumption, and customs (Charles Camp, *American Foodways: What, When, Why, and How We Eat in America* [Little Rock, AR: August House, 1989]; Joe Gray Taylor, "Foodways," in *Encyclopedia of Southern Culture*, ed. Charles Reagan Wilson and William Ferris [Chapel Hill: University of North Carolina Press, 1989], 613–16). The Southern Foodways Alliance, with its annual symposium, was established in 1977 by the Center for the Study of Southern Culture at the University of Mississippi.

3. Joseph E. Dabney, *Smokehouse Ham, Spoon Bread, & Scuppernong Wine: The Folklore and Art of Southern Appalachian Cooking* (Nashville, TN: Cumberland House, 1998), 263–71.

4. John Egerton, *Southern Food: At Home, on the Road, in History* (New York: Alfred A. Knopf, 1987), 2–3, 173.

5. "Turnip Greens," from Vance Randolph, *Ozark Folksongs*, ed. Norm Cohen (Urbana: University of Illinois Press, 1982), 243–45. The song may have begun life on the blackface minstrel stage and was recorded by Mississippi bluesman Bo Chatmon in 1928.

6. Quoted in Sam Bowers Hilliard, *Hog Meat and Hoecake: Food Supply in the Old South 1840–1860* (Carbondale: Southern Illinois University Press, 1972), 42.

7. Steven Raichlen, *The Barbeque! Bible* (New York: Workman Publishing, 1998); Lolis Eric Elie, ed., *Cornbread Nation 2: The United States of Barbeque* (Chapel Hill: University of North Carolina Press, 2004); James Auchmutey and Susan Puckett, *The Ultimate Barbeque Sauce Cookbook* (Atlanta: Longstreet Press, 1995); John T. Edge, *Southern Belly: The Ultimate Food Lover's Companion to the South* (Athens, GA: Hill Street Press, 2000); Dabney, 187–204; Egerton, 147–67; Howard Wight Marshall, "Meat Preservation on the Farm in Missouri's 'Little Dixie,'" *Journal of American Folklore* 92, no. 366 (1979): 400–417.

8. Eliot Wigginton, ed., *The Foxfire Book* (Garden City, NY: Anchor/Doubleday, 1972), 189–207; Linda Garland Page and Eliot Wigginton, eds., *The Foxfire Book of Appalachian Cookery: Regional Memorabilia and Recipes* (New York: E. P. Dutton, 1984), ch. 9; Hilliard, ch. 5; Dabney, 173–204.

9. "Chitlin Cookin' Time in Cheatham County," recorded by the Arthur Smith Trio

in 1936, reissued on *Smoky Mountain Ballads*, RCA Victor LP V–507. Cheatham County, Tennessee, lies just northwest of Nashville. *Chitlins*, a contraction of *chitterlings*, are considered a defining element of "soul food," inspiring the name "Chitlin Circuit" for the string of clubs and juke joints patronized by African Americans, for which see LaMonda Horton-Stallings, "Chitlin Circuit" and idem, "Chitterlings," in Anand Prahlad, ed., *The Greenwood Encyclopedia of African American Folklore* (Westport, CT: Greenwood Press, 2006), 228–31.

10. Bill Neal, *Biscuits, Spoonbread, and Sweet Potato Pie* (New York: Alfred A. Knopf, 1996), 4–28; Egerton, 226–31; Dabney, 96–112.

11. Joseph Earl Dabney, *Mountain Spirits: A Chronicle of Corn Whiskey from King James' Ulster Plantation to America's Appalachians and the Moonshine Life* (New York: Charles Scribner's Sons, 1974); Wigginton, 301–45.

12. "Mountain Dew" was written in 1920 by Bascom Lamar Lunsford, revised by fellow North Carolinian Scott Wiseman (Loyal Jones, *Minstrel of the Appalachians: The Story of Bascom Lamar Lunsford* [Boone, NC: Appalachian Consortium Press, 1984], 34–39), and is related to the Irish song "The Real Old Mountain Dew" (Colm O Lochlainn, *Irish Street Ballads* [Dublin: Three Candles, 1965], 128–29).

13. Maryann Byrd, *The Biscuit Dive Guide* and accompanying documentary video, *The Rise of the Southern Biscuit* (Nashville, TN: Byrdword Productions, 2006); Neal, 33–51; Dabney, *Smokehouse Ham*, 113–22; Egerton, 217–21.

14. J. L. Herring, *Saturday Night Sketches: Stories of Old Wiregrass Georgia* (1918; reprint, Tifton, GA: Sunny South Press, 1978), 117–22; Eliot Wigginton, ed., *Foxfire 3* (Garden City, NY: Anchor/Doubleday, 1975), 424–36; Dabney, *Smokehouse Ham*, 423–32. As the title of a Confederate folk song, "Sorghum Molasses," suggests (John A. Burrison, *Brothers in Clay: The Story of Georgia Folk Pottery* [Athens: University of Georgia Press, 1983], 53), in folk usage the distinction between syrup and molasses is not always clear; properly, molasses is a thicker by-product of sugar refining.

15. Fred Brown and Sherri M. L. Smith, *The Best of Georgia Farms Cookbook and Tour Book* (Atlanta: Georgia Department of Agriculture, 1998), 250–51.

16. "Goober Peas," Manly Wade Wellman, *The Rebel Songster: Songs the Confederates Sang* (Charlotte, NC: Heritage House, 1959), 42–43.

17. John M. Hunter, "Geophagy in Africa and in the United States: A Culture-Nutrition Hypothesis," *Geographical Review* 63, no. 2 (1973): 170–95; Robert W. Twyman, "The Clay Eater: A New Look at an Old Southern Enigma," *Journal of Southern History* 37 (August 1971): 439–48; Donald E. Vermeer and Dennis A. Frate, "Geophagy in a Mississippi County," *Annals of American Geographers* 65 (September 1975): 414–24; Margaret V. Clayton, "A Study of Geophagy among Negroes in the Alabama Black Belt," M.A. thesis (Athens: University of Georgia, 1965); Gordon L. Jones, "'A Morbid Appetite': Dirt-Eating and Cachexia Africana in the Southern United States, 1830–1860," M.A. thesis (Columbia: University of South Carolina, 1990). For southeastern Indian clay-eating, see Frank G. Speck, "Catawba Texts," *Columbia University Contributions to Anthropology* 24 (1934): 47–48.

18. J. S. Bradford, "Crackers," *Lippincott's Magazine of Literature, Science and Education* 6 (November 1870): 465.

19. "The Clay-Eaters of Georgia," *China, Glass and Lamps* (1893): 24.

20. Thomas Spencer, "Dirt-Eating Persists in Rural South" (http://www.newhouse news.com/archive/story1c012502, as of July 18, 2006).

21. John A. Burrison, "Brunswick Stew," in *The New Georgia Encyclopedia* (http:// www.georgiaencyclopedia.org/nge/Article.jsp?path=/Folklife/Foodways&id=h-555); Dabney, *Smokehouse Ham*, 211–16. These stews are the subject of three documentary videos produced by Woodward Studio of Greenville, South Carolina: *Brunswick Stew: A Virginia Treasure* (1998), *Southern Stews: A Taste of the South* (2002), and *Brunswick Stew: Georgia Named Her, Georgia Claims Her* (2005).

22. Sweet iced tea is mainly a twentieth-century phenomenon, perhaps an echo of antebellum upperclass lemonade; the first published recipe appears in Marion Cabell Tyree's *Housekeeping in Old Virginia* (1879). In Georgia I heard a folk joke about a storekeeper who'd gotten in his first shipment of tea and offered free samples to his farmer customers. When one of them returned a week later, he was asked how he liked this novelty. "Well," he replied, "I didn't much care for it; they were the bitterest greens I ever et!" These essentially homemade beverages should be distinguished from mass-produced and -marketed soft drinks such as Coca–Cola, Royal Crown Cola, and Dr Pepper, that also contribute to regional identity and have spawned their own folklore (e.g., http://www.snopes.com/ cokelore/cokelore.asp#santa, as of January 10, 2007; Gary Alan Fine, *Manufacturing Tales: Sex and Money in Contemporary Legends* [Knoxville: University of Tennessee Press, 1992], ch. 4).

23. Floyd C. Watkins and Charles Hubert Watkins, *Yesterday in the Hills* (1963; reprint, Athens: University of Georgia Press, 1973), 46; Susan Tucker and Sharon Stallworth Nossiter, "Food," in *The Greenwood Encyclopedia of American Regional Cultures: The South*, ed. Rebecca Mark and Rob Vaughan (Westport, CT: Greenwood Press, 2004), 291; Burrison, *Brothers in Clay*, 123, 151–53.

24. For an international introduction to the subject see Henry Glassie, *Vernacular Architecture* (Bloomington: Indiana University Press, 2000).

25. Frank Lawrence Owsley, *Plain Folk of the Old South* (1949; reprint, Baton Rouge: Louisiana State University Press, 1982), 104–108; Everett Dick, *The Dixie Frontier* (1948; reprint, New York: Capricorn Books, 1964), 127–28; John C. Campbell, *The Southern Highlander and His Homeland* (New York: Russell Sage Foundation, 1921), 143; Herring, 268–74.

26. For traditional wood construction in general, see Fred B. Kniffin and Henry Glassie, "Building in Wood in the Eastern United States: A Time-Place Perspective," in *Common Places: Readings in American Vernacular Architecture*, ed. Dell Upton and John Michael Vlach (Athens: University of Georgia Press, 1986), 159–81.

27. Watkins and Watkins, 37; Mitchell B. Garrett, *Horse and Buggy Days on Hatchet Creek* (University, AL: University of Alabama Press, 1957), 102. Some mountaineers believed that the fieldstone foundation piers should be at least eighteen inches high, as termites could climb no higher (Wigginton, 55).

28. Jocelyn Hazelwood Donlon, *Swinging in Place: Porch Life in Southern Culture* (Chapel Hill: University of North Carolina Press, 2001); Sue Bridwell Beckham, "Porches," in Wilson and Ferris, 515. Folklorist John Michael Vlach suggests that the sitting porch was introduced by slaves from West Africa in his *The Afro-American Tradition in Decorative Arts*, rev. ed. (Athens: University of Georgia Press, 1990), 136–38, and idem,

"Afro-Americans," in *America's Architectural Roots: Ethnic Groups That Built America*, ed. Dell Upton (Washington, D.C.: Preservation Press, 1986), 45. Before the open porch migrated to the North, porches there, like those of Britain, were enclosed or covered entranceways.

29. Surveys of southern folk architecture are included in Henry Glassie, *Pattern in the Material Folk Culture of the Eastern United States* (Philadelphia: University of Pennsylvania Press, 1968), 64–121, and Allen G. Noble, *Wood, Brick, and Stone: The North American Settlement Landscape* (Amherst: University of Massachusetts Press, 1984). Studies of specific building types or places include Henry Glassie, *Folk Housing in Middle Virginia: A Structural Analysis of Historic Artifacts* (Knoxville: University of Tennessee Press, 1975); John Michael Vlach, *Back of the Big House: The Architecture of Plantation Slavery* (Chapel Hill: University of North Carolina Press, 1993); George W. McDaniel, *Hearth and Home: Preserving a People's Culture* (Philadelphia: Temple University Press, 1982); William Lynwood Montell and Michael Lynn Morse, *Kentucky Folk Architecture* (Lexington: University Press of Kentucky, 1995); Charles E. Martin, *Hollybush: Folk Building and Social Change in an Appalachian Community* (Knoxville: University of Tennessee Press, 1984); Michael Ann Williams, *Homeplace: The Social Use and Meaning of the Folk Dwelling in Southwestern North Carolina* (Athens: University of Georgia Press, 1991); John Morgan, *The Log House in East Tennessee* (Knoxville: University of Tennessee Press, 1990); Marian Moffett and Lawrence Wodehouse, *East Tennessee Cantilever Barns* (Knoxville: University of Tennessee Press, 1993); Ronald W. Haase, *Classic Cracker: Florida's Wood-Frame Vernacular Architecture* (Sarasota, FL: Pineapple Press, 1992); Eugene M. Wilson, *Alabama Folk Houses* (Montgomery: Alabama Historical Commission, 1975); Jean Sizemore, *Ozark Vernacular Houses: A Study of Rural Homeplaces in the Arkansas Ozarks 1830–1930* (Fayetteville: University of Arkansas Press, 1994); Howard W. Marshall, *Folk Architecture in Little Dixie: A Regional Culture in Missouri* (Columbia: University of Missouri Press, 1981); Jay Dearborn Edwards and Nicolas Kariouk Pecquet du Bellay de Verton, *A Creole Lexicon: Architecture, Landscape, People* (Baton Rouge: Louisiana State University Press, 2004); Terry G. Jordan, *Texas Log Buildings: A Folk Architecture* (Austin: University of Texas Press, 1978). An example of coffee-table books on southern architecture, which tend to feature neoclassical-style homes of the wealthy, is Mills Lane, *Architecture of the Old South: Georgia* (Savannah: Beehive Press, 1986).

30. Vlach, *Afro-American Tradition in Decorative Arts*, 123–31; idem, "The Shotgun House: An African Architectural Legacy," in Upton and Vlach, 58–78; idem, "Afro-Americans," in Upton, 42–47.

31. Quoted in Elizabeth Kytle, *Willie Mae* (New York: Alfred A. Knopf, 1959), 38.

32. The Friends of the Shotgun House was formed to preserve Santa Monica, California's last surviving example, built in 1898 (http://shotgunhouse.org/index.html, as of January 10, 2007).

33. Herring, 269–70.

34. Mark Twain, *The Autobiography of Mark Twain*, ed. Charles Neider (New York: Harper & Row, 1959), 4.

35. Glassie suggests the Tennessee Valley as the home of the dogtrot (*Pattern in the Material Folk Culture of the Eastern United States*, 88–99), but similar houses have been found in Pennsylvania, one reputedly dating to 1698 (Terry G. Jordan and Matti Kaups,

The American Backwoods Frontier: An Ethnic and Ecological Interpretation [Baltimore: Johns Hopkins University Press, 1989], 179–92; Richard H. Hulan, "The Dogtrot House and Its Pennsylvania Associations," *Pennsylvania Folklife* 26 [Summer 1977]: 25–32). Jerah Johnson reviews the dogtrot origin debate and adds his own suggestion in "The Vernacular Architecture of the South: Log Buildings, Dog-Trot Houses, and English Barns," in *Plain Folk of the South Revisited*, ed. Samuel C. Hyde Jr. (Baton Rouge: Louisiana State University Press, 1997), 62–72. Some dogtrot-like houses occurred when a second single-pen cabin was grafted to an existing one with a space left between the two.

36. http://www.fresnoflatsmuseum.org/vtour.html (as of January 10, 2007).

37. David C. Barrow Jr., "A Georgia Corn-Shucking," in *The Negro and His Folklore in Nineteenth-Century Periodicals*, ed. Bruce Jackson, Publications of the American Folklore Society Bibliographical and Special Series 18 (Austin: University of Texas Press, 1967), 169.

38. Fred Kniffin, "Folk Housing: A Key to Diffusion," in Upton and Vlach, 17–18; Glassie, *Pattern in the Material Folk Culture of the Eastern United States*, 88–93; Noble, 2: 2–5, 10–14.

39. Richard Westmacott, *African-American Gardens and Yards in the Rural South* (Knoxville: University of Tennessee Press, 1992). The swept yard as a tradition for the white population is documented by Watkins and Watkins, 38, and in a 2006 interview with Mr. and Mrs. Jerald Williams of Buford, Georgia, by Nicole Mullen for the GFA: "Everybody back in my childhood days had swept yards. In the mid-'50s to late '60s everyone in the neighborhood started putting grass in; we got citified. . . . The brooms were made out of dogwood; you'd go to the woods and get a bunch of limbs and tie them together." Normally, sweeping was confined to the front yard (which still could be punctuated by flowerbeds), with vegetable and herb gardens placed at the back and sides of the house.

40. "Everyday Use," in Alice Walker, *In Love and Trouble: Stories of Black Women* (New York: Harcourt Brace Jovanovich, 1973), 47.

41. John W. Heisey, *A Checklist of American Coverlet Weavers* (Charlottesville: University Press of Virginia for Colonial Williamsburg Foundation, 1978); Guy F. Reinert, *Coverlets of the Pennsylvania Germans* (Allentown, PA: Pennsylvania German Folklore Society, 1949), 35–41.

42. John A. Burrison, *Shaping Traditions: Folk Arts in a Changing South* (Athens: University of Georgia Press, 2000), 10–11, 76–77, 137; Allen H. Eaton, *Handicrafts of the Southern Highlands* (1937; reprint, New York: Dover Publications, 1973), chs. 5–6; Frances Louisa Goodrich, *Mountain Homespun* (1931; reprint, Knoxville: University of Tennessee Press, 1989); Sadye Tune Wilson and Doris Finch Kennedy, *Of Coverlets: The Legacies, the Weavers* (Nashville, TN: Tunstede, 1983); Kathleen Curtis Wilson, *Textile Art from Southern Appalachia: The Quiet Work of Women* (Johnson City, TN: Overmountain Press, 2001).

43. Eaton, chs. 3–4; Philis Alvic, *Weavers of the Southern Highlands* (Lexington: University Press of Kentucky, 2003).

44. Laurel Horton, correspondence with author, May 23, 2006; the "Pineapple" pattern is featured on the cover of her *Social Fabric: South Carolina's Traditional Quilts* (Columbia: McKissick Museum, University of South Carolina, [1986]). See also idem, *Mary Black's Family Quilts: Memory and Meaning in Everyday Life* (Columbia: University

of South Carolina Press, 2005); Jonathan Holstein and John Finley, *Kentucky Quilts, 1800–1900* (Louisville: Kentucky Quilt Project, 1982); Bets Ramsey and Merikay Waldvogel, *The Quilts of Tennessee: Images of Domestic Life Prior to 1930* (Nashville, TN: Rutledge Hill Press, 1986); Ruth Haislip Roberson, ed., *North Carolina Quilts* (Chapel Hill: University of North Carolina Press, 1988); Anita Zaleski Weinraub, ed., *Georgia Quilts: Piecing Together a History* (Athens: University of Georgia Press, 2006); Nancilu B. Burdick, *Legacy: The Story of Talula Gilbert Bottoms and Her Quilts* (Nashville, TN: Rutledge Hill Press, 1988); Gail Andrews Trechsel, "Covering Alabama: Nineteenth-Century Quilts and Needlework," in *Made in Alabama: A State Legacy*, ed. E. Bryding Adams (Birmingham, AL: Birmingham Museum of Art, 1995), 99–133; Mary Elizabeth Johnson Huff and J. D. Schwalm, *Mississippi Quilts* (Jackson: University Press of Mississippi, 2002); John Rice Irwin, *A People [Appalachia] and Their Quilts* (West Chester, PA: Schiffer Publishing, 1984); Jan Arnow, *By Southern Hands: A Celebration of Craft Traditions in the South* (Birmingham, AL: Oxmoor House and Roundtable Press, 1987), 104–11. Yvonne J. Milspaw considered "Regional Style in [American] Quilt Design" in *Journal of American Folklore* 110, no. 438 (1997): 363–90.

45. Vlach, *Afro-American Tradition in Decorative Arts*, ch. 4; Gladys-Marie Fry, *Stitched from the Soul: Slave Quilts from the Antebellum South* (Chapel Hill: University of North Carolina Press, 2002); John Beardsley et al., *Gee's Bend* [Alabama]*: The Women and Their Quilts* (Atlanta: Tinwood Press, 2002); Questa Benberry, *Always There: The African-American Presence in American Quilts* (Louisville: Kentucky Quilt Project, 1992); Roland L. Freeman, *A Communion of the Spirits: African-American Quilters, Preservers, and Their Stories* (Nashville, TN: Rutledge Hill Press, 1996); Regenia A. Perry, *Harriet Powers's Bible Quilts* (New York: St. Martin's/Rizzoli International, 1994); Jacqueline L. Tobin and Raymond G. Dobard, *Hidden In Plain View: A Secret Story of Quilts and the Underground Railroad* (New York: Doubleday, 1999); Laurel Horton, "The Underground Railroad Quilt Code: Traditional Narrative Strategies in Promoting a 'Good Story,'" paper (American Folklore Society annual meeting, Atlanta, 2005).

46. Bill McCarthy, "Clothing," in Wilson and Ferris, 466–68; Helen Bradley Foster, *New Raiments of Self: African American Clothing in the Antebellum South* (New York: Berg Publishers, 1997), ch. 6; Michael P. Smith, *Mardi Gras Indians* (Gretna, LA: Pelican Publishing, 1994); Kalamu ya Salaam, *"He's the Prettiest": A Tribute to Big Chief Allison "Tuttie" Montana's 50 Years of Mardi Gras Indian Suiting* (New Orleans: New Orleans Museum of Art, 1997); Carl Lindahl and Carolyn Ware, *Cajun Mardi Gras Masks* (Jackson: University Press of Mississippi, 1997); Arnow, 116–19; Dorothy Downs, *Art of the Florida Seminole and Miccosukee Indians* (Gainesville: University Press of Florida, 1995), chs. 1–3, 12; Burrison, *Shaping Traditions*, 51, color pl. 19.

47. Burrison, *Brothers in Clay*, 29.

48. Ibid., ch. 2.

49. Ibid., 68, 125–26, 154–55, 209; H. E. Comstock, *The Pottery of the Shenandoah Valley Region* (Chapel Hill: University of North Carolina Press for Museum of Early Southern Decorative Arts, 1994), 205, 280–81, 331, 387; *The Pottery of Charles F. Decker: A Life Well Made* (Jonesborough, TN: Jonesborough/Washington County History Museum and Historic Jonesborough Visitors Center, 2004), 14; Charles G. Zug III, *Turners and Burners: The Folk Potters of North Carolina* (Chapel Hill: University of North Carolina Press,

1986), 355–62, 369–70; Mark Hewitt and Nancy Sweezy, *The Potter's Eye: Art and Tradition in North Carolina Pottery* (Chapel Hill: University of North Carolina Press for North Carolina Museum of Art, 2005), 98–101, 200–201; Cinda K. Baldwin, *Great and Noble Jar: Traditional Stoneware of South Carolina* (Athens: University of Georgia Press, 1993), 182–85; Joey Brackner, *Alabama Folk Pottery* (Tuscaloosa: University of Alabama Press with Birmingham Museum of Art, 2006), 30–31, 35–39, 137–38, 147, 183–84; *Made By Hand: Mississippi Folk Art* (Jackson: State Historical Museum, 1980), 52, 66. Clay grave markers also were made to a limited extent in southwestern Pennsylvania, New Jersey, and the Midwest; examples are known for the British Isles, Germany, and Africa, but probably were not an influence on the southern tradition.

50. Burrison, *Brothers in Clay*, 58–62; Baldwin, 16–20, 144–47; Georgeanna H. Greer, *American Stonewares: The Art and Craft of Utilitarian Potters* (Exton, PA: Schiffer Publishing, 1981), 202–10; Daisy Wade Bridges, *Ash Glaze Traditions in Ancient China and the American South* (Charlotte, NC: Ceramic Circle of Charlotte and Southern Folk Pottery Collectors Society, 1997); Hewitt and Sweezy, 103–63 (see 106–7 for an alkaline–glazed bottle dated 1820 and signed by Abner Landrum of Edgefield District, South Carolina).

51. Georgeanna H. Greer, "Groundhog Kilns—Rectangular American Kilns of the Nineteenth and Early Twentieth Centuries," *Northeast Historical Archaeology* 6, nos. 1–2 (1977): 42–54; David Gaimster, *German Stoneware 1200–1900: Archaeology and Cultural History* (London: British Museum Press, 1997), 44–47; Comstock, 36–37; Baldwin, 20–21, 121, 161–62; Zug, 202–34; Burrison, *Brothers in Clay*, 91–96, 149, 179, 260, 280, color pl. 10; Brackner, 62–63. Studio potters use the term *crossdraft* differently to mean a kiln fired from the side.

52. Arnow, 12–47; Sarah H. Hill, *Weaving New Worlds: Southeastern Cherokee Women and Their Basketry* (Chapel Hill: University of North Carolina Press, 1997); Betty J. Duggan and Brett H. Riggs, *Studies in Cherokee Basketry* (Knoxville: Frank H. McClung Museum, University of Tennessee, and Qualla Arts and Crafts Mutual, 1991); Marshall Gettys, ed., *Basketry of Southeastern Indians* (Idabel, OK: Potsherd Press, Museum of the Red River, 1984); Vlach, *Afro-American Tradition in Decorative Arts*, ch. 1; Dale Rosengarten, *Row upon Row: Sea Grass Baskets of the South Carolina Lowcountry* (Columbia: McKissick Museum, University of South Carolina, 1986); Eaton, ch. 10; Rachel Nash Law and Cynthia W. Taylor, *Appalachian White Oak Basketmaking: Handing Down the Basket* (Knoxville: University of Tennessee Press, 1991); John Rice Irwin, *Baskets and Basket Makers in Southern Appalachia* (Exton, PA: Schiffer Publishing, 1982); J. Geraint Jenkins, *Traditional* [British] *Country Craftsmen* (New York: Frederick A. Praeger, 1966), opp. 45, 47–50.

53. Mary G. Jones and Lily Reynolds, *Coweta County Chronicles for One Hundred Years* (Newnan, GA: Sarah Dickinson Chapter, Daughters of the American Revolution, 1928), 48.

54. Frances Anne Kemble, *Journal of a Residence on a Georgian Plantation in 1838–1839*, ed. John A. Scott (New York: Alfred A. Knopf, 1961), 63. Pierce Butler was a Philadelphian who inherited his wealthy father's plantations on the Georgia coast. Four years after his marriage to Fanny Kemble, she visited them and kept a journal of the experience; the visit strengthened her abolitionist beliefs, causing clashes with her slaveholding husband that led to their divorce.

55. *Neat Pieces: The Plain-Style Furniture of Nineteenth-Century Georgia*, rev. ed. (Athens: University of Georgia Press, 2006), 44, 113–26.

56. Betsy K. White, *Great Road Style: The Decorative Arts Legacy of Southwest Virginia and Northeast Tennessee* (Charlottesville: University of Virginia Press, 2006), 23–25, 48–67; Derita Coleman Williams and Nathan Harsh, *The Art and Mystery of Tennessee Furniture and Its Makers Through 1850* (Nashville: Tennessee Historical Society and Tennessee State Museum Foundation, 1988), 83, 161–67.

57. *Neat Pieces*, 126; Anne S. McPherson, "'That Article of Household Furniture Peculiar to Earlier Days in the South': Sugar Chests in Middle Tennessee and Central Kentucky, 1800–1835," *Journal of Early Southern Decorative Arts* 23, no. 2 (1997): 1–65; Robert Hicks and Benjamin H. Caldwell Jr., "A Short History of the Tennessee Sugar Chest," *The Magazine Antiques* 164 (September 2003): 128–33; Williams and Harsh, 52, 74–76, 137–46.

58. *Neat Pieces*, 139–41; Williams and Harsh, 136. Several Internet sites that attribute the lazy Susan's invention to Thomas Jefferson seem to be confusing it with the dumbwaiter he installed at Monticello to convey food to the dining room from the kitchen below, or with his small, revolving-top reading tables built at his joinery. According to the *Oxford English Dictionary*, the first reference to the term *lazy Susan* appears in a 1917 advertisement in *Vanity Fair*.

59. http://www.oldcharlestonjogglingboard.com/ (as of January 10, 2007).

60. Glassie, *Pattern in the Material Folk Culture of the Eastern United States*, 228–34; Ralph and Terry Kovel, *American Country Furniture 1780–1875* (New York: Crown Publishers, 1965), chs. 6–7.

61. Burrison, *Shaping Traditions*, 7–8, 66–68, 129–32. For more on Appalachian chairs and makers, see Eaton, 151–61; Michael Owen Jones, *Craftsman of the Cumberlands: Tradition and Creativity* (Lexington: University Press of Kentucky, 1989); Jerry Israel, "The Mace Family of Chair Makers," in *May We All Remember Well: A Journal of the History and Cultures of Western North Carolina*, vol. 1, ed. Robert S. Brunk (Asheville: Robert S. Brunk Auction Services, 1997), 176–200; Adam Sanders, "Mace Chairs," and Curtis Buchanan, "Chair Making," in *Encyclopedia of Appalachia*, ed. Rudy Abramson and Jean Haskell (Knoxville: University of Tennessee Press, 2006), 810, 786–87; Jock Lauterer, *Wouldn't Take Nothin' for My Journey Now* (Chapel Hill: University of North Carolina Press, 1980), 68–74.

62. George Pullen Jackson, *White and Negro Spirituals: Their Life Span and Kinship* (1943; reprint, New York: Da Capo Press, 1975); William Francis Allen, Charles Pickard Ware, and Lucy McKim Garrison, *Slave Songs of the United States* (1867; reprint, Baltimore, MD: Clearfield Press, 1992); James Weldon Johnson and J. Rosamond Johnson, *The Books of American Negro Spirituals* (1925–26; reprint, New York: Da Capo Press, 1977); Dena J. Epstein, *Sinful Tunes and Spirituals: Black Folk Music to the Civil War* (Urbana: University of Illinois Press, 1977); Lydia Parrish, *Slave Songs of the Georgia Sea Islands* (1942; reprint, Hatboro, PA: Folklore Associates, 1965); Art Rosenbaum and Margo Newmark Rosenbaum, *Shout Because You're Free: The African American Ring Shout Tradition in Coastal Georgia* (Athens: University of Georgia Press, 1998).

63. A select list of blues publications would include Bruce Bastin, *Red River Blues: The Blues Tradition in the Southeast* (Urbana: University of Illinois Press, 1986); Samuel

B. Charters, *The Country Blues* (1959; reprint, New York: Da Capo Press, 1975); David Evans, *Big Road Blues: Tradition and Creativity in the Folk Blues* (Berkeley: University of California Press, 1982); William R. Ferris, *Blues from the Delta* (Garden City, NY: Anchor Press, 1978); B. B. King and David Ritz, *Blues All Around Me: The Autobiography of B. B. King* (New York: Avon Books, 1996); Sandra R. Lieb, *Mother of the Blues: A Study of Ma Rainey* (Amherst: University of Massachusetts Press, 1981); Albert Murray, *Stomping the Blues*, rev. ed. (New York: Da Capo Press, 2000); Paul Oliver, *Blues Fell This Morning: Meaning in the Blues* (Cambridge, Eng.: Cambridge University Press, 1990); Harry Oster, *Living Country Blues* (Detroit: Folklore Associates, 1969); Barry Lee Pearson, *"Sounds So Good to Me": The Bluesman's Story* (Philadelphia: University of Pennsylvania Press, 1984); idem, *Virginia Piedmont Blues: The Lives and Art of Two Virginia Bluesmen* (Philadelphia: University of Pennsylvania Press, 1990); idem and Bill McCulloch, *Robert Johnson Lost and Found* (Urbana: University of Illinois Press, 2003); Jeff Todd Titon, *Early Downhome Blues: A Musical and Cultural Analysis*, rev. ed. (Chapel Hill: University of North Carolina Press, 1994); and *Living Blues Magazine* (published by the Center for the Study of Southern Culture at the University of Mississippi).

64. The bibliographies for jazz and bluegrass are extensive, but a starter kit might include Marshall W. Stearns, *The Story of Jazz* (London: Oxford University Press, 1970); Alan Lomax, *Mister Jelly Roll: The Fortunes of Jelly Roll Morton, New Orleans Creole and "Inventor of Jazz"* (1950; reprint, Berkeley: University of California Press, 2001); Colin Larkin, ed., *The Virgin Encyclopedia of Jazz*, rev. ed. (London: Virgin, 2004); Robert Cantwell, *Bluegrass Breakdown: The Making of the Old Southern Sound* (Urbana: University of Illinois Press, 1984); Neil V. Rosenberg, *Bluegrass: A History* (Urbana: University of Illinois Press, 1985); Richard D. Smith, *Can't You Hear Me Callin': The Life of Bill Monroe, Father of Bluegrass* (Boston: Little, Brown, 2000).

65. Bill C. Malone, *Country Music U.S.A.: A Fifty-Year History*, 2nd rev. ed. (Austin: University of Texas Press, 2002); Paul Oliver, *Songsters and Saints: Vocal Traditions on Race Records* (Cambridge, Eng.: Cambridge University Press, 1984); Gene Busnar, *The Rhythm and Blues Story* (New York: Julian Messner, 1985).

66. Richard Middleton, *Popular Music and the Blues: A Study of the Relationship and Its Significance* (London: Victor Gollancz, 1972); Bob Brunning, *Blues: The British Connection* (Poole, Eng.: Blandford Press, 1986); Michael Bertrand, *Race, Rock, and Elvis* (Urbana: University of Illinois Press, 2000); Vernon Chadwick, ed., *In Search of Elvis: Music, Race, Art, Religion* (Boulder, CO: Westview Press, 1997).

67. Charles Joyner, *Shared Traditions: Southern History and Folk Culture* (Urbana: University of Illinois Press, 1999), 204–6; Malone, 87, 104–9, 324; Mark Zwonitzer and Charles Hirshberg, *Will You Miss Me When I'm Gone: The Carter Family and Their Legacy in American Music* (New York: Simon & Schuster, 2002), 127–28, 132–33, 137–38.

68. Thomas Jefferson, *Thomas Jefferson's Notes on the State of Virginia*, ed. William Peden (Chapel Hill: University of North Carolina Press, 1954), 288.

69. Philip F. Gura and James F. Bollman, *America's Instrument: The Banjo in the Nineteenth Century* (Chapel Hill: University of North Carolina Press, 1999); Cecilia Conway, *African Banjo Echoes in Appalachia: A Study of Folk Traditions* (Knoxville: University of Tennessee Press, 1995); Glassie, *Pattern in the Material Folk Culture of the Eastern United States*, 22–24.

70. L. Allen Smith, *A Catalogue of Pre-Revival Appalachian Dulcimers* (Columbia: University of Missouri Press, 1983); Ralph Lee Smith, *Appalachian Dulcimer Traditions* (Lanham, MD: Scarecrow Press, 1997); R. Gerald Alvey, *Dulcimer Maker: The Craft of Homer Ledford* (Lexington: University Press of Kentucky, 1984).

71. Paula Hathaway Anderson-Green, *A Hot-Bed of Musicians: Traditional Music in the Upper New River Valley–Whitetop Region* (Knoxville: University of Tennessee Press, 2002); Fred C. Fussell, *Blue Ridge Music Trails: Finding a Place in the Circle* (Chapel Hill: University of North Carolina Press, 2003); Joe Wilson, *A Guide to the Crooked Road: Virginia's Heritage Music Trail* (Winston-Salem, NC: John F. Blair Publisher, 2006); Kevin Donleavy, *Strings in Life: Conversations with Old-Time Musicians from Virginia and North Carolina* (Blacksburg, VA: Pocahontas Press, 2004); Marty McGee, *Traditional Musicians of the Central Blue Ridge* (Jefferson, NC: McFarland, 2000); John Rice Irwin, *Musical Instruments of the Southern Appalachian Mountains* (West Chester, PA: Schiffer Publishing, 1983); *Blue Ridge Folk Instruments and Their Makers . . .* (Ferrum, VA: Blue Ridge Institute, Ferrum College, 1992).

72. Barry Jean Ancelet, *Cajun and Creole Music Makers* (Jackson: University Press of Mississippi, 1999); Ann Allen Savoy, *Cajun Music: A Reflection of a People*, vol. 1 (Eunice, LA: Bluebird Press, 1984); Charles J. Stivale, *Disenchanting les Bons Temps: Identity and Authenticity in Cajun Music and Dance* (Durham, NC: Duke University Press, 2003); Michael Tisserand, *The Kingdom of Zydeco* (New York: Arcade Publishing, 1998); Ben Sandmel, *Zydeco!* (Jackson: University Press of Mississippi, 1999).

73. Tristram P. Coffin, *The British Traditional Ballad in North America*, rev. ed. (Philadelphia: American Folklore Society, 1963); Evelyn Kendrick Wells, *The Ballad Tree: A Study of British and American Ballads, Their Folklore, Verse, and Music* (New York: Ronald Press, 1950), 286–97; G. Malcolm Laws Jr., *Native American Balladry: A Descriptive Study and Bibliographical Syllabus*, rev. ed. (Philadelphia: American Folklore Society, 1964), 39; W. K. McNeil, ed., *Southern Folk Ballads* (Little Rock, AR: August House, 1987).

74. Francis James Child, ed., *The English and Scottish Popular Ballads* (1882–1898; reprint, New York: Dover Publications, 1965). A literary scholar, Child was not much concerned with the melodies of the ballads; Bertrand Harris Bronson, in *The Traditional Tunes of the Child Ballads . . .* (Princeton, NJ: Princeton University Press, 1959–1972) later did for the melodies what Child did for their texts, while considering American variants collected since the 1920s.

75. G. Malcolm Laws, *American Balladry from British Broadsides: A Guide for Students and Collectors of Traditional Song* (Philadelphia: American Folklore Society, 1957). Broadside ballads were cheaply printed (without music, but meant to be sung) on one side of a paper sheet. Composed with recycled formulas by professional "gutter poets," they treated current events or fictional situations, the latter enduring in an oral singing tradition. The British broadside trade carried over to America; Benjamin Franklin wrote two "street ballads" for his printer brother in Boston ca. 1720, and by the 1850s New York was the largest production center. So far as I can learn, the last gasp of American broadside ballad printing occurred in Atlanta in the 1930s.

76. *Child Ballads in America Sung By Jean Ritchie*, vol. 1 (New York: Folkways Records, 1961, FA 2301), album booklet, 1. Ritchie provides social contexts for some of her songs in her early autobiography, *Singing Family of the Cumberlands* (1955; reprint, Lexington: Uni-

versity Press of Kentucky, 1988). For other exemplary mountain ballad singers, see Roger D. Abrahams, ed., *A Singer and Her Songs: Almeda Riddle's Book of Ballads* (Baton Rouge: Louisiana State University Press, 1970); Betty N. Smith, *Jane Hicks Gentry: A Singer among Singers* (Lexington: University Press of Kentucky, 1998); and Thomas G. Burton, *Some Ballad Folks* (Johnson City: East Tennessee State University Research Development Committee, 1978).

77. *Frank Proffitt Sings Folk Songs*, recorded by Sandy Paton (New York: Folkways Records, 1962, FA 2360), album booklet, 4.

78. "Little Mary Phagan," recorded in 1968 from Mrs. R. H. (who at age twelve sold printed broadsides of the ballad on the streets of Marietta) by Roger Cochran for the GFA. See John A. Burrison, "Fiddlers in the Alley: Atlanta As an Early Country Music Center," *Atlanta Historical Bulletin* 21, no. 2 (1977): 68–70, and Gene Wiggins, *Fiddlin' Georgia Crazy: Fiddlin' John Carson, His Real World, and the World of His Songs* (Urbana: University of Illinois Press, 1987), 34–43. Laws, *Native American Balladry*, 201–2 (no. F 20), documents the ballad's distribution throughout the South.

79. Burrison, "Fiddlers in the Alley," 82–83; Laws, *Native American Balladry*, 223–24 (no. G 22). Other ballads by Jenkins that entered oral tradition include "Kenny Wagner" (Laws, E 7), "Frank Dupree" (Laws, E 24), and "Billy the Kid" (Laws, 277), all dealing with outlaws. The Floyd Collins tragedy, detailed in Robert K. Murray and Roger W. Brucker, *Trapped! The Story of Floyd Collins*, rev. ed. (Lexington: University Press of Kentucky, 1982), inspired the 1951 movie *Ace in the Hole*, directed by Billy Wilder and starring Kirk Douglas.

80. Laws, *Native American Balladry*, 255 (no. I 17). An African American ballad, "The Boll Weevil" was a favorite of the great Louisiana-Texas songster Leadbelly (Huddie Ledbetter), but was also sung by whites.

81. "John Henry," as sung by John Cephas on *Virginia Traditions: Non-Blues Secular Black Music*, Blue Ridge Institute BRI–001. This African American ballad—also known to white singers—describes a legendary worker said to have hammered dynamite holes for blasting the Big Bend Tunnel on the Chesapeake and Ohio Railroad near Hinton, West Virginia; however, no conclusive evidence of his existence, or of such a contest with a steam drill, has been found. See Laws, *Native American Balladry*, 246 (no. I 1); Guy B. Johnson, *John Henry: Tracking Down a Negro Legend* (1929; reprint, New York: AMS Press, 1974); Louis W. Chappell, *John Henry: A Folk-Lore Study* (1933; reprint, Port Washington, NY: Kennikat Press, 1968); Brett Williams, *John Henry: A Bio-Bibliography* (Westport, CT: Greenwood Press, 1983); Scott Reynolds Nelson, *Steel Drivin' Man: John Henry, the Untold Story of an American Legend* (New York: Oxford University Press, 2006). Norm Cohen's *Long Steel Rail: The Railroad in American Folksong*, rev. ed. (Urbana: University of Illinois Press, 2000), offers a survey of train songs.

82. William L. Andrews, gen. ed., *The Literature of the American South* (New York: W. W. Norton, 1998): "Among the dialogues we believe important to reckon with in the development of southern literature is that between writing and oral artistry" (xxii). To that end, this anthology includes a section and accompanying audio CD on "Vernacular Traditions" with examples of folk songs, sermons, and storytelling.

83. For books on southern folk narratives, see the bibliography in my *Storytellers: Folktales and Legends from the South* (Athens: University of Georgia Press, 1989 [paper ed.,

1991]), to which add these subsequent publications: Thomas E. Barden, ed., *Virginia Folk Legends* (Charlottesville: University Press of Virginia, 1991); William Bernard McCarthy, ed., *Jack in Two Worlds: Contemporary North American Tales and Their Tellers* (Chapel Hill: University of North Carolina Press, 1994); Robert Isbell, *Ray Hicks: Master Storyteller of the Blue Ridge* (Chapel Hill: University of North Carolina Press, 1996); Alan Brown, *The Face in the Window and Other Alabama Ghostlore* (Tuscaloosa: University of Alabama Press, 1996); Carl Lindahl, Maida Owens, and C. Renée Harvison, eds., *Swapping Stories: Folktales from Louisiana* (Jackson: University Press of Mississippi, 1997); and Barbara R. Duncan, *Living Stories of the Cherokee* (Chapel Hill: University of North Carolina Press, 1998).

84. "John and the Coon," recorded in 1968 from Cassie Mae Copeland, 51, a black resident of Atlanta reared in Stockbridge, Georgia, by Laree Morgan for the GFA. This tale ironically turns a racist epithet into salvation for Master's favorite slave. In other Master and John folktales, John's wit allows him to narrowly escape punishment for his misdeeds; he is the human heir to Brer Rabbit's trickery. For another variant of the same story, see my *Storytellers* (paper ed.), 237, and the note on 367 for further references.

85. Jan Harold Brunvand, *The Study of American Folklore*, 4th ed. (New York: W. W. Norton, 1998), 123–24.

86. Mountain riddles, recorded in 1966 from Ab Jones, 88, of Blue Ridge, Georgia, by David Goeckel for the GFA. For more on southern riddles, see Michael Montgomery, "Speech Play," in Abramson and Haskell, 1029–30; James Still, *Rusties and Riddles and Gee-Haw Whimmy-Diddles* (Lexington: University Press of Kentucky, 1989); May Justus, *The Complete Peddler's Pack: Games, Songs, Rhymes, and Riddles from Mountain Folklore* (Knoxville: University of Tennessee Press, 1967), 10–13; Linda Garland Page and Hilton Smith, *The Foxfire Book of Toys and Games: Reminiscences and Instructions from Appalachia* (New York: E. P. Dutton, 1985), 103–4; Richard M. Dorson, *Buying the Wind: Regional Folklore in the United States* (Chicago: University of Chicago Press, 1964), 205–6, 213–14 (pretended-obscene examples), 270–71; Tristram P. Coffin and Hennig Cohen, eds., *Folklore in America* (Garden City, NY: Doubleday, 1966), 160–70; Daryl Cumber Dance, ed., *From My People: 400 Years of African American Folklore* (New York: W. W. Norton, 2002), 541–44.

87. Vance Randolph, *Ozark Superstitions* (1947; reprint, New York: Dover Publications, 1964), ch. 12; Jeffrey E. Anderson, *Conjure in African American Society* (Baton Rouge: Louisiana State University Press, 2005); Harry Middleton Hyatt, *Hoodoo—Conjuration— Witchcraft—Rootwork* (Hannibal, MO: Western Publishing, 1970–78); Sharla M. Fett, *Working Cures: Healing, Health, and Power on Southern Slave Plantations* (Chapel Hill: University of North Carolina Press, 2002), ch. 4; Newbell Niles Puckett, *Folk Beliefs of the Southern Negro* (1926; reprint, New York: Dover Publications, 1969), chs. 3–4; Savannah Unit, Georgia Writers' Project, *Drums and Shadows: Survival Studies among the Georgia Coastal Negroes* (1940; reprint, Athens: University of Georgia Press, 1986).

88. Robert Tallant, *Voodoo in New Orleans* (1946; reprint, New York: Collier Books, 1962); Zora Neale Hurston, *Mules and Men: Negro Folktales and Voodoo Practices in the South* (1935; reprint, New York: Harper & Row, 1970), part 2; Martha Ward, *Voodoo Queen: The Spirited Lives of Marie Laveau* (Jackson: University Press of Mississippi, 2004); Jessie Ruth Gaston, "The Case of Voodoo in New Orleans," in *Africanisms in American Culture,*

ed. Joseph E. Holloway, 2nd ed. (Bloomington: Indiana University Press, 2005), 111–51; Carolyn Morrow Long, *Spiritual Merchants: Religion, Magic, and Commerce* (Knoxville: University of Tennessee Press, 2001); Michael Atwood Mason, *Living Santería: Rituals and Experiences in an Afro-Cuban Religion* (Washington, D.C.: Smithsonian Institution Press, 2002). The slave populations of both New Orleans and Haiti were drawn from the Yoruba, Fon, and Kongo peoples of West Africa, but Senegambians were added to the New Orleans mix, partly accounting for variations in voodoo worship.

89. Thomas G. Burton, *Serpent-Handling Believers* (Knoxville: University of Tennessee Press, 1993); David L. Kimbrough, *Taking Up Serpents: Snake Handlers of Eastern Kentucky* (Chapel Hill: University of North Carolina Press, 1995); Dennis Covington, *Salvation on Sand Mountain: Snake Handling and Redemption in Southern Appalachia* (New York: Penguin Books, 1995); Weston La Barre, *They Shall Take Up Serpents: Psychology of the Southern Snake-Handling Cult* (New York: Schocken Books, 1969).

90. Ted Olson, *Blue Ridge Folklife* (Jackson: University Press of Mississippi, 1998), 116–17; John B. Rehder, *Appalachian Folkways* (Baltimore: Johns Hopkins University Press, 2004), 237–39; Alan Jabbour, Philip E. Coyle, and Paul Webb, *North Shore Cemetery Decoration Project Report* (Gatlinburg, TN: Great Smoky Mountains National Park, 2005).

91. William H. Wiggins Jr., *Oh Freedom! Afro-American Emancipation Celebrations* (Knoxville: University of Tennessee Press, 1990).

92. Barry Jean Ancelet, *"Capitaine, Voyage Ton Flag": The Traditional Cajun Country Mardi Gras* (Lafayette: Center for Louisiana Studies, University of Southwest Louisiana, 1989); Carl Lindhal, ed., "Southwestern Louisiana Mardi Gras Traditions," *Journal of American Folklore* 114, no. 452 (2001); Carolyn E. Ware, *Cajun Women and Mardi Gras: Reading the Rules Backward* (Urbana: University of Illinois Press, 2007); Pat Mire (producer), *Dance for a Chicken: The Cajun Mardi Gras*, videocassette 58 (Eunice, LA: Attakapas Productions, 1993).

93. Watkins and Watkins, 62; Garrett, 117–18, who also notes that "Young men of courting age took great pains to protect their skin from suntan. . . . A skin free from suntan and palms free from calluses were considered the hallmarks of gentility" (116); Anthony Cavender, *Folk Medicine in Southern Appalachia* (Chapel Hill: University of North Carolina Press, 2003), 105.

94. John Egerton, "Grits," in Wilson and Ferris, 688–89; Dabney, *Smokehouse Ham*, 315–22; *It's Grits*, documentary video (Greenville, SC: Woodward Studio, 1981). Hasty pudding, New England's maize translation of England's oatmeal porridge, once was such a staple that in 1793 Joel Barlow wrote a sort of epic poem to praise it; all that remains is Harvard University's Hasty Pudding Theatricals and Award. Cornmeal mush is still eaten by more traditional Pennsylvania Germans (e.g., the Amish) in the Mid-Atlantic and Midwest, and took root prior to grits in parts of Appalachia.

95. George Pullen Jackson, *White Spirituals in the Southern Uplands* (1933; reprint, New York: Dover Publications, 1965); idem, "Some Factors in the Diffusion of American Religious Folksongs," *Journal of American Folklore* 65, no. 258 (1952): 365–69.

96. Hugh McGraw et al., eds., *The Sacred Harp, 1991 Edition* (Bremen, GA: Sacred Harp Publishing, 1991); Jackson, *White Spirituals in the Southern Uplands*; John Beall, *Public Worship, Private Faith: Sacred Harp and American Folksong* (Athens: University of Georgia Press, 1997); Buell E. Cobb Jr., *The Sacred Harp: A Tradition and Its Music*

(Athens: University of Georgia Press, 1978); Dorothy D. Horn, *Sing to Me of Heaven: A Study of Folk and Early American Materials in Three Old Harp Books* (Gainesville: University Press of Florida, 1970). A 2006 documentary video, *Awake, My Soul: The Story of the Sacred Harp*, was produced by my former students Matt and Erica Hinton (http://www.awakemysoul.com). In 1934 Judge Jackson of Ozark, Alabama, published *The Colored Sacred Harp*, the 1992 edition of which is used today by Alabama's African American Wiregrass Sacred Harp Singers. Songbooks using other shape-note systems include William Walker's *The Southern Harmony and Musical Companion*, ed. Glenn C. Wilcox (Lexington: University Press of Kentucky, 1993); John G. McCurry's *The Social Harp*, ed. Daniel W. Patterson and John F. Garst (Athens: University of Georgia Press, 1973); and those published by the Stamps-Baxter and Vaughn music companies supporting gospel harmony singing, both white and black.

97. Steve Siporin, *American Folk Masters: The National Heritage Fellows* (New York: Harry N. Abrams and Museum of International Folk Art, 1992), 37, 171–72, 234–35.

98. Burrison, *Brothers in Clay*; Zug; Brackner; Eliot Wigginton and Margie Bennett, eds., *Foxfire 8* (Garden City, NY: Anchor/Doubleday, 1984), 71–384; Nancy Sweezy, *Raised in Clay: The Southern Pottery Tradition*, rev. ed. (Chapel Hill: University of North Carolina Press, 1994); Charles R. Mack, *Talking with the Turners: Conversations with Southern Folk Potters* (Columbia: University of South Carolina Press, 2006). For the Native American living pottery tradition in the Carolinas (less vital than that of the Southwest's Pueblo Indians), see Thomas John Blumer, *Catawba Indian Pottery: The Survival of a Folk Tradition* (Tuscaloosa: University of Alabama Press, 2004) and Rodney L. Leftwich, *Arts and Crafts of the Cherokee* (Cherokee, N.C.: Cherokee Publications, 1970), 63–86.

3. An Early International Crossroads: The Diverse Roots of Southern Folk Culture

1. This chapter is revised from my article "Transported Traditions: Transatlantic Foundations of Southern Folk Culture," *Studies in the Literary Imagination* 36, no. 2 (2003): 1–24.

2. Walt Whitman, *Leaves of Grass*, ed. Emory Holloway (Garden City, NY: Doubleday, 1943). Whitman liked this line so much he used it twice: in his 1855 Preface (488) and in an individual poem in this collection, "By Blue Ontario's Shore" (288). The Smithsonian Institution's National Museum of American History borrowed the line for the title of its 1976–91 exhibition *A Nation of Nations*, a sophisticated presentation of America's cultural pluralism.

3. John F. Kennedy, *A Nation of Immigrants*, rev. ed. (New York: Harper & Row, 1964).

4. Israel Zangwill, *The Melting Pot: A Drama in Four Acts* (1908), in *The Works of Israel Zangwill* (New York: AMS Press, 1969), 33.

5. Michael D'Innocenzo and Josef P. Sirefman, eds., *Immigration and Ethnicity: American Society—"Melting Pot" or "Salad Bowl"?* (Westport, CT: Greenwood Press with Hofstra University, 1992).

6. Joko M. Sengova, "Gullah," in *The Greenwood Encyclopedia of African American Folklore*, ed. Anand Prahlad (Westport, CT: Greenwood Press, 2006), 555–59; Patricia Jones-Jackson, *When Roots Die: Endangered Traditions on the Sea Islands* (Athens: University of Georgia Press, 1987), especially ch. 4; Charles Joyner, *Shared Traditions: Southern History and Folk Culture* (Urbana: University of Illinois Press, 1999), 14–15, 196–98; David

Buisseret and Steven G. Reinhardt, eds., *Creolization in the Americas* (College Station: Texas A&M University, 2000).

7. Carolyn Kolb, "Gumbo," in *Encyclopedia of Southern Culture*, ed. Charles Reagan Wilson and William Ferris (Chapel Hill: University of North Carolina Press, 1989), 502–3. Gumbo is known elsewhere in the coastal South but usually is just okra-based, lacking the French and Native American elements (e.g., Sallie Ann Robinson, *Gullah Home Cooking the Daufuskie Way* [Chapel Hill: University of North Carolina Press, 2003], 46–48).

8. Michael H. Crawford, *The Origins of Native Americans: Evidence from Anthropological Genetics* (Cambridge, Eng.: Cambridge University Press, 1998); Charles Hudson, *The Southeastern Indians* (Knoxville: University of Tennessee Press, 1976), 36–37.

9. Peter Nabokov and Robert Easton, *Native American Architecture* (New York: Oxford University Press, 1989); idem, "Native Americans," in *America's Architectural Roots: Ethnic Groups That Built America*, ed. Dell Upton (Washington, D.C.: Preservation Press, 1986), 16–35.

10. Don L. Shadburn, *Cherokee Planters in Georgia, 1832–1838* (Roswell, GA: W. H. Wolfe Associates, 1990).

11. Celeste Ray, "Ethnicity: American Indians," in *The Greenwood Encyclopedia of American Regional Cultures: The South*, ed. Rebecca Mark and Rob Vaughan (Westport, CT: Greenwood Press, 2004), 114–22.

12. John H. Goff, *Placenames of Georgia* (Athens: University of Georgia Press, 1975), 55–58.

13. Kay K. Moss, *Southern Folk Medicine 1750–1820* (Columbia: University of South Carolina Press, 1999); Anthony Cavender, *Folk Medicine in Southern Appalachia* (Chapel Hill: University of North Carolina Press, 2003), 66.

14. Quoted in John A. Burrison, *Shaping Traditions: Folk Arts in a Changing South* (Athens: University of Georgia Press, 2000), 114 (cat. no. 100).

15. Dorothy Downs, *Art of the Florida Seminole and Miccosukee Indians* (Gainesville: University Press of Florida, 1995), 242.

16. Joseph Earl Dabney, *Smokehouse Ham, Spoon Bread, & Scuppernong Wine: The Folklore and Art of Southern Appalachian Cooking* (Nashville, TN: Cumberland House, 1998), 198.

17. John Michael Vlach, *The Afro-American Tradition in Decorative Arts*, rev. ed. (Athens: University of Georgia Press, 1990), 97–107; Jan Arnow, *By Southern Hands: A Celebration of Craft Traditions in the South* (Birmingham, AL: Oxmoor House and Roundtable Press, 1987), 95–97.

18. Kenneth S. Goldstein, "'The Texas Rangers' in Aberdeenshire," in *A Good Tale and a Bonnie Tune*, ed. Mody C. Boatright et al., Texas Folklore Society Publications 32 (Dallas: Southern Methodist University Press, 1964), 188–98; A. L. Lloyd, *Folk Song in England* (New York: International Publishers, 1967), 387–88. See Georgia mountain ballad singer Lillie West's variant of "The Texas Rangers" in chapter five.

19. Francis James Child, ed., *The English and Scottish Popular Ballads* (1882–1898; reprint, New York: Dover Publications, 1965); Cecil J. Sharp, *English Folk Songs from the Southern Appalachians*, ed. Maud Karpeles (London: Oxford University Press, 1932); Maud Karpeles, *Cecil Sharp: His Life and Work* (Chicago: University of Chicago Press, 1967), chs. 12–13.

20. A hallmark of folklore methodology since the nineteenth century, comparative

research of this sort cannot always "prove" descent but, if properly done, can strongly suggest it; see W. Edson Richmond, "The Comparative Approach: Its Aims, Techniques, and Limitations," in *Folksong and Folksong Scholarship*, ed. Roger D. Abrahams (Dallas, TX: Southern Methodist University Press, 1964), 19–29, and Linda Dégh, ed., "The Comparative Method in Folklore," *Journal of Folklore Research* 23, nos. 2/3 (1986). This essay's conclusions, many of which are supported by scholarly consensus, are made more speculative by the divergence of southern culture from its Old World roots over the intervening centuries, as well as reliance on some later reports in the belief that these traditions have been continuous since early settlement.

21. David Hackett Fischer, *Albion's Seed: Four British Folkways in America*, vol. 1, *America, A Cultural History* (New York: Oxford University Press, 1989), especially 207–418, 605–782; Duane G. Meyer, *The Highland Scots of North Carolina, 1732–1776* (Chapel Hill: University of North Carolina Press, 1961); Anthony W. Parker, *Scottish Highlanders in Colonial Georgia: The Recruitment, Emigration, and Settlement at Darien, 1735–1748* (Athens: University of Georgia Press, 1997); Celeste Ray, *Highland Heritage: Scottish Americans in the American South* (Chapel Hill: University of North Carolina Press, 2001).

22. Sharp; Tristram P. Coffin, *The British Traditional Ballad in North America*, rev. ed. (Philadelphia: American Folklore Society, 1963).

23. "Dividing the Walnuts," recorded in 1970 from Emily Ellis of Cedartown, Georgia, by Betsy Ostrander and Kay Long for the GFA, from John A. Burrison, ed., *Storytellers: Folktales and Legends from the South* (Athens: University of Georgia Press, 1991 [paper ed.]), 71–72; for other variants, see 54–55, 147–48. For British origins, see Hazel Harrod, "A Tale of Two Thieves," in *The Sky Is My Tipi*, ed. Mody C. Boatright, Texas Folklore Society Publications 22 (Dallas, TX: Southern Methodist University Press, 1949), 207–14, and Katharine M. Briggs, *A Dictionary of British Folk-Tales* (London: Routledge, 1970), A2: 14–17.

24. Harnett T. Kane, *The Southern Christmas Book* (New York: David McKay, 1958), 127–28, 152; Max E. White, "Sernatin': A Traditional Christmas Custom in Northeast Georgia," *Southern Folklore Quarterly* 45 (1981): 89–99; Eliot Wigginton, ed., *A Foxfire Christmas: Appalachian Memories and Traditions* (New York: Doubleday, 1990), 26–41; Ronald Hutton, *The Stations of the Sun: A History of the Ritual Year in Britain* (Oxford, Eng.: Oxford University Press, 1996), 11–12, 95–96.

25. Newman Ivey White, gen. ed., *The Frank C. Brown Collection of North Carolina Folklore* (Durham, NC: Duke University Press, 1952–64), 6: 517–18; Vance Randolph, *Ozark Superstitions* (1947; reprint, New York: Dover Publications, 1964), 79; Hutton, 50–52.

26. Fischer, 282; C. W. Sullivan III, "'Jumping the Broom': A Further Consideration of the Origins of an African American Wedding Custom," *Journal of American Folklore* 110, no. 436 (1997): 203–4; idem, "'Jumping the Broom': Possible Welsh Origins of an African-American Custom," *Southern Folklore* 55, no. 1 (1998): 15–23.

27. A. B. Longstreet, *Georgia Scenes . . .* (1835; reprint, New York: Sagamore Press, 1957), 62–70; Richard Malcolm Johnston and William Hand Browne, *Life of Alexander H. Stephens* (Philadelphia: Lippincott, 1878), 26–27; Fischer, 724–26; Keith V. Thomas, *Rule and Misrule in the Schools of Early Modern England* (Reading, Eng.: University of Reading, Department of History, 1976).

28. J. L. Herring, *Saturday Night Sketches: Stories of Old Wiregrass Georgia* (1918; reprint,

Tifton, GA: Sunny South Press, 1978), 163–68; Mitchell B. Garrett, *Horse and Buggy Days on Hatchet Creek* (Tuscaloosa: University of Alabama Press, 1957), 188–90; Fischer, 150–51.

29. White, *Frank C. Brown Collection of North Carolina Folklore*, 1: 56–57, 89–93; May Justus, *The Complete Peddler's Pack: Games, Songs, Rhymes, and Riddles from Mountain Folklore* (Knoxville: University of Tennessee Press, 1967), 54, 46–47; Alice Bertha Gomme, *The Traditional Games of England, Scotland, and Ireland* (1894–98; reprint, New York: Dover Publications, 1964), 1: 170–83, 2: 233–55.

30. Henry Glassie, "The Types of the Southern Mountain Cabin," in Jan Harold Brunvand, *The Study of American Folklore: An Introduction*, 3rd ed. (New York: W. W. Norton, 1986), 542–45; idem, *Folk Housing in Middle Virginia: A Structural Analysis of Historic Artifacts* (Knoxville: University of Tennessee Press, 1975), 74–81.

31. John A. Burrison, *Brothers in Clay: The Story of Georgia Folk Pottery* (Athens: University of Georgia Press, 1983), 65–66, color pl. 2; idem, *Handed On: Folk Crafts in Southern Life* (Atlanta: Atlanta Historical Society, 1993), 41; Peter C. D. Brears, *The English Country Pottery: Its History and Techniques* (Rutland, VT: Charles E. Tuttle, 1971), 63–65, 104. See also the discussion of syrup jugs in chapter four.

32. Laurel Horton, *Social Fabric: South Carolina's Traditional Quilts* (Columbia: McKissick Museum, University of South Carolina, [1986]); Ruth Haislip Roberson, ed., *North Carolina Quilts* (Chapel Hill: University of North Carolina Press, 1988); Gail Andrews Trechsel, "Textiles," in *Southern Folk Art*, ed. Cynthia Elyce Rubin (Birmingham, AL: Oxmoor House, 1985), 180–99; Janet Rae, *Quilts of the British Isles* (London: Constable, 1987).

33. John Hope Franklin and Alfred A. Moss Jr., *From Slavery to Freedom: A History of African Americans*, 8th ed. (New York: Alfred A. Knopf, 2000), ch. 1; Paul Oliver, *Savannah Syncopators: African Retentions in the Blues*, reprinted in Paul Oliver et al., *Yonder Come the Blues: The Evolution of a Genre* (Cambridge, Eng.: Cambridge University Press, 2001), ch. 5.

34. Melville J. Herskovits, *The Myth of the Negro Past* (1941; reprint, Boston: Beacon Press, 1958).

35. Lorenzo Dow Turner, *Africanisms in the Gullah Dialect* (1949; reprint, Ann Arbor: University of Michigan Press, 1974); J. L. Dillard, *Black English: Its History and Usage in the United States* (New York: Vintage Books/Random House, 1973), 116–18.

36. Florence E. Baer, *Sources and Analogues of the Uncle Remus Tales*, Folklore Fellows Communications 228 (Helsinki: Academia Scientiarum Fennica, 1980), 29–31; Joel Chandler Harris, *Nights with Uncle Remus: Myths and Legends of the Old Plantation*, ed. John T. Bickley and R. Bruce Bickley Jr. (New York: Penguin Books, 2003), Introduction. The most famous of these, "The Tar Baby," is first reported among Oklahoma Cherokees in 1845, thirty–two years before its earliest documentation in African American tradition; but there would have been many opportunities for southern Indians to borrow it from slaves in their more than a century of contact prior to 1845. For possible Native American influences, see David Elton Gay, "On the Interaction of Traditions: Southeastern Rabbit Tales as African-Native American Folklore" and Sandra K. Baringer, "Brer Rabbit and His Cherokee Cousin: Moving Beyond the Appropriation Paradigm," in *When Brer Rabbit Meets Coyote: African-Native American Literature*, ed. Jonathan Brennan (Urbana: University of Illinois Press, 2003), 101–38.

37. Philip F. Gura and James F. Bollman, *America's Instrument: The Banjo in the Nineteenth Century* (Chapel Hill: University of North Carolina Press, 1999), 11–17; Cecilia Conway, *African Banjo Echoes in Appalachia* (Knoxville: University of Tennessee Press, 1995), Introduction and ch. 1. The *bania*, a Senegal lute with three or four strings, probably gave its name to the banjo; the *halam*, a five–stringed lute of the Wolof and other Senegambian peoples, is played with three open strings.

38. Richard Alan Waterman, "African Influence on the Music of the Americas," in *Mother Wit from the Laughing Barrel: Readings in the Interpretation of Afro-American Folklore*, ed. Alan Dundes (Englewood Cliffs, NJ: Prentice-Hall, 1973), 81–94; Art Rosenbaum, *Shout Because You're Free: The African American Ring Shout Tradition in Coastal Georgia* (Athens: University of Georgia Press, 1998), 17–25; Oliver; Samuel B. Charters, *The Roots of the Blues: An African Search* (Boston: M. Boyars, 1981).

39. Walter Rucker, "Grave Decorations," in *The Greenwood Encyclopedia of African American Folklore*, ed. Anand Prahlad (Westport, CT: Greenwood Press, 2006), 543–45; Robert Farris Thompson, "Kongo Influences on African American Artistic Culture," in *Africanisms in American Culture*, ed. Joseph E. Holloway, 2nd ed. (Bloomington: Indiana University Press, 2005), 305–19; Vlach, *Afro-American Tradition in Decorative Arts*, 139–47, 7–16; Lydia Parrish, *Slave Songs of the Georgia Sea Islands* (1942; reprint, Hatboro, PA: Folklore Associates, 1965), 47–48; Burrison, *Shaping Traditions*, 43, 46; Dale Rosengarten, *Row upon Row: Sea Grass Baskets of the South Carolina Lowcountry* (Columbia: McKissick Museum, University of South Carolina, 1986). A similar type of log mortar and pestle was used by southern Indians for milling corn, but the mortar's concave bowl was shallow and the working end of the pestle narrow, while the African American mortar bowl is deeper and the pestle wedge-shaped at both ends as is often the case in West Africa. Coiled straw baskets were made in England ("lipwork"), but on coastal rice plantations it is more likely that the technique was an African carryover (coiled-grass baskets are still made in Senegal). The cast-net has not yet been generally recognized as an Africanism and awaits further research.

40. Jessica B. Harris, *Iron Pots and Wooden Spoons: Africa's Gifts to New World Cooking* (New York: Simon & Schuster, 1989), xvii; John Egerton, *Southern Food: At Home, on the Road, in History* (New York: Alfred A. Knopf, 1987), 13. Peanuts and chile peppers (the latter gracing today's southern table as hot sauce), introduced to Africa from Latin America by the early slave trade, were later brought to the South ingrained in African culinary practice. Collard (colewort) greens are said to be another African gift to southern cuisine, but are documented in England as early as the eighteenth century.

41. James G. Leyburn, *The Scotch-Irish: A Social History* (Chapel Hill: University of North Carolina Press, 1962); Grady McWhiney, *Cracker Culture: Celtic Ways in the Old South* (Tuscaloosa: University of Alabama Press, 1988); Rodger Cunningham, *Apples on the Flood: The Southern Mountain Experience* (Knoxville: University of Tennessee Press, 1987). "Scotch-Irish" (alternatively "Scots-Irish") is the term adopted by their American descendants; "Ulster Scots" is preferred in the British Isles. Predominantly Catholic Irish immigrants arrived in the nineteenth century; although their numbers were greatest in the North, their presence in the South is reflected in the massive St. Patrick's Day celebration in Savannah, Georgia (David T. Gleeson, *The Irish in the South, 1815–1877* [Chapel Hill: University of North Carolina Press, 2001]).

42. Joseph Earl Dabney, *Mountain Spirits: A Chronicle of Corn Whiskey from King James'*

Ulster Plantation to America's Appalachians and the Moonshine Life (New York: Charles Scribner's Sons, 1974); John McGuffin, *In Praise of Poteen* (Belfast, N. Ire.: Appletree Press, 1978); Kevin Danaher, *In Ireland Long Ago*, rev. ed. (Cork: Mercier Press, 1964), 58–63. Similar distilling technologies were known to Germanic and Finno-Swedish settlers of the Mid-Atlantic, but the Ulster connection was undoubtedly the strongest, hence the survival in the South of the Anglo-Irish terms "moonshine" and "mountain dew" (the Gaelic equivalent is *poitín*).

43. Glassie, "Types of the Southern Mountain Cabin," 545–49; idem, "Irish," in *America's Architectural Roots: Ethnic Groups That Built America*, ed. Dell Upton (Washington, D.C.: Preservation Press, 1986), 74–79; E. Estyn Evans, *Irish Folk Ways* (1957; reprint, London: Routledge, 1988), 41–46.

44. Evans, 78 and pl. 1; Danaher, 30; Claudia Kinmonth, *Irish Country Furniture, 1700–1950* (New Haven, CT: Yale University Press, 1993), 129–31; the oatmeal chest (*gàirneal* in Gaelic) is mentioned in William Butler Yeats's 1886 poem, "The Stolen Child." A common and highly utilitarian item of furniture in the upland South, the meal bin seems to have escaped the notice of writers, including those in the decorative arts who publish on southern furniture. Irish examples tend to be larger than southern ones, with as many as three compartments; in both cultures some have only a single compartment, although two is the norm. Irish meal chests typically have a perpendicular front, except for those of County Cork which taper inward towards the base, like most southern examples; this design feature facilitates reaching the inside bottom.

45. Burrison, *Shaping Traditions*, 12, 32, 108 (cat. nos. 17–19), color pl. 2; Evans, 74, 98–99; John Rice Irwin, *Alex Stewart: Portrait of a Pioneer* (West Chester, PA: Schiffer Publishing, 1985).

46. Joyce H. Cauthen, *With Fiddle and Well-Rosined Bow: Old-Time Fiddling in Alabama* (Tuscaloosa: University of Alabama Press, 1989), 3–4; Samuel P. Bayard, *Dance to the Fiddle, March to the Fife: Instrumental Folk Tunes in Pennsylvania* (University Park: Pennsylvania State University Press, 1982), nos. 332, 328, 238–39, 334.

47. In *Country Music U.S.A.: A Fifty-Year History* (Austin: University of Texas Press for American Folklore Society, 1968), Bill C. Malone describes the southern "high, lonesome" singing style (12, 15), but I find no mention of a possible Irish connection in print.

48. Burrison, *Storytellers*, 4, 137–52; Richard Chase, *The Jack Tales* (Cambridge, MA: Houghton Mifflin, 1943); Charles L. Perdue Jr., ed., *Outwitting the Devil: Jack Tales from Wise County, Virginia* (Santa Fe, NM: Ancient City Press, 1987); Carl Lindahl, ed., *Perspectives on the Jack Tales and Other North American Märchen* (Bloomington: Folklore Institute, Indiana University, 2001); Briggs, A1: 313–36; Henry Glassie, ed., *Irish Folk Tales* (New York: Pantheon, 1985), 257–311; *Told in Ireland: The Stories of Frank McKenna*, Tape 002 (Holywood, N. Ire.: Ulster Folk and Transport Museum, [n.d., ca. 1989]).

49. Terry G. Jordan and Matti Kaups, *The American Backwoods Frontier: An Ethnic and Ecological Interpretation* (Baltimore: Johns Hopkins University Press, 1989), chs. 5–6. The largest element of the Pennsylvania-German population came from the Rhineland-Palatinate in west-central Germany, where exposed-timber framing (*fachwerk*), not horizontal logs, was the predominant building technique.

50. L. Allen Smith, *A Catalogue of Pre-Revival Appalachian Dulcimers* (Columbia: University of Missouri Press, 1983).

51. Joseph Earl Dabney, *Smokehouse Ham, Spoon Bread, & Scuppernong Wine: The Folk-*

lore and Art of Southern Appalachian Cooking (Nashville, TN: Cumberland House, 1998), 336; Linda Garland Page and Eliot Wigginton, eds., *The Foxfire Book of Appalachian Cookery: Regional Memorabilia and Recipes* (New York: E. P. Dutton and Foxfire Press, 1984), 272–73; Don Yoder, "Sauerkraut in the Pennsylvania Folk-Culture," *Pennsylvania Folklife* 12 (Summer 1961): 56–69; William Woys Weaver, *Sauerkraut Yankees: Pennsylvania German Food and Foodways* (Philadelphia: University of Pennsylvania Press, 1983), 174–76.

52. Rubin, ed., *Southern Folk Art*, 79–91, 139, 141, 150; John Bivins Jr., *Longrifles of North Carolina* (York, PA: George Shumway, 1968).

53. Charles van Ravenswaay, *The Arts and Architecture of German Settlements in Missouri: A Survey of Vanishing Culture* (Columbia: University of Missouri Press, 1977); Catherine W. Bishir, *North Carolina Architecture* (Chapel Hill: University of North Carolina Press, 1990), 30–32; John Bivins Jr., *The Moravian Potters in North Carolina* (Chapel Hill: University of North Carolina Press for Old Salem, 1972). Another possible Germanic influence on architecture of the South and Mid–Atlantic is the smokehouse (*Räucherhaus* in German), an outbuilding dedicated to meat preservation and documented in Virginia by 1716 (Carl R. Lounsbury, ed., *An Illustrated Glossary of Early Southern Architecture and Landscape* [New York: Oxford University Press, 1994], 337; Allen G. Noble, *Wood, Brick, and Stone: The North American Settlement Landscape* [Amherst: University of Massachusetts Press, 1984], 2: 89–90; Dabney, *Smokehouse Ham*, 188–91).

54. Walter L. Robbins, "Christmas Shooting Rounds in America and Their Background," *Journal of American Folklore* 86, no. 339 (1973): 48–52; White, *Frank C. Brown Collection of North Carolina Folklore*, 1: 241–43; Fischer, 745. Not yet published at the time of this writing, Gerald L. Milnes's *Signs, Cures, and Witchery: German Appalachian Folklore* (Knoxville: University of Tennessee Press, 2007) should further our understanding of central European influence on southern folk culture.

55. Samuel Kinser, *Carnival, American Style: Mardi Gras at New Orleans and Mobile* (Chicago: University of Chicago Press, 1990); Roger D. Abrahams, et al., *Blues for New Orleans: Mardi Gras and America's Creole Soul* (Philadelphia: University of Pennsylvania Press, 2006); Barry Jean Ancelet, *Cajun and Creole Folktales: The French Oral Tradition of South Louisiana* (New York: Garland Publishers, 1994), 78–81.

56. Cajuns and Creoles are predominantly Catholic; French Protestants (Huguenots) came to the Carolinas, but their impact on southern folk culture has yet to be determined. There was also a small Huguenot element in the Scotch-Irish population.

57. Colin Brooker, "Tabby: Its Origin and Evolution as a Structural System," paper (Vernacular Architecture Forum, St. Louis, Missouri, May 1989); Kathleen Deagan, "Southeastern Spanish," in Upton, 87, 89.

58. Kenneth S. Goldstein, liner notes for Jean Ritchie, *Singing Family of the Cumberlands*, Riverside RLP 12–653 (1957). The album includes readings from, and has the same title as, her early autobiography, published in 1955 (and reprinted by University Press of Kentucky in 1988).

59. Jean Ritchie, correspondence to the author, October 13, 2006. Two long-playing albums were produced from her many hours of tape recordings: *Field Trip—England*, Folkways FW 8871 (1959), and *As I Roved Out: Field Trip—Ireland*, Folkways FW 8872 (1960). A *Field Trip—Scotland* CD is scheduled to be issued in 2007 on her Greenhays label; see Susan Hendrix Brumfield, *Jean Ritchie's Field Trip—Scotland, Recordings Collected in Scotland, 1952–53*, Ph.D. dissertation (Norman: University of Oklahoma, 2000).

60. The documentary films *Family across the Sea* (Columbia: South Carolina Educational Television, 1990), produced and written by Tim Carrier, and *The Language You Cry In* (Alicante, Spain: Inko Producciones [now based in Seville], 1998), produced and directed by Alvaro Toepke and Angel Serrano, are distributed by California Newsreel.

61. *Salm & Soul*, Gaelic Psalm Singing CD (2005); *Siubhal nan Salm* (Journey of the Psalms), Scottish television documentary (in Gaelic) presented by Mary Ann Kennedy and produced by Eyeline Media; Margaret Bennett, "Afro-Gaelic Roots? Blackening the Line and Singing in the Spirit," paper (American Folklore Society, Atlanta, October 2005); Ben McConville, "Black Music from Scotland? It Could Be the Gospel Truth," *Scotland on Sunday*, August 31, 2003; Jeff Todd Titon, "Lined Singing," in Abramson and Haskell, 1322–23.

62. Burrison, *Shaping Traditions*, 40, 65–68, cat. nos. 43, 92, 309.

63. Overshot coverlets once were woven in the North as well, with one of the last practitioners, William "Weaver" Rose, dying in 1913 (Isadora M. Safner, *The Weaving Roses of Rhode Island* [Loveland, CO: Interweave Press, 1985]).

64. Publications I've seen on Scottish weaving emphasize tartans, but the fact that Canadian overshot weaving was concentrated in the Scottish-settled Maritime Provinces is suggestive (Harold B. Burnham and Dorothy K. Burnham, *Keep Me Warm One Night: Early Handweaving in Eastern Canada* [Toronto: University of Toronto Press, 1972], 10–11, 13, 52–53, 174–263).

65. An institution that tangibly addresses these processes for the southern backcountry is the Frontier Culture Museum (a.k.a. Museum of American Frontier Culture) at Staunton, Virginia. It reconstructs three historic Old World farmsteads—English, Irish, and German—to compare with one from the Valley of Virginia, as described in the museum's 1997 *Guidebook*.

66. A few such pioneers have been identified, however. For example, Moravian records reveal that the central European earthenware tradition was transplanted to North Carolina in 1755 by Gottfried Aust, who had trained as a potter under Andreas Dober at Herrnhut in eastern Germany (Bivins, *Moravian Potters in North Carolina*, 16–23). Aust's tradition was built upon, in turn, by his apprentices, and *their* apprentices, in Piedmont North Carolina.

67. John Shelton Reed, *Minding the South* (Columbia: University of Missouri Press, 2003), 7; Joyner, 9, 149.

4. Journey of the Jug: An Artifact-Based Case Study

1. This chapter is a revision of my article "Fluid Vessel: Journey of the Jug," *Ceramics in America* [6] (2006): 93–121.

2. "Ham Rachel, of Alabama," in Harden E. Taliaferro ("Skitt"), *Fisher's River (North Carolina) Scenes and Characters* (1859; reprint, New York: Arno Press, 1977), 267.

3. John A. Burrison, *Brothers in Clay: The Story of Georgia Folk Pottery* (Athens: University of Georgia Press, 1983).

4. Bengt Olsson, *Memphis Blues and Jug Bands* (London: Studio Vista, 1970); Laurie Wright and Fred Cox, *The Jug Bands of Louisville* (Chigwell, Eng.: Storyville Publications, 1993).

5. The word *jug* was in use by 1538, according to the *Oxford English Dictionary*, but its

etymology is unknown; the suggestion of Josiah Wedgwood, late-1700s "father" of England's pottery industry, that it came from the pet name for Joan or Judith is inadequate as an explanation.

6. This quote is first attributed to Shaw in "Picturesque Speech and Patter," *Reader's Digest* 41 (November 1942): 100, but I have not been able to trace it to a specific work of his.

7. E.g., R. K. Henrywood, *An Illustrated Guide to British Jugs: From Medieval Times to the Twentieth Century* (Woodbridge, Eng.: Antique Collectors' Club, 1997).

8. "The Brown Jug," written in 1761 by Francis Fawkes, describes the corpse of corpulent toper Toby Filpot (inspired by real-life big drinker and fellow Yorkshireman Henry Elwes, who died that same year) moldering into clay, to be recycled by a potter into "this brown jug, / Now sacred to friendship, to mirth and mild ale." The poem, along with printed images, is thought to have inspired, in turn, Staffordshire's Toby character mug. "The Little Brown Jug" was written by Philadelphian Joseph Eastburn Winner in 1869, later becoming a Glenn Miller jazz standard: "Me and my wife live all alone / In a little log hut we call our own; / She loves gin and I love rum, / And don't we have a lot of fun! / Ha, ha, ha, you and me, / Little brown jug, don't I love thee!" The narrator's diction suggests that Winner intended the song as a spoof of Quaker support for temperance.

9. Henry Hodges, *Technology in the Ancient World* (New York: Alfred A. Knopf, 1972), 114–17, 156–57, 179–81, 185–87.

10. Charles Burney, *The Ancient Near East* (Ithaca, NY: Cornell University Press, 1977), 107; Ruth Amiran, *Ancient Pottery of the Holy Land from Its Beginnings in the Neolithic Period to the End of the Iron Age* (Rutgers, NJ: Rutgers University Press, 1970), 58 ff.; Robert J. Charleston, ed., *World Ceramics* (London and New York: Paul Hamlyn, 1968), 23 (no. 32); Trudy S. Kawami, *Ancient Iranian Ceramics from the Arthur M. Sackler Collections* (New York: Arthur M. Sackler Foundation and Harry N. Abrams, 1992), 94, 110, 217–18; A. D. Lacy, *Greek Pottery in the Bronze Age* (London: Methuen, 1967), 75 (e), 178 (a); James Whitley, *Style and Society in Dark Age Greece: The Changing Face of a Pre-Literate Society 1100–700 B.C.* (Cambridge, Eng.: Cambridge University Press, 1991), pl. 11; *Meisterwerke Altägyptischer Keramik: 5000 Jahre Kunst und Kunsthandwerk aus Ton und Fayence* (Höhr-Grenzhausen, Germany: Rastal-Haus, 1978), 179 (no. 298), 182 (no. 311).

11. John W. Hayes, *Handbook of Mediterranean Roman Pottery* (Norman: University of Oklahoma Press, 1997), 22 (pl. 5 left), 25 (pl. 7), 55 (fig. 20, no. 9), 56 (fig. 21, no. 3), 61 (fig. 25, no. 7), 75 (pl. 28), 93 (pl. 39, top); Val Rigby and Ian Freestone, "Ceramic Changes in Late Iron Age Britain," in *Pottery in the Making: Ceramic Traditions*, ed. Ian Freestone and David Gaimster (Washington, D.C.: Smithsonian Institution Press, 1997), 61 (fig. 6); Vivien G. Swan, *Pottery in Roman Britain* (Princes Risborough, Eng.: Shire Publications, 1975), 38 (pl. 30 center), 43 (no. 21); K. J. Barton, *Pottery in England from 3500 B.C.–A.D. 1730* (Newton Abbot, Eng.: David & Charles, 1975), 96 (nos. 26–27); Ivor Noël Hume, *If These Pots Could Talk: Collecting 2,000 Years of British Household Pottery* (Hanover, NH: University Press of New England for Chipstone Foundation, 2001), 20, 28. Greek and Roman potters also made amphoras, related to jugs but typically larger with an elongated, tapering body and two loop handles.

12. Earthenware—the world's earliest ceramic type—is made from a coarse-grained, impure (typically reddish-brown) clay; from the Middle Ages on, lead was commonly

used to flux, or melt, the silica contributor—usually flint—in the glaze. For medieval German earthenware jugs, see Charleston, 116 (no. 339b), and Bernhard Beckmann, "The Main Types of the First Four Production Periods of Siegburg Pottery," in *Medieval Pottery from Excavations*, ed. Vera I. Evison et al. (New York: St. Martin's Press, 1974), 194, 209–10 (nos. 44–52). The German language adds to semantic confusion: while certain vessel types are given very specific names, what Americans call a jug is referred to variously as a *Krug, Flasche,* or *Pulle.* The latter two terms translate as "bottle," while the more generic *Krug* can mean "jug," "tankard or mug," "jar or crock," and "pitcher."

13. Stoneware is made from a fine-grained, relatively pure clay that fires gray or tan at 2300° F. Fifteenth-century German potters began to glaze their stoneware by throwing common salt in the kiln, the vaporized sodium combining with the molten alumina and silica on the pots' surface to create a clear coating of glass. See David Gaimster, *German Stoneware 1200–1900: Archaeology and Cultural History* (London: British Museum Press, 1997), 85 ff.; Peter Seewaldt, *Rheinisches Steinzeug* (Trier, Germany: Rheinischen Landesmuseums, 1990), 37 ff.

14. Called Bellarmines by English writers, these anthropomorphized jugs were thought to be caricatures of Cardinal Roberto Bellarmino (1542–1621), an opponent of Protestantism in central Europe. However, the earliest dated example was made in 1550, while some with hand-modeled faces predate 1500 (Anthony Thwaite, "The Chronology of the Bellarmine Jug," *The Connoisseur* 182 [April 1973]: 255–62; Margaret Thomas, *German Stoneware: A Catalogue of the Frank Thomas Collection* [Woodbridge, Eng.: Antique Collectors' Club, 2003]). Another theory is that the bearded face represents the Wild Man of the Woods, a northern European folklore figure (Gaimster, 209). In England, graybeard jugs filled with magical items were buried under hearths to ward off witches, for which see Ralph Merrifield, *The Archaeology of Ritual and Magic* (New York: New Amsterdam Books, 1988), 163–75, and Hume, 118–26. Some sixteenth-century Bartmanns have a wider mouth than jugs as we're defining them and probably were drinking, not storage, vessels (e.g., Gaimster, 67 [no. 3.21] and color pl. 12).

15. For example, Wilhelm Elling's *Steinzeug aus Stadtlohn und Vreden* (Vreden, Germany: Hamaland-Museum, 1994) documents a tradition of salt-glazed jug-making near the Dutch border, west of Münster, continuous from the seventeenth century to the present. Germany's living tradition of salt-glazed stoneware is concentrated, however, in several Westerwald towns collectively known as *Kannenbäckerland* (the mug-baking district), west of Frankfurt, where jugs remain part of the ceramic repertoire.

16. J. N. L. Myres, *Anglo-Saxon Pottery and the Settlement of England* (Oxford, Eng.: Clarendon Press, 1969); Cathy Haith, "Pottery in Early Anglo-Saxon England," in Freestone and Gaimster, 146–51. Globular-bodied, narrow-necked bottles—jugs minus a handle—from Kent burial sites, if English-made, may mark the reintroduction of the potter's wheel from the Continent as early as the seventh century; see Vera I. Evison, "The Asthall Type of Bottle," in Evison, 77–92 and pls. 2–4.

17. Barton, 109; Michael R. McCarthy and Catherine M. Brooks, *Medieval Pottery in Britain A.D. 900–1600* (Leicester, Eng.: Leicester University Press, 1988), 231 (no. 667), 248 (no. 782), 261 (no. 861), 278 (no. 983), 279 (no. 985), 383 (no. 1615), 384 (no. 1623), 397 (nos. 1700, 1706).

18. E.g., Hume, 166. For English non-delft earthenware jugs of the 1600s, see R.

Coleman–Smith and T. Pearson, *Excavations in the Donyatt* [Somerset] *Potteries* (Chichester, Eng.: Phillimore, 1988), 80, 148, 156, showing jugs that are actually called jugs!

19. Peter C. D. Brears, *The English Country Pottery: Its History and Techniques* (Rutland, VT: Charles E. Tuttle, 1971), 70; Andrew McGarva, *Country Pottery: The Traditional Earthenware of Britain* (London: A & C Black, 2000), 24–26, 29; John Manwaring Baines, *Sussex Pottery* (Brighton, Eng.: Fisher Publications, 1980), 15, 45. Puzzle and West Country harvest "jugs" were not jugs by our definition but drinking vessels, the former a trick mug, the latter essentially a pitcher.

20. Gaimster, 309–17; Jonathan Horne, "John Dwight, 'The Master Potter' of Fulham," *The Magazine Antiques* 143, no. 4 (1993): 562–71; Adrian Oswald et al., *English Brown Stoneware 1670–1900* (London: Faber and Faber, 1982); Robin Hildyard, *Browne Muggs: English Brown Stoneware* (London: Victoria and Albert Museum, 1985).

21. One way of determining when the American meaning arose is to find early illustrations of jugs associated with the word, as in potters' price lists such as those reproduced in Harold F. Guilland, *Early American Folk Pottery* (Philadelphia: Chilton Book Co., 1971), 41 (Clarkson Crolius pottery, Manhattan, 1809), William C. Ketchum Jr., *Early Potters and Potteries of New York State* (New York: Funk & Wagnalls, 1970), 179 (John Burger pottery, Rochester, 1857), and Lura Woodside Watkins, *Early New England Potters and Their Wares* (Cambridge, MA: Harvard University Press, 1950), 147 (Norton pottery, Bennington, Vermont, 1856), 149 and 151 (Farrar pottery, Fairfax, Vermont, 1840 and 1851), as well as in literary publications such as Taliaferro, 266–67.

22. Diana Stradling and J. Garrison Stradling, in editing *The Art of the Potter* (New York: Main Street/Universe Books, 1977) from *The Magazine Antiques*, organized the articles on American redware into two sections, "The Germanic Influence" and "The English Influence."

23. Watkins, 235.

24. Ibid., figs. 13, 37, 39–41, 73, 84; Guilland, 155, 228, color pl. [11]; Stradling and Stradling, 43, 47, 51, 57, 65, 66–69; Joseph Johnson Smith, *Regional Aspects of American Folk Pottery* (York, PA: Historical Society of York County, 1974), figs. 1, 3, 56, 57, 59, 60; Brian Cullity, *Slipped and Glazed: Regional American Redware* (Hyannis, MA: Patriot Press for Heritage Plantation of Sandwich, 1991), 31 (no. 48), 32 (no. 51), 37 (no. 63), 50 (no. 99), color pls. 1–2, 4, and 6; Arthur E. James, *The Potters and Potteries of Chester County, Pennsylvania* (Exton, PA: Schiffer Publishing, 1978), 88; Jeannette Lasansky, *Central Pennsylvania Redware Pottery 1780–1904* (University Park: Pennsylvania State University Press for Keystone Books, 1979), 42; Anthony W. Butera Jr., "'Informed Conjecture': Collecting Long Island Redware," *Ceramics in America* [3] (2003): 214, 219; Barbara H. Magid and Bernard K. Means, "In the Philadelphia Style: The Pottery of Henry Piercy," *Ceramics in America* [3] (2003): 56 (fig. 25); Don Horvath and Richard Duez, "The Potters and Pottery of Morgan's Town, Virginia: The Earthenware Years, Circa 1796–1854," *Ceramics in America* [4] (2004): 103 (fig. 5), 113–14 (figs. 28–32); H. E. Comstock, *The Pottery of the Shenandoah Valley Region* (Chapel Hill: University of North Carolina Press for Museum of Early Southern Decorative Arts, 1994), 72 (figs. 3.14–15), 89 (fig. 4.13), 104 (fig. 4.60), 119 (fig. 4.109), 204 (fig. 5.14); John Bivins Jr., *The Moravian Potters in North Carolina* (Chapel Hill: University of North Carolina Press for Old Salem, 1972), 124; Charles G. Zug III, *Turners and Burners: The Folk Potters of North Carolina* (Chapel Hill: University of North Carolina Press, 1986), color pl. 3; Bill Beam et al., eds., *Two Centuries of Potters: A Catawba*

Valley Tradition (Lincolnton, NC: Lincoln County Historical Association, 1999), 14 (fig. 1) and front cover. Perhaps due to its emphasis on decorated pieces, there are no jugs in the catalog of the finest public display of Pennsylvania redware, Beatrice B. Garvan's *The Pennsylvania German Collection* (Philadelphia: Philadelphia Museum of Art, 1982).

25. Early American stoneware potters working largely in the German tradition include the Crolius and Remmey families, Thomas Commereau, and David Morgan, all of Manhattan, James Morgan of New Jersey, and Jonathan Fenton of Boston. Those working more in the English tradition include William Rogers of Yorktown, Virginia, Frederick Carpenter of Charlestown, Massachusetts, and Branch Green of Philadelphia. English-born Anthony Duche of colonial Philadelphia made stoneware in both the German and English styles (Robert L. Giannini III, "Anthony Duche, Sr., Potter and Merchant of Philadelphia," *The Magazine Antiques* 119 [January 1981]: 198–203).

26. Guilland, 237, 249, 252, 255–56, 260; Georgeanna H. Greer, *American Stonewares: The Art and Craft of Utilitarian Potters* (Exton, PA: Schiffer Publishing, 1981), 155–56, 182, 225; Donald Blake Webster, *Decorated Stoneware Pottery of North America* (Rutland, VT: Charles E. Tuttle, 1971), 65–66, 98, 160; Stradling and Stradling, 81–90, 106–7, 114–16, 119–22; James R. Mitchell, "The Potters of Cheesequake, New Jersey," in *Ceramics in America*, ed. Ian M. G. Quimby, Winterthur Conference Report 1972 (Charlottesville: University Press of Virginia, 1973), 319–38; Robert Hunter and Hank D. Lutton, "A Yankee Jug in Dixie," *Ceramics in America* [6] (2006): 240–42; Comstock, 318 (fig. 6.6); Norman F. Barka, "Archaeology of a Colonial Pottery Factory: The Kilns and Ceramics of the 'Poor Potter' of Yorktown," *Ceramics in America* [4] (2004): 16, 32; Quincy J. Scarborough Jr., *North Carolina Decorated Stoneware: The Webster School of Folk Potters* (Fayetteville, NC: Scarborough Press, 1986).

27. E.g., Cinda K. Baldwin, *Great and Noble Jar: Traditional Stoneware of South Carolina* (Athens: University of Georgia Press, 1993), 35, 37, 39, 40, 45, 53, 100, 147, 150, 153, 154–56, 159, 169, color pls. 2–4, 6, 12; Greer, 170, 173; Arthur F. Goldberg and James P. Witkowski, "Beneath His Magic Touch: The Dated Vessels of the African-American Slave Potter Dave," *Ceramics in America* [6] (2006): 74, 84. The double-collared neck sometimes migrated west on jugs made by Edgefield-trained potters (e.g., Baldwin, 64, by J. S. Nash in Texas; Burrison, 123, attributed to Cyrus Cogburn in Georgia).

28. Greer, 76; Guilland, 83; Cornelius Osgood, *The Jug and Related Stoneware of Bennington* (Rutland, VT: Charles E. Tuttle, 1971), 116.

29. A glaring historical inaccuracy of certain films portraying the colonial or frontier era is the inclusion of these late-nineteenth-century shouldered jugs. The earliest examples are two-toned, with salt-glazed wall and (since the stacking dish blocked the salt glazing) Albany slip-glazed shoulder, neck, and interior. Later examples, often molded on a jolly machine rather than thrown, either carried on the two-tone effect with Bristol glaze replacing the salt or were fully Bristol glazed. For a sample of such jugs, see Lyndon C. Viel, *The Clay Giants: The Stoneware of Red Wing, Goodhue County, Minnesota* (Des Moines, IA: Wallace–Homestead Book Co., 1977–87).

30. John McGuffin, *In Praise of Poteen* (Belfast, N. Ire.: Appletree Press, 1978); Joseph Earl Dabney, *Mountain Spirits: A Chronicle of Corn Whiskey from King James' Ulster Plantation to America's Appalachians and the Moonshine Life* (New York: Charles Scribner's Sons, 1974).

31. Quoted in Burrison, 132.

32. Jim Broom in North Carolina and Horace Brown and Norman Smith in Alabama, besides the previously mentioned "Jughead" for Georgia's Lanier Meaders.

33. Catawba-Lincoln counties and Buncombe County, North Carolina; Greenville County, South Carolina; Upson-Pike counties, Georgia; White County, Tennessee; and Shelby County, Alabama. The famed Jugtown Pottery of Seagrove, Moore County, North Carolina, was founded in 1921, but it is not clear if the community itself had been known by that name.

34. E.g., Stradling and Stradling, 94 (twenty gallons, Vermont); Greer, 107 (twelve gallons, Ohio).

35. Earthenware "cider jars" were a specialty of Halifax-area, West Yorkshire, potters. They typically have a spigot hole in the lower wall; some were lead-glazed only halfway down the outside so the temperature differential would cause the hard cider to "roll," hastening fermentation. The same basic shape in brown salt-glazed stoneware as made in the Liverpool area apparently was used in transatlantic trade. Dating from the late eighteenth through mid-nineteenth centuries, these large English jugs rarely have been published, but see *A History of Local Potteries* (Bradford, Eng.: Bradford Art Galleries and Museums, 1981), 11 (B); Zug, 31; Stradling and Stradling, 154 (center); John A. Burrison, *Handed On: Folk Crafts in Southern Life* (Atlanta: Atlanta Historical Society, 1993), 41 (no. 4).

36. E.g., Stradling and Stradling, 131 (fig. 1, New York); Greer, 107 (Ohio); Webster, 67 and 165 (New York State), 94 (Ohio); Baldwin, 172, 149 (South Carolina). Stoneware "fountain" and keg forms also were used as coolers.

37. Greer, 42–43, 178; Baldwin, 37, 45, 49, 150–51, 153, 155–56, 169, color pls. 3–4; Zug, 46, 48, 77, 87, 307, color pls. 7, 16; Beam, 14–15, 33, 36, 39, 75, 80–81, 87, 90; Burrison, *Brothers in Clay*, 23, 65, 123–25, 127, 145, 175, 268; Joey Brackner, *Alabama Folk Pottery* (Tuscaloosa: University of Alabama Press with Birmingham Museum of Art, 2006), 45, 103, 113 (right), 134, 158 (below).

38. Burrison, *Brothers in Clay*, 66 (pl. 35), 116–17, 255, color pl. 6; Zug, 368 (fig. 12–14).

39. Lacy, 218 (fig. 90d), a Mycenaean example dating to 1200 B.C.; for German stoneware examples dating to the 1500s–1600s, see Otto Von Falke, *Das Rheinische Steinzeug* (Osnabrück, Germany: Otto Zeller, 1977), 1: 89, 2: 59–61, 109.

40. Zug, 375–77; "Lin Craven Making a Ring Jug," video clip supporting John A. Burrison, "Folk Pottery," in *The New Georgia Encyclopedia* (http://www.georgiaencyclopedia.org/nge/Article.jsp?path=/Folklife/FolkArt&id=h–461).

41. Burrison, *Brothers in Clay*, 184–85.

42. Lacy, 259 (fig. 102e), an example of 1800 B.C.

43. Museo del Botijo in Toral de los Guzmanes, León; Museo del Botijo in Villena, Valencia; Museu del Càntir d' Argentona, Cataluña. For recent Spanish jugs, "monkey" and otherwise, see J. Llorens Artigas and J. Corredor-Matheos, *Spanish Folk Ceramics of Today* (New York: Watson-Guptill Publications, 1974).

44. Guilland, 193 (left, Vermont); Cullity, 26 (no. 34, Massachusetts); Lasansky, 43; Greer, 162 and 196 (Ohio); Nigel Barley, *Smashing Pots: Works of Clay from Africa* (Washington, D.C.: Smithsonian Institution Press, 1994), 27, 50, 118, 122; John Michael Vlach, *The Afro-American Tradition in Decorative Arts*, rev. ed. (Athens: University of Georgia Press, 1990), 86–90. Monkey jugs were not made in England, with the exception of the "Sarum kettle" manufactured by Doulton of Lambeth around 1900, based on an African example in the Salisbury Museum.

45. Barton, 99; Griselda Lewis, *A Collector's History of English Pottery* (New York: Viking Press, 1969), 15 (fig. 9), 18 (figs. 18, 20, 21), 57 (fig. 106), 123 (fig. 227); McCarthy and Brooks, 229, 269, 337, 367; Jacqueline Pearce and Alan Vince, *Surrey Whitewares* (London: Museum of London and London and Middlesex Archaeological Society, 1988), 24, 78, 127, 129–31; Desmond Eyles, *"Good Sir Toby": The Story of Toby Jugs and Character Jugs Through the Ages* (London: Doulton, 1955); Vic Schuler, *Collecting British Toby Jugs . . . 1780 to the Present Day* (London: Francis Joseph, 1997); Hume, 310.

46. Susan C. Power, *Early Art of the Southeastern Indians: Feathered Serpents and Winged Beings* (Athens: University of Georgia Press, 2004), color pls. 6, 19–20; Roy S. Dickens Jr., *Of Sky and Earth: Art of the Early Southeastern Indians* (Atlanta: High Museum of Art, 1982), 28, 52–53, 58, 82–84; Michael J. O'Brien, *Cat Monsters and Head Pots: The Archaeology of Missouri's Pemiscot Bayou* (Columbia: University of Missouri Press, 1994), xxxiv, xxxix.

47. A face pitcher attributed to Henry Remmey Jr. is dated 1838; a two-faced monkey jug likely by him or his son Richard is dated 1858. Both are salt-glazed stoneware, with cobalt blue–highlighted facial hair as with some German graybeards. For the Remmeys, see Stradling and Stradling, 114–18; Ketchum, 30–32; Susan H. Myers, *Handcraft to Industry: Philadelphia Ceramics in the First Half of the Nineteenth Century* (Washington, D.C.: Smithsonian Institution Press, 1980), 22–25.

48. For antebellum and later African American face vessels from South Carolina, see Vlach, 81–92; Baldwin, 79–87, 108–9, color pls. 12–13; and Mark M. Newell with Peter Lenzo, "Making Faces: Archaeological Evidence of African-American Face Jug Production," *Ceramics in America* [6] (2006): 122–38.

49. Edwin AtLee Barber, *Pottery and Porcelain of the United States* (New York: G. P. Putnam, 1909), 466. Stereoscopic cards issued in 1882 by photographer J. A. Palmer of Aiken, South Carolina (in Edgefield District), depict a Negro boy and girl pondering a monkey-form face jug, the earliest known illustrations of a locally made face vessel; titled *An Aesthetic Darkey*, the images likely were inspired by W. H. Beard's painting *The Aesthetic Monkey*, satirizing Oscar Wilde's American lecture tour and published in 1882 in *Harper's Weekly* (Jill Beute Koverman, *Making Faces: Southern Face Vessels from 1840–1990* [Columbia: McKissick Museum, University of South Carolina, 2000], 15–16).

50. Robert Farris Thompson, "African Influence on the Art of the United States," in *Black Studies in the University*, ed. Armstead L. Robinson et al. (New York: Bantam Books, 1969), 141.

51. Marla C. Berns, "Pots as People: Yungur Ancestral Portraits," *African Arts* 23 (July 1990): 50–60 and front cover. The Mangbetu of Zaire made juglike figural pots with vertical loop handles, but too late (late 1800s) to have influenced South Carolina slaves (Barley, 148–49).

52. Koverman, 6–7; Baldwin, 47, 51–54.

53. This scenario is not so far-fetched; a later potter, Charles Decker, began his career at the Remmey Pottery in Philadelphia before establishing northeast Tennessee's Keystone Pottery in 1871, where he and his son William made Remmey-style face jugs (*The Pottery of Charles F. Decker: A Life Well Made* [Jonesborough, TN: Jonesborough/Washington County History Museum, 2004], 52–53, 58).

54. A review of recent issues of *Ceramics Monthly*, *The Studio Potter*, *Ceramics Art and*

Perception, and *American Craft* suggests that the jug is not among the forms privileged by contemporary studio potters.

55. Koverman; William W. Ivey, *North Carolina and Southern Folk Pottery* (Seagrove, NC: Museum of North Carolina Traditional Pottery, 1992); Robert C. Lock, *The Traditional Potters of Seagrove, North Carolina* (Greensboro, NC: Antiques and Collectibles Press, 1994), 184–90; Barry G. Huffman, *Catawba Clay: Contemporary Southern Face Jug Makers* (Hickory, NC: A. W. Huffman, 1997); Michael A. Crocker and W. Newton Crouch Jr., *The Folk Pottery of Cheever, Arie, and Lanier Meaders: A Pictorial Legacy* (Griffin, GA: C&C Productions, 1994).

5. Georgia on My Mind: A Place-Based Case Study

1. This chapter is revised from my essay "Folklife" in *The New Georgia Encyclopedia* (http://www.georgiaencyclopedia.org/nge/Article.jsp?path=/Folklife/General&id=h–704). More than thirty entries are currently online in the encyclopedia's folklife section.

2. Stephen Vincent Benét's 1925 poem "The Mountain Whippoorwill; How Hill-Billy Jim Won the Great Fiddlers' Prize (A Georgia Romance)" was inspired by a news report of young Lowe Stokes beating veteran Fiddlin' John Carson by playing the tune "Hell's Broke Loose in Georgia" at the 1924 Fiddlers' Convention in downtown Atlanta (Eugene Wiggins, "Benét's 'Mountain Whippoorwill': Folklore atop Folklore," *Tennessee Folklore Society Bulletin* 41 [September 1975]: 99–114).

3. George Mitchell, *In Celebration of a Legacy: The Traditional Arts of the Lower Chattahoochee Valley* (Columbus, GA: Columbus Museum of Arts and Sciences, 1981). Other parts of Georgia that share traditions across state lines are the south-central Wiregrass section, shared with Alabama and Florida (Jerrilyn McGregory, *Wiregrass Country* [Jackson: University Press of Mississippi, 1997]), and the northeast Georgia mountains, shared with North Carolina and represented in the Foxfire publications.

4. John A. Burrison, *Brothers in Clay: The Story of Georgia Folk Pottery* (Athens: University of Georgia Press, 1983).

5. Charles H. Smith, *The Farm and the Fireside: Sketches of Domestic Life in War and in Peace* (Atlanta: Constitution Publishing, 1892), 11–15. George Featherstonhaugh and Henry Fearon described gander pullings in their early 1800s travels through the South (David Hackett Fischer, *Albion's Seed: Four British Folkways in America*, vol. 1, *America, A Cultural History* [New York: Oxford University Press, 1989], 363–64); the last reference to the sport I've found for Georgia occurred "soon after the Civil War" in the southeastern part of the state (Lucile Hodges, *A History of Our Locale, Mainly Evans County, Georgia* [Macon, GA: Southern Press, 1965], 94–95).

6. David C. Barrow Jr., "A Georgia Corn-Shucking," in *The Negro and His Folklore in Nineteenth-Century Periodicals*, ed. Bruce Jackson (Austin: University of Texas Press for American Folklore Society, 1967), 168–76; Roger D. Abrahams, *Singing the Master: The Emergence of African-American Culture in the Plantation South* (New York: Pantheon Books, 1992).

7. Recorded in 1967 from Lillie Mulkey West, 79, of Lower Young Cane, Georgia, by Barbara Sampson for the GFA.

8. Lillie West was brought to my attention by student Barbara Sampson, who, with

her mother, Blairsville resident Barbara Ruth Sampson, recorded the first interview in 1967; the following year student Judy Nelson, with her husband, Craig, made a follow-up visit in which most of the songs were recorded, and several months later I made a final recording. Background information on Lillie was gleaned from Kim Dyer, "The Land of an Uncloudy Day," *Moonshadow: Appalachia Past, Present and Future By Union County Students* 6 (1982): 120–21; Jane Ross Davis, "Twenty-Five Sheep Bells," in *The Heritage of Gilmer County, Georgia, 1832–1996* (Belmont, CA: Wadsworth Publishing, 1996), 415–16; Philip Mulkey West, *The Mulkeys of America* (Portland, OR: The Mulkey Book, 1982), 725–51; and Hedy West, "No Fiddle in My Home, Lillie West Recalls," *Sing Out!* 26, no. 5 (1978): 2–6. Don West's quotes are from the introduction to his book of poetry, *Clods of Southern Earth* (New York: Boni and Gaer, 1946), 11–12; his daughter, Hedy West (who died in 2005), is included in Kristine Baggelaar and Donald Milton, *Folk Music: More Than a Song* (New York: Thomas Y. Crowell, 1976), 401–2.

9. Memories of Music Making. Lillie's father, Kim, was a deacon at Clear Creek Baptist Church; many fundamentalist Protestants regard the fiddle as the "devil's instrument," since it is used mainly for "sinful" dance music. In the version of this story given by Hedy West in her *Sing Out!* article, Lillie's father and uncle Bob had also blamed fiddling and drinking at dances for a number of local deaths. "The Unclouded Day" is a gospel song written by the Reverend Josiah K. Alwood in 1890.

10. "A Woman's Confession (Frankie Silver)." G. Malcolm Laws Jr., *Native American Balladry: A Descriptive Study and a Bibliographic Syllabus*, rev. ed. (Philadelphia: American Folklore Society, 1964), 182–83 (no. E 13); Lillie's melody is ascribed to Alexander Johnson and associated with Isaac Watts's "Devotion" in Hugh McGraw et al., eds., *The Sacred Harp, 1991 Edition* (Bremen, GA: Sacred Harp Publishing, 1991), 48. In the tradition of British broadside "last goodnights," the ballad was composed in the first person as if written by the criminal awaiting execution. For more on the song and its background, see Daniel W. Patterson, *A Tree Accurst: Bobby McMillon and Stories of Frankie Silver* (Chapel Hill: University of North Carolina Press, 2000), and Fred C. Fussell, *Blue Ridge Music Trails: Finding a Place in the Circle* (Chapel Hill: University of North Carolina Press, 2003), 134–41. Frankie Silver was hanged for the murder of her husband, Charles (Lillie recalled his name as John), at Morganton, North Carolina, on July 12, 1833. Hedy West performed her grandmother's variant in 1966 on *Pretty Saro*, Topic 12T 146.

11. "The Little Old Man That Lived Out West (The Wife Wrapped in Wether's Skin)." Lillie learned this variant of Child no. 277 (Francis James Child, ed., *The English and Scottish Popular Ballads* [1882–1898; reprint, New York: Dover Publications, 1965], 5: 104–7, 304–5; Tristram P. Coffin, *The British Traditional Ballad in North America*, rev. ed. [Philadelphia: American Folklore Society, 1963], 146–48), also known as "The Wee Cooper o' Fife," from her mother. The old Scottish ballad may have been inspired by the "Taming of the Shrew" and "Wife Lapped in Morrel's Skin" folktales; for the former, see my *Storytellers: Folktales and Legends from the South* (Athens: University of Georgia Press, 1991 [paper ed.]), 275–76). A wether is a gelded male sheep; some variants make it clearer that wrapping the wife in its skin is the husband's lame ploy to answer her family's reaction should she complain about being beaten. Hedy West sang her grandmother's variant on *Hedy West, Vol. 2*, Vanguard VRS 9162, and *Old Times and Hard Times*, Folk Legacy FSA–032.

12. "A Fair Maid in the Garden." G. Malcolm Laws Jr., *American Balladry from British Broadsides* (Philadelphia: American Folklore Society, 1957), 224–25 (no. N 42). Probably originating as an Irish street ballad in the early nineteenth century, this is the most widely reported "broken token"–type ballad in the South. Like the Greek myth of Odysseus and Penelope, the protagonist (his appearance altered or disguised) returns to test his sweetheart's fidelity, the "surprise" revelation never failing to delight listeners. This ballad, which Lillie learned from a cousin, offers an antidote to the cynicism of the previous songs.

13. "When I Was Single." As handwritten by Lillie in 1968, with slight corrections from her recorded singing. This misogynistic—or is it misogamistic?—song has its origins in seventeenth-century England (Vance Randolph, *Ozark Folksongs*, ed. Norm Cohen [Urbana: University of Illinois Press, 1982], 329–31). Lillie also sang "I Wish I was a Single Girl Again," expressing similar sentiments but from the woman's perspective.

14. "The Drunkard's Child." Related to "The Drunkard's Lone Child," a favorite temperance song of the 1860s, for which see Randolph, 257–59, and Sigmund Spaeth, *Weep Some More My Lady* (Garden City, NY: Doubleday, 1927), 191–92. Lillie also sang or wrote down two other sentimental ballads, "The Orphan Girl" (for which see H. M. Belden, ed., *Ballads and Songs Collected by the Missouri Folk-Lore Society*, rev. ed. [Columbia: University of Missouri Press, 1955], 277–78) and "The Blind Child." As Lillie indicates in her introduction, in some areas it was customary, as a learning aid, to write down the words of these otherwise orally transmitted songs; such manuscripts are referred to as "song-ballets."

15. "Joe Bowers." Laws, *Native American Balladry*, 139–40 (no. B 14). Although sometimes ascribed to San Francisco entertainer John Woodward, a more likely author of this comic take on the California gold rush is John A. Stone, also thought to have written the more famous and equally cynical "Sweet Betsy from Pike" (Laws B 9). Lillie's variant, learned from her father, omits the last straw for Joe, the concluding stanzas that describe the child of Sal and the butcher as also being red-haired. Hedy West recorded it on *Pretty Saro*.

16. "The Texas Ranger." Lillie's handwritten text and introduction. Laws, *Native American Balladry*, 123 (no. A 8). Her Civil War version is from the Confederate point of view; there is another version with Indians as the enemy. Lillie also knew a third western ballad, "The Lone Prairie (Dying Cowboy)," Laws B 2.

17. "The Honest Farmer." From Lillie's handwritten text and introduction of 1968, but also recorded. This agricultural protest song is modeled on John B. Matthias's sacred song of 1836, "Palms of Victory (The Wayworn Traveler)." Compare Fiddlin' John Carson's rewrite, partially quoted in chapter one. Hedy West performed her grandmother's variant on *Hedy West, Vol. 2*.

18. Art Rosenbaum and Margo Newmark Rosenbaum, *Folk Visions and Voices: Traditional Music and Song in North Georgia* (Athens: University of Georgia Press, 1983), 58.

19. Newman Ivey White, gen. ed., *The Frank C. Brown Collection of North Carolina Folklore* (Durham, NC: Duke University Press, 1952–64).

20. Since the publication of Steve Siporin's *American Folk Masters: The National Heritage Fellows* (New York: Harry N. Abrams and Museum of International Folk Art, 1992),

two more National Heritage Fellowships have been awarded to Georgians: the McIntosh County Shouters and Catawba Indian potter Georgia Harris.

21. In addition to these subcultures, Georgia has had its share of smaller ethnic enclaves, including Sephardic (Iberian) and Ashkenazic (German) Jews in Savannah beginning in 1733; Salzburgers at Ebenezer, Effingham County, in 1734; Highland Scots at Darien, McIntosh County, 1735; New England Puritans (via South Carolina) at Midway and Sunbury, Liberty County, 1752; Scotch-Irish at Queensborough, Jefferson County, late 1760s; Welsh slate miners at Van Wert and Rockmart, Polk County, late 1830s; Finns (via New England) at Jesup, Wayne County, 1920s; Beachy Amish Mennonites (via Virginia) at Montezuma, Macon County, 1950s.

6. Branches and New Shoots: Southern Folk Culture Today and Tomorrow

1. "Goodbye, God," recorded in 1975 from Henry T. Malone of Atlanta by Vicki McGaughey for the GFA. This folk joke reflects the view of some southerners that the big city of Atlanta is godless—and unsouthern.

2. E.g., David E. Whisnant, *All That Is Native and Fine: The Politics of Culture in an American Region* (Chapel Hill: University of North Carolina Press, 1983); Jane S. Becker, *Selling Tradition: Appalachia and the Construction of an American Folk, 1930–1940* (Chapel Hill: University of North Carolina Press, 1998).

3. Douglas DeNatale et al., eds., *New Ways for Old Jugs: Tradition and Innovation at the Jugtown Pottery* (Columbia: McKissick Museum, University of South Carolina, 1994).

4. Quoted in John A. Burrison, *Brothers in Clay: The Story of Georgia Folk Pottery* (Athens: University of Georgia Press, 1983), 269.

5. Pam Durban Porter, ed., *Cabbagetown Families, Cabbagetown Food* (Atlanta: Patch Publications, 1976), developed by R. Cary Bynum into the play *Cabbagetown, Three Women*; Oraien E. Catledge, *Cabbagetown* (Austin: University of Texas Press, 1985).

6. "Orchestra at Hotel Put Out of Business by Fiddlers' Playing," *Atlanta Constitution*, February 7, 1915, quoted in John A. Burrison, "Fiddlers in the Alley: Atlanta As an Early Country Music Center," *Atlanta Historical Bulletin* 21, no. 2 (1977): 65; see also Wayne W. Daniel, *Pickin' on Peachtree: A History of Country Music in Atlanta, Georgia* (Urbana: University of Illinois Press, 1990).

7. "Dreadful Memories," from John Greenway, *American Folksongs of Protest* (1953; reprint, New York: A. S. Barnes/Perpetua, 1960), 273–75; see also Shelly Romalis, *Pistol Packin' Mama: Aunt Molly Jackson and the Politics of Folksong* (Urbana: University of Illinois Press, 1998). Aunt Molly's composition is modeled on Tennessean J. B. F. Wright's 1925 gospel song, "Precious Memories."

8. "Babies in the Mill," from Archie Green, ed., *Babies in the Mill: Nancy Dixon, Dorsey Dixon, Howard Dixon*, Testament Records T–3301.

9. "A Camper's Exposé," recorded in 1975 from Edgar A. Tillman of Blackshear, Georgia, by Catherine Cash for the GFA. For "The Nude in the RV," see Jan Harold Brunvand, *The Vanishing Hitchhiker: American Urban Legends and Their Meanings* (New York: W. W. Norton, 1981), 132–36.

10. Interview recorded in 2006 with "Anonymous Artist" of Atlanta, Georgia, by Rebecca M. Vitt for the GFA.

11. "Shooting the Bird," recorded in 1999 from "Ted" of Decatur, Georgia, by Joshua Elrod for the GFA. The description of Trackside's patrons is from Amy Winn's "Nightshift" column in the Atlanta weekly newspaper *Creative Loafing* (October 2–8, 2003): 82. Although generated by an actual event, in its telling the tale was shaped by the old, widespread folk–literature theme of "the trickster tricked."

12. D. A. Duchon et al., *Globalizing Georgia: Atlanta Ethnicity Atlas and Multicultural Directory of Georgia, 2003–2004* (Atlanta: CARA Publications, Department of Anthropology and Geography, Georgia State University, 2003); Celeste Ray, "Ethnicity," in *The Greenwood Encyclopedia of American Regional Cultures: The South*, ed. Rebecca Mark and Rob Vaughan (Westport, CT: Greenwood Press, 2004), 142–48; Margaret R. Dittemore and Fred J. Hay, eds., *Documenting Cultural Diversity in the Resurgent American South: Collectors, Collecting, and Collections* (Chicago: Association of College and Research Libraries, 1997); Barbara Lau, *From Cambodia to Greensboro: Tracing the Journeys of New North Carolinians* (Greensboro, NC: Greensboro Historical Museum, 2004). For the integration of recent immigrant traditions in the folk culture of a southern state, see Kristin G. Congdon and Tina Bucavalas, *Just Above the Water: Florida Folk Art* (Jackson: University Press of Mississippi, 2006).

13. Sally Peterson discusses story cloths as "key texts" for Hmong culture in "Translating Experience and the Reading of a Story Cloth," *Journal of American Folklore* 101, no. 399 (1988): 6–22; see also Deborah A. Duchon, *Home Is Where You Make It: Hmong Refugees in Georgia*, M.A. thesis (Atlanta: Georgia State University, 1993).

14. Charles Joyner, *Shared Traditions: Southern History and Folk Culture* (Urbana: University of Illinois Press, 1999), 189. See also Theodore Rosengarten and Dale Rosengarten, eds., *A Portion of the People: Three Hundred Years of Southern Jewish Life* (Columbia: University of South Carolina Press with McKissick Museum, 2002); Marcie Cohen Ferris, *Matzoh Ball Gumbo: Culinary Tales of the Jewish South* (Chapel Hill: University of North Carolina Press, 2005); and *Shalom Y'all*, a documentary video directed by Brian Bain and produced by Susan Levitas (http://www.shalomyall.com, 2002).

15. Leslie Gordon, "Passover Foodways in a Savannah, Georgia, Family," 2001, research paper deposited in the GFA.

16. Sheila Kay Adams has written a book of reminiscent stories, *Come Go Home with Me* (Chapel Hill: University of North Carolina Press, 1995), and has recorded a number of cassettes and CDs on the Ivy Creek label; her Internet homepage address (as of January 11, 2007) is http://www.jimandsheila.com/SheilasPages/SheilaHome.html. Rick Stewart is included in my *Shaping Traditions: Folk Arts in a Changing South* (Athens: University of Georgia Press, 2000), 32, 108 (cat. no. 18); his homepage (as of January 11, 2007) is http://www.rickstewart.20m.com/.

17. Quoted in Henry Glassie, *The Stars of Ballymenone* (Bloomington: Indiana University Press, 2006), epigraph and 29.

18. Author's interview with Lillie Mulkey West, 80, of Lower Young Cane, Georgia, 1968.

BOOKS ON SOUTHERN FOLK CULTURE

Music and Song

Abrahams, Roger D., ed. 1970. *A Singer and Her Songs: Almeda Riddle's Book of Ballads*. Baton Rouge: Louisiana State University Press.

———. 1992. *Singing the Master: The Emergence of African-American Culture in the Plantation South*. New York: Pantheon Books.

Allen, William Francis, Charles Pickard Ware, and Lucy McKim Garrison. 1867; reprint, 1992. *Slave Songs of the United States*. Baltimore: Clearfield Press.

Ancelet, Barry Jean. 1999. *Cajun and Creole Music Makers*. Jackson: University Press of Mississippi.

Anderson-Green, Paula Hathaway. 2002. *A Hot-Bed of Musicians: Traditional Music in the Upper New River Valley–Whitetop Region*. Knoxville: University of Tennessee Press.

Bastin, Bruce. 1986. *Red River Blues: The Blues Tradition in the Southeast*. Urbana: University of Illinois Press.

Bayard, Samuel P. 1982. *Dance to the Fiddle, March to the Fife: Instrumental Folk Tunes in Pennsylvania* (southwestern Pennsylvania and neighboring West Virginia, on the upper edge of southern Appalachia). University Park: Penn State University Press.

Beall, John. 1997. *Public Worship, Private Faith: Sacred Harp and American Folksong*. Athens: University of Georgia Press.

Belden, H. M., ed. Rev. ed., 1955. *Ballads and Songs Collected By the Missouri Folk-Lore Society*. Columbia: University of Missouri Press.

Burton, Thomas G. 1978. *Some Ballad Folks*. Johnson City: East Tennessee State University Research Development Committee.

Cantwell, Robert. 1984. *Bluegrass Breakdown: The Making of the Old Southern Sound*. Urbana: University of Illinois Press.

Cauthen, Joyce H. 1989. *With Fiddle and Well-Rosined Bow: Old-Time Fiddling in Alabama*. Tuscaloosa: University of Alabama Press.

Chappell, Louis W. 1933; reprint, 1968. *John Henry: A Folk-Lore Study*. Port Washington, NY: Kennikat Press.

Charters, Samuel B. 1959; reprint, 1975. *The Country Blues*. New York: Da Capo Press.

———. 1981. *The Roots of the Blues: An African Search*. Boston: M. Boyars.

Cobb, Buell E., Jr. 1978. *The Sacred Harp: A Tradition and Its Music*. Athens: University of Georgia Press.

Cohen, Norm. Rev. ed., 2000. *Long Steel Rail: The Railroad in American Folksong*. Urbana: University of Illinois Press.

Conway, Cecilia. 1995. *African Banjo Echoes in Appalachia: A Study of Folk Traditions*. Knoxville: University of Tennessee Press.

Daniel, Wayne W. 1990. *Pickin' on Peachtree: A History of Country Music in Atlanta, Georgia*. Urbana: University of Illinois Press.

Epstein, Dena J. 1977. *Sinful Tunes and Spirituals: Black Folk Music to the Civil War*. Urbana: University of Illinois Press.

Evans, David. 1982. *Big Road Blues: Tradition and Creativity in the Folk Blues*. Berkeley: University of California Press.

Ferris, William R. 1978. *Blues from the Delta*. Garden City, NY: Anchor Press.

Fussell, Fred C. 2003. *Blue Ridge Music Trails: Finding a Place in the Circle*. Chapel Hill: University of North Carolina Press.

Goff, James R., Jr. 2002. *Close Harmony: A History of Southern Gospel*. Chapel Hill: University of North Carolina Press.

Gordon, Robert. 2002. *Can't Be Satisfied: The Life and Times of Muddy Waters*. Boston: Little, Brown.

Green, Archie. 1972. *Only a Miner: Studies in Recorded Coal-Mining Songs*. Urbana: University of Illinois Press.

Greenway, John. 1953; reprint, 1960. *American Folksongs of Protest*. New York: A. S. Barnes/ Perpetua.

Gura, Philip F., and James F. Bollman. 1999. *America's Instrument: The Banjo in the Nineteenth Century*. Chapel Hill: University of North Carolina Press.

Harris, Michael W. 1992. *The Rise of Gospel Blues: The Music of Thomas Andrew Dorsey in the Urban Church*. New York: Oxford University Press.

Horn, Dorothy D. 1970. *Sing to Me of Heaven: A Study of Folk and Early American Materials in Three Old Harp Books*. Gainesville: University Press of Florida.

Jackson, George Pullen. 1933; reprint, 1965. *White Spirituals in the Southern Uplands*. New York: Dover Publications.

———. 1943; reprint, 1975. *White and Negro Spirituals: Their Life Span and Kinship*. New York: Da Capo Press.

Johnson, Guy B. 1929; reprint, 1974. *John Henry: Tracking Down a Negro Legend*. New York: AMS Press.

Johnson, James Weldon, and J. Rosamond Johnson. 1925–26; reprint, 1977. *The Books of American Negro Spirituals*. New York: Da Capo Press.

Jones, Loyal. 1984. *Minstrel of the Appalachians: The Story of Bascom Lamar Lunsford*. Boone, NC: Appalachian Consortium Press.

King, B. B., and David Ritz. 1996. *Blues All Around Me: The Autobiography of B. B. King*. New York: Avon Books.

Lieb, Sandra R. 1981. *Mother of the Blues: A Study of Ma Rainey*. Amherst: University of Massachusetts Press.

Lomax, Alan. 1950. *Mister Jelly Roll: The Fortunes of Jelly Roll Morton, New Orleans Creole and "Inventor of Jazz."* New York: Grosset & Dunlap/Universal Library.

Lomax, John A., and Alan Lomax. 1936. *Negro Folk Songs As Sung By Lead Belly . . .* New York: Macmillan.

Malone, Bill C. 2nd rev. ed., 2002. *Country Music U.S.A.: A Fifty-Year History.* Austin: University of Texas Press.

McNeil, W. K., ed. 1987. *Southern Folk Ballads.* Little Rock, AR: August House.

————, ed. 1993. *Southern Mountain Folksongs: Traditional Songs from the Appalachians and the Ozarks.* Little Rock, AR: August House.

————, ed. 2005. *Encyclopedia of American Gospel Music.* New York: Routledge.

Murray, Albert. Rev. ed., 2000. *Stomping the Blues.* New York: Da Capo Press.

Oliver, Paul. 1990. *Blues Fell This Morning: Meaning in the Blues.* Cambridge, Eng.: Cambridge University Press.

————, et al. 2001. *Yonder Come the Blues: The Evolution of a Genre.* Cambridge, Eng.: Cambridge University Press.

Olsson, Bengt. 1970. *Memphis Blues and Jug Bands.* London: Studio Vista.

Oster, Harry. 1969. *Living Country Blues.* Detroit: Folklore Associates.

Parrish, Lydia. 1942; reprint, 1965. *Slave Songs of the Georgia Sea Islands.* Hatboro, PA: Folklore Associates.

Patterson, Beverly Bush. 1995. *The Sound of the Dove: Singing in Appalachian Primitive Baptist Churches.* Urbana: University of Illinois Press.

Patterson, Daniel W. 2000. *A Tree Accurst: Bobby McMillon and Stories of Frankie Silver* (the ballad and its historical background). Chapel Hill: University of North Carolina Press.

Pearson, Barry Lee. 1984. *"Sounds So Good to Me": The Bluesman's Story.* Philadelphia: University of Pennsylvania Press.

————. 1990. *Virginia Piedmont Blues: The Lives and Art of Two Virginia Bluesmen.* Philadelphia: University of Pennsylvania Press.

————, and Bill McCulloch. 2003. *Robert Johnson Lost and Found.* Urbana: University of Illinois Press.

Randolph, Vance. 1982. *Ozark Folksongs.* Ed. Norm Cohen. Urbana: University of Illinois Press.

Ritchie, Jean. 1955; reprint, 1988. *Singing Family of the Cumberlands.* Lexington: University Press of Kentucky.

Rosenbaum, Art, and Margo Newmark Rosenbaum. 1983. *Folk Visions and Voices: Traditional Music and Song in North Georgia.* Athens: University of Georgia Press.

————. 1998. *Shout Because You're Free: The African American Ring Shout Tradition in Coastal Georgia.* Athens: University of Georgia Press.

Rosenberg, Neil V. 1985; reprint, 1993. *Bluegrass: A History.* Urbana: University of Illinois Press.

Sandmel, Ben. 1999. *Zydeco!* Jackson: University Press of Mississippi.

Savoy, Ann Allen. 1984. *Cajun Music: A Reflection of a People,* vol. 1. Eunice, LA: Bluebird Press.

Sharp, Cecil J. 1932. *English Folk Songs from the Southern Appalachians.* Ed. Maud Karpeles. London: Oxford University Press.

Smith, Betty N. 1998. *Jane Hicks Gentry: A Singer among Singers.* Lexington: University Press of Kentucky.

Smith, Richard D. 2000. *Can't You Hear Me Callin': The Life of Bill Monroe, Father of Bluegrass.* Boston: Little, Brown.

Stearns, Marshall W. 1970. *The Story of Jazz*. London: Oxford University Press.

Stivale, Charles J. 2003. *Disenchanting les Bons Temps: Identity and Authenticity in Cajun Music and Dance*. Durham, NC: Duke University Press.

Tisserand, Michael. 1998. *The Kingdom of Zydeco*. New York: Arcade Publishing.

Titon, Jeff Todd. Rev. ed., 1994. *Early Downhome Blues: A Musical and Cultural Analysis*. Chapel Hill: University of North Carolina Press.

Wiggins, Gene. 1987. *Fiddlin' Georgia Crazy: Fiddlin' John Carson, His Real World, and the World of His Songs*. Urbana: University of Illinois Press.

Williams, Brett. 1983. *John Henry: A Bio-Bibliography*. Westport, CT: Greenwood Press.

Wilson, Joe. 2006. *A Guide to the Crooked Road: Virginia's Heritage Music Trail*. Winston-Salem, NC: John F. Blair Publisher.

Wolfe, Charles. 1997. *The Devil's Box: Masters of Southern Fiddling*. Nashville, TN: Vanderbilt University Press.

———, and Kip Lornell. 1992. *The Life and Legend of Leadbelly*. New York: HarperCollins Publishers.

Zwonitzer, Mark, and Charles Hirshberg. 2002. *Will You Miss Me When I'm Gone: The Carter Family and Their Legacy in American Music*. New York: Simon & Schuster.

Architecture, Crafts, and Food

Adams, E. Bryding, ed. 1995. *Made in Alabama: A State Legacy*. Birmingham, AL: Birmingham Museum of Art.

Alvey, R. Gerald. 1984. *Dulcimer Maker: The Craft of Homer Ledford*. Lexington: University Press of Kentucky.

Baldwin, Cinda K. 1993. *Great and Noble Jar: Traditional Stoneware of South Carolina*. Athens: University of Georgia Press.

Beam, Bill, et al., eds. 1999. *Two Centuries of Potters: A Catawba Valley Tradition*. Lincolnton, NC: Lincoln County History Association.

Beardsley, John, et al. 2002. *Gee's Bend: The Women and Their Quilts*. Atlanta: Tinwood Press.

Becker, Jane S. 1998. *Selling Tradition: Appalachia and the Construction of an American Folk, 1930–1940*. Chapel Hill: University of North Carolina Press.

Benberry, Questa. 1992. *Always There: The African-American Presence in American Quilts*. Louisville: Kentucky Quilt Project, 1992.

Bivins, John, Jr. Rev. ed., 1988. *Longrifles of North Carolina*. York, PA: George Shumway.

———. 1972. *The Moravian Potters in North Carolina*. Chapel Hill: University of North Carolina Press for Old Salem.

Blumer, Thomas John. 2004. *Catawba Indian Pottery: The Survival of a Folk Tradition*. Tuscaloosa: University of Alabama Press.

Brackner, Joey. 2006. *Alabama Folk Pottery*. Tuscaloosa: University of Alabama Press with Birmingham Museum of Art.

Burdick, Nancilu B. 1988. *Legacy: The Story of Talula Gilbert Bottoms and Her Quilts*. Nashville, TN: Rutledge Hill Press.

Burrison, John A. Rev. ed., 1995. *Brothers in Clay: The Story of Georgia Folk Pottery*. Athens: University of Georgia Press.

———. 2000. *Shaping Traditions: Folk Arts in a Changing South.* Athens: University of Georgia Press.

Comstock, H. E. 1994. *The Pottery of the Shenandoah Valley Region.* Chapel Hill: University of North Carolina Press for Museum of Early Southern Decorative Arts.

Congdon, Kristin G., and Tina Bucavalas. 2006. *Just Above the Water: Florida Folk Art.* Jackson: University Press of Mississippi.

Dabney, Joseph Earl. 1974. *Mountain Spirits: A Chronicle of Corn Whiskey from King James' Ulster Plantation to America's Appalachians and the Moonshine Life.* New York: Charles Scribner's Sons.

———. 1998. *Smokehouse Ham, Spoon Bread, & Scuppernong Wine: The Folklore and Art of Southern Appalachian Cooking.* Nashville, TN: Cumberland House.

Downs, Dorothy. 1995. *Art of the Florida Seminole and Miccosukee Indians.* Gainesville: University Press of Florida.

Eaton, Allen H. 1937; reprint, 1973. *Handicrafts of the Southern Highlands.* New York: Dover Publications.

Edge, John T. 2000. *Southern Belly: The Ultimate Food Lover's Companion to the South.* Athens, GA: Hill Street Press.

Edwards, Jay Dearborn, and Nicolas Kariouk Pecquet du Bellay de Verton. 2004. *A Creole Lexicon: Architecture, Landscape, People.* Baton Rouge: Louisiana State University Press.

Egerton, John. 1987. *Southern Food: At Home, on the Road, in History.* New York: Alfred A. Knopf.

Elie, Lolis Eric, ed. 2004. *Cornbread Nation 2: The United States of Barbeque.* Chapel Hill: University of North Carolina Press.

Ferris, Marcie Cohen. 2005. *Matzoh Ball Gumbo: Culinary Tales of the Jewish South.* Chapel Hill: University of North Carolina Press.

Foster, Helen Bradley. 1997. *New Raiments of Self: African American Clothing in the Antebellum South.* New York: Berg Publishers.

Fry, Gladys-Marie. 2002. *Stitched from the Soul: Slave Quilts of the Antebellum South.* Chapel Hill: University of North Carolina Press.

Glassie, Henry. 1968. *Pattern in the Material Folk Culture of the Eastern United States.* Philadelphia: University of Pennsylvania Press.

———. 1975. *Folk Housing in Middle Virginia: A Structural Analysis of Historic Artifacts.* Knoxville: University of Tennessee Press.

Goodrich, Frances Louisa. 1931; reprint, 1989. *Mountain Homespun.* Knoxville: University of Tennessee Press.

Harris, Jessica B. 1989. *Iron Pots and Wooden Spoons: Africa's Gifts to New World Cooking.* New York: Simon & Schuster.

Haase, Ronald W. 1992. *Classic Cracker: Florida's Wood-Frame Vernacular Architecture.* Sarasota, FL: Pineapple Press.

Hewitt, Mark, and Nancy Sweezy. 2005. *The Potter's Eye: Art and Tradition in North Carolina Pottery.* Chapel Hill: University of North Carolina Press for North Carolina Museum of Art.

Hill, Sarah H. 1997. *Weaving New Worlds: Southeastern Cherokee Women and Their Basketry.* Chapel Hill: University of North Carolina Press.

Horton, Laurel. [1986]. *Social Fabric: South Carolina's Traditional Quilts*. Columbia: McKissick Museum, University of South Carolina.

―――. 2005. *Mary Black's Family Quilts: Memory and Meaning in Everyday Life*. Columbia: University of South Carolina Press.

Huff, Mary Elizabeth Johnson, and J. D. Schwalm. 2002. *Mississippi Quilts*. Jackson: University Press of Mississippi.

Irwin, John Rice. 1982. *Baskets and Basket Makers in Southern Appalachia*. Exton, PA: Schiffer Publishing.

―――. 1983. *Guns and Gunmaking Tools of Southern Appalachia*. Exton, PA: Schiffer Publishing.

―――. 1983. *Musical Instruments of the Southern Appalachian Mountains*. West Chester, PA: Schiffer Publishing.

―――. 1984. *A People and Their Quilts*. West Chester, PA: Schiffer Publishing.

―――. 1985. *Alex Stewart: Portrait of a Pioneer*. West Chester, PA: Schiffer Publishing.

Jones, Michael Owen. 1989. *Craftsman of the Cumberlands: Tradition and Creativity*. Lexington: University Press of Kentucky.

Jordan, Terry G. 1978. *Texas Log Buildings: A Folk Architecture*. Austin: University of Texas Press.

―――, and Matti Kaups. 1989. *The American Backwoods Frontier: An Ethnic and Ecological Interpretation*. Baltimore: Johns Hopkins University Press.

Law, Rachel Nash, and Cynthia W. Taylor. 1991. *Appalachian White Oak Basketmaking: Handing Down the Basket*. Knoxville: University of Tennessee Press.

Leftwich, Rodney L. 1970. *Arts and Crafts of the Cherokee*. Cherokee, NC: Cherokee Publications.

Little, M. Ruth. 1998. *Sticks & Stones: Three Centuries of North Carolina Gravemarkers*. Chapel Hill: University of North Carolina Press.

Mack, Charles R. 2006. *Talking with the Turners: Conversations with Southern Folk Potters*. Columbia: University of South Carolina Press.

Marshall, Howard W. 1981. *Folk Architecture in Little Dixie: A Regional Culture in Missouri*. Columbia: University of Missouri Press.

Martin, Charles E. 1984. *Hollybush: Folk Building and Social Change in an Appalachian Community*. Knoxville: University of Tennessee Press.

McDaniel, George W. 1982. *Hearth and Home: Preserving a People's Culture*. Philadelphia: Temple University Press.

Moffett, Marian, and Lawrence Wodehouse. 1993. *East Tennessee Cantilever Barns*. Knoxville: University of Tennessee Press.

Morgan, John. 1990. *The Log House in East Tennessee*. Knoxville: University of Tennessee Press.

Nabokov, Peter, and Robert Easton. 1989. *Native American Architecture*. New York: Oxford University Press.

Neat Pieces: The Plain-Style Furniture of Nineteenth-Century Georgia. Rev. ed., 2006. Athens: University of Georgia Press.

Noble, Allen G., 1984. *Wood, Brick, and Stone: The North American Settlement Landscape*. Amherst: University of Massachusetts Press.

Page, Linda Garland, and Eliot Wigginton, eds. 1984. *The Foxfire Book of Appalachian*

Cookery: Regional Memorabilia and Recipes. New York: E. P. Dutton and Foxfire Press.

Perry, Reginia A. 1994. *Harriet Powers's Bible Quilts*. New York: St. Martin's Press/Rizzoli International.

Power, Susan C. 2006. *Art of the Cherokee: Prehistory to the Present*. Athens: University of Georgia Press.

Ramsey, Bets, and Merikay Waldvogel. 1986. *The Quilts of Tennessee: Images of Domestic Life Prior to 1930*. Nashville, TN: Rutledge Hill Press.

Roberson, Ruth Haislip, ed. 1988. *North Carolina Quilts*. Chapel Hill: University of North Carolina Press.

Rosengarten, Dale. 1986. *Row upon Row: Sea Grass Baskets of the South Carolina Lowcountry*. Columbia: McKissick Museum, University of South Carolina.

Rubin, Cynthia Elyce, ed. 1985. *Southern Folk Art*. Birmingham, AL: Oxmoor House.

Sizemore, Jean. 1994. *Ozark Vernacular Houses: A Study of Rural Homeplaces in the Arkansas Ozarks 1830–1930*. Fayetteville: University of Arkansas Press.

Smith, L. Allen. 1983. *A Catalogue of Pre-Revival Appalachian Dulcimers*. Columbia: University of Missouri Press.

Sweezy, Nancy. Rev. ed., 1994. *Raised in Clay: The Southern Pottery Tradition*. Chapel Hill: University of North Carolina Press.

Upton, Dell, ed. 1986. *America's Architectural Roots: Ethnic Groups That Built America*. Washington, D.C.: Preservation Press.

Vlach, John Michael. Rev. ed., 1990. *The Afro-American Tradition in Decorative Arts*. Athens: University of Georgia Press.

———. 1993. *Back of the Big House: The Architecture of Plantation Slavery*. Chapel Hill: University of North Carolina Press.

Weinraub, Anita Zaleski, ed. 2006. *Georgia Quilts: Piecing Together a History*. Athens: University of Georgia Press.

Westmacott, Richard. 1992. *African-American Gardens and Yards in the Rural South*. Knoxville: University of Tennessee Press.

White, Betsy K. 2006. *Great Road Style: The Decorative Arts Legacy of Southwest Virginia and Northeast Tennessee*. Charlottesville: University of Virginia Press.

Williams, Derita Coleman, and Nathan Harsh. 1988. *The Art and Mystery of Tennessee Furniture and Its Makers Through 1850*. Nashville: Tennessee Historical Society and Tennessee State Museum Foundation.

Williams, Michael Ann. 1991. *Homeplace: The Social Use and Meaning of the Folk Dwelling in Southwestern North Carolina*. Athens: University of Georgia Press.

Wilson, Eugene M. 1975. *Alabama Folk Houses*. Montgomery: Alabama Historical Commission.

Wilson, Kathleen Curtis. 2001. *Textile Art from Southern Appalachia: The Quiet Work of Women*. Johnson City, TN: Overmountain Press.

Wilson, Sadye Tune, and Doris Finch Kennedy. 1983. *Of Coverlets: The Legacies, the Weavers*. Nashville, TN: Tunstede.

Zug, Charles G., III. 1986. *Turners and Burners: The Folk Potters of North Carolina*. Chapel Hill: University of North Carolina Press.

Storytelling, Beliefs, Customs, Speech, and Surveys

Abrahams, Roger D., et al. 2006. *Blues for New Orleans: Mardi Gras and America's Creole Soul*. Philadelphia: University of Pennsylvania Press.

Ancelet, Barry Jean.1989. *"Capitaine, Voyage ton Flag": The Traditional Cajun Country Mardi Gras*. Lafayette: Center for Louisiana Studies, University of Southwest Louisiana.

———. 1994. *Cajun and Creole Folktales: The French Oral Tradition of South Louisiana*. New York: Garland Publishers.

———, Jay D. Edwards, and Glen Pitre. 1991. *Cajun Country*. Jackson: University Press of Mississippi.

Anderson, Jeffrey E. 2005. *Conjure in African American Society*. Baton Rouge: Louisiana State University Press.

Ballard, William L. 1978. *The Yuchi Green Corn Ceremonial: Form and Meaning*. Los Angeles: University of California American Indian Studies Center.

Barden, Thomas E., ed. 1991. *Virginia Folk Legends*. Charlottesville: University Press of Virginia.

Botkin, B. A., ed. 1945. *Lay My Burden Down: A Folk History of Slavery*. Chicago: University of Chicago Press.

Brown, Alan. 1996. *The Face in the Window and Other Alabama Ghostlore*. Tuscaloosa: University of Alabama Press.

Burrison, John A., ed. 1991 (paperback ed.). *Storytellers: Folktales and Legends from the South*. Athens: University of Georgia Press. See bibliography for prior publications on southern storytelling.

Burton, Thomas G. 1993. *Serpent-Handling Believers*. Knoxville: University of Tennessee Press.

Cavender, Anthony. 2003. *Folk Medicine in Southern Appalachia*. Chapel Hill: University of North Carolina Press.

Dance, Daryl Cumber, ed. 2002. *From My People: 400 Years of African American Folklore*. New York: W. W. Norton.

Duncan, Barbara R. 1998. *Living Stories of the Cherokee*. Chapel Hill: University of North Carolina Press.

Fett, Sharla M. 2002. *Working Cures: Healing, Health, and Power on Southern Slave Plantations*. Chapel Hill: University of North Carolina Press.

Garrett, Mitchell B. 1986. *Horse and Buggy Days on Hatchet Creek*. University, AL: University of Alabama Press.

Herring, J. L. 1918; reprint, 1978. *Saturday Night Sketches: Stories of Old Wiregrass Georgia*. Tifton, GA: Sunny South Press.

Holloway, Joseph E., ed. Rev. ed., 2005. *Africanisms in American Culture*. Bloomington: Indiana University Press.

Hurston, Zora Neale. 1935; reprint, 1970. *Mules and Men: Negro Folktales and Voodoo Practices in the South*. New York: Harper & Row.

Hyatt, Harry Middleton. 1970–78. *Hoodoo—Conjuration—Witchcraft—Rootwork*. Hannibal, MO: Western Publishing.

Isbell, Robert. 1996. *Ray Hicks: Master Storyteller of the Blue Ridge*. Chapel Hill: University of North Carolina Press.

Jackson, Jason Baird. 2003. *Yuchi Ceremonial Life: Performance, Meaning, and Tradition in a Contemporary American Indian Community*. Lincoln: University of Nebraska Press.

Jones, Bessie. 1983; reprint, 1989. *For the Ancestors: Autobiographical Memories*. Ed. John Stewart. Athens: University of Georgia Press.

Jones-Jackson, Patricia. 1987. *When Roots Die: Endangered Traditions on the Sea Islands*. Athens: University of Georgia Press.

Joyner, Charles. 1984. *Down By the Riverside: A South Carolina Slave Community*. Urbana: University of Illinois Press.

———. 1999. *Shared Traditions: Southern History and Folk Culture*. Urbana: University of Illinois Press.

Justus, May. 1967. *The Complete Peddler's Pack: Games, Songs, Rhymes, and Riddles from Mountain Folklore*. Knoxville: University of Tennessee Press.

Kane, Harnett T. 1958. *The Southern Christmas Book*. New York: David McKay.

Kimbrough, David L. 1995. *Taking Up Serpents: Snake Handlers in Eastern Kentucky*. Chapel Hill: University of North Carolina Press.

Kinser, Samuel. 1990. *Carnival, American Style: Mardi Gras at New Orleans and Mobile*. Chicago: University of Chicago Press.

Lindahl, Carl, ed. 2001. *Perspectives on the Jack Tales and Other North American Märchen*. Bloomington: Folklore Institute, Indiana University.

———, and Carolyn Ware. 1997. *Cajun Mardi Gras Masks*. Jackson: University Press of Mississippi.

———, Maida Owens, and C. Renée Harvison, eds. 1997. *Swapping Stories: Folktales from Louisiana*. Jackson: University Press of Mississippi.

Long, Carolyn Morrow. 2001. *Spiritual Merchants: Religion, Magic, and Commerce*. Knoxville: University of Tennessee Press.

McCarthy, William Bernard, ed. 1994. *Jack in Two Worlds: Contemporary North American Tales and Their Tellers*. Chapel Hill: University of North Carolina Press.

McGregory, Jerrilyn. 1997. *Wiregrass Country*. Jackson: University Press of Mississippi.

Milnes, Gerald C. 2007. *Signs, Cures, and Witchery: German Appalachian Folklore*. Knoxville: University of Tennessee Press.

Montgomery, Michael B., and Joseph S. Hall. 2004. *Dictionary of Smoky Mountain English*. Knoxville: University of Tennessee Press.

Moss, Kay K. 1999. *Southern Folk Medicine 1750–1820*. Columbia: University of South Carolina Press.

Olson, Ted. 1998. *Blue Ridge Folklife*. Jackson: University Press of Mississippi.

Patterson, Daniel W., and Charles G. Zug III, eds. 1990. *Arts in Earnest: North Carolina Folklife*. Durham, NC: Duke University Press.

Prahlad, Anand, ed. 2006. *The Greenwood Encyclopedia of African American Folklore*. Westport, CT: Greenwood Press.

Puckett, Newbell Niles. 1926; reprint, 1969. *Folk Beliefs of the Southern Negro*. New York: Dover Publications.

Pyatt, Sherman E., and Alan Johns. 1999. *A Dictionary and Catalog of African American Folklife of the South*. Westport, CT: Greenwood Press.

Randolph, Vance. 1947; reprint, 1964. *Ozark Superstitions*. New York: Dover Publications.

———, and George P. Wilson. 1953. *Down in the Holler: A Gallery of Ozark Folk Speech*. Norman: University of Oklahoma Press.

Ray, Celeste, ed. 2003. *Southern Heritage on Display: Public Ritual and Ethnic Diversity within Southern Regionalism*. Tuscaloosa: University of Alabama Press.

Rehder, John B. 2004. *Appalachian Folkways*. Baltimore: Johns Hopkins University Press.

Roberts, John W. 1989. *From Trickster to Badman: The Black Folk Hero in Slavery and Freedom*. Philadelphia: University of Pennsylvania Press.

Rosenberg, Bruce A. Rev. ed., 1988. *Can These Bones Live? The Art of the American Folk Preacher*. Urbana: University of Illinois Press.

Savannah Unit, Georgia Writers' Project. 1940; reprint, 1986. *Drums and Shadows: Survival Studies among the Georgia Coastal Negroes*. Athens: University of Georgia Press.

Siporin, Steve. 1992. *American Folk Masters: The National Heritage Fellows*. New York: Harry N. Abrams and Museum of International Folk Art.

Tallant, Robert. 1946; reprint, 1962. *Voodoo in New Orleans*. New York: Collier Books.

Tullos, Allen, ed. 1977. *Long Journey Home: Folklife in the South*. Chapel Hill, NC: Southern Exposure.

Turner, Lorenzo Dow. 1949; reprint, 1974. *Africanisms in the Gullah Dialect*. Ann Arbor: University of Michigan Press.

Ward, Martha. 2004. *Voodoo Queen: The Spirited Lives of Marie Laveau*. Jackson: University Press of Mississippi.

Ware, Carolyn E. 2007. *Cajun Women and Mardi Gras: Reading the Rules Backward*. Urbana: University of Illinois Press.

Watkins, Floyd C., and Charles Hubert Watkins. 1963; reprint, 1973. *Yesterday in the Hills*. Athens: University of Georgia Press.

Whisnant, David E. 1983. *All That Is Native and Fine: The Politics of Culture in an American Region*. Chapel Hill: University of North Carolina Press.

White, Newman Ivey, gen. ed. 1952–64. *The Frank C. Brown Collection of North Carolina Folklore*. Durham, NC: Duke University Press.

Wiggins, William H., Jr. 1990. *Oh, Freedom! Afro-American Emancipation Celebrations*. Knoxville: University of Tennessee Press.

Wigginton, Eliot, ed. 1972. *The Foxfire Book* (first in a series of 12). Garden City, NY: Anchor/Doubleday.

———, ed. 1990. *A Foxfire Christmas: Appalachian Memories and Traditions*. New York: Doubleday.

Wolfram, Walt. 1976. *Appalachian Speech*. Arlington, VA: Center for Applied Linguistics.

INDEX

Included in parentheses are folklore practitioners' specialties and genres of titled folklore items; page numbers in *italics* refer to illustrations.

A

accordion, 71

Adams, Sheila Kay (singer and storyteller), *176*

Africa, influence from, 44–46, 51, 54, 57, 61, 70, 77, 84–85, 95–98, 107, 128–30, 161

Alabama, 22, 34–35, 40, *42*, *51*, 60, 77, 81, 86, 108, 110, 134, 174

Alderman, Clint (potter), 60

Appalachia, *4*, 8–9, 14–17, *16*, 20–22, 25, 27–29, *28*, 32, 38, *42*, *44*, *51*, 55–*56*, 61, *67*, 70–*71*, *75*–78, *79*, *87*, 89, *93*–94, *98*–103, *99*–*100*, *102*–3, 105–7, 108, 110, *120*–*21*, *125*–26, *131*, *137*–59, *138*, *141*, 165, 167, *176*–77, *plates 5, 7, 14*

Appalachian South Folklife Center (Pipestem, West Virginia), 141

architecture, *5*, 48–55, 86, *93*–94. *See also* barn, transverse-crib; cabins; *chickee*; chimney, external; corn crib; dogtrot house; *fachwerk*; fence, worm/snake; foundation, pier-and-sill; Frontier Culture Museum; hall-and-parlor house; kitchen, detached; logs, horizontal; porch, sitting; "raisings," house and barn; Rural Life Museum; shotgun house; smokehouse; tabby; Vermilionville; yard, swept

Archive of Folk Culture (Library of Congress), 160

Arkansas, 74

Arp, Bill (literary character), 136–37

Arthur Smith Trio (singers and musicians), 185–86n9

Atlanta History Center and Museum, 14, 29, 165

Aust, Gottfried (potter), 205n66

Averett, Eddie (potter), *122*

B

"Babies in the Mill" (song), 168–69

bagpipes, 98, *106*

ballads, 72–74, 140–59; American, 73–74, 88–89, 144–48, 155–57; British broadside, 72, 151–52; "Child," 72–73, 90, 149–50; sentimental, 153–55

banjo, 9, 15–17, 20, 70, *96*–*97*, 142

"Barbara Allen" (song), 90

barbeque, 43, 88, 165, *plate 1*

Barber, Edwin AtLee, 129–30

barn, transverse-crib, 52–54, *53*

Barrow, David C., Jr., 52

Bartmannkrug (German graybeard jug), *115*, 129

Bartram, William, 5

baskets, 61–*62*; hamper, *26*–*27*, 61; rib, 61–*62*; rivercane, 22, 61–*62*; sweetgrass, 61–*62*, *97*

Bayard, Samuel, 7–8

Beatles, 69

clothing, 57–58; "dough face" (mask), 91; headwrap, 57–58, 68; Mardi Gras costumes, 57, *plate 8*; Seminole patchwork, 57–58; sunbonnet, *42*, 79

coal mining, 38, 89, 167–69

coffee, 47–48

Cold Mountain (motion picture), 165

Coleman, Milton (storyteller), 30, 182n23

Collins Clement, Ethel (weaver), 55–56

Collins, Floyd. *See* "Death of Floyd Collins, The"

Commereau, Thomas (potter), *plate 11*

comparative research method, 90

Continental Europe, influence from, 101–5

Coolidge, Calvin, 25

coopering (wood craft), 98, *100*, 177

Copeland, Cassie Mae (storyteller), 75–76

corn (maize), importance of, 43–44, 86–*87*

corn breads, 42–43, 165, 174, *plate 1*

corn crib, 108, *138*

corn shucking, *138*–39

Cotten, Elizabeth (singer), 69

cotton (cash crop), 26–27, 38–39, 56

coverlets, overshot, 55–*56*, 108. *See also* weaving

Coxe, Tench, 55

crackers (poor whites), 46, 90, 137

Craig, Burlon (potter), *plate 6*

crawfish, 72

Creoles, 25, *58*, 71–72, 78, 102

creolization (cultural blending), 84, 102

Crocker, Dwayne (potter), *113*

Crocker, Michael (potter), 22

Crolius, Clarkson, Sr., and Clarkson, Jr. (potters), *118*, *plate 11*

D

Dalhart, Vernon (Marion Try Slaughter), 73

Davidson potters, 60

Davies, Thomas (pottery shop owner), *129*

Davis, Jimmie (singer, musician, and song writer), 35

Davis, R. M. (carpenter), *53*

"Death of Floyd Collins, The" (song), 73

Decker, Charles and William (potters), 211n53

Decoration Day, 78, *plate 7*

Delaware Valley, 4–5, 88, 90, 101–2

D'Entrecolles, Père, 61

"Devil's Dream, The" (tune), 98

devolutionary premise (folklore in decline), 158–59

Dial, Jonathan (potter), *31*

dialects, 24–25, 38, 40, 95. *See also* Gullah dialect

"Dividing the Walnuts" (story), 90–91, 171

Dixon, Dorsey (singer, musician, and song writer), 168–69

dogtrot house, *51*–52, *plate 2*

Dorsey, David (potter), *120*

"Dreadful Memories" (song), 167–68

drinks, soft (southern mass-produced), 187n22

"Drunkard's Child, The" (song), 153–55

Duche, Andrew (potter), *5*

Du Halde, Jean-Baptiste, 61, 65

dulcimer, Appalachian, 8–9, 70–*71*, 101, *103*

Dwight, John (English potter), 117

E

earthenware (redware), *5*, 60, *94*, *114*–17, 119, 206–7n12, *plates 9–10*, *14*

Eaton, Allen, 8

economy, agrarian. *See* farming

Edgefield District, South Carolina (pottery center), 60–61, *94*, *119*, *124*, *129*–*32*

Eller, Lawrence (singer), 3, 179n1

Ellis, Emily (storyteller), 90–91, 171

England. *See* Britain

English Folk Dance and Song Society, 107

Ennis, Seamus (Irish musician and singer), *106*

"Evangelical Cabby, The" (story), 36–37

F

face jugs. *See* jugs: face

fachwerk (German half-timber
 construction), 101, *104*, 203n49
"Fair Maid in the Garden, A" (song),
 151–52
farming, 25–29, 38–39, 167, 177
"Fast-Running Dog" (story), 20–21
Faulkner, William, 3, 38
fence, worm/snake, 101–2
Ferguson, Bobby (potter), *132*
Ferguson, William (potter), *31*
Ferris, Marcie Cohen, *175*
fiddle, 35, *39*, 70–71, 98, 142–44
fiddlers' conventions: Atlanta, Georgia,
 166–67; Elk Creek, Virginia, 71; Galax,
 Virginia, 71
Finno-Swedes, 101–2
Fischer, David Hackett, 89–90
flag, Confederate, 40
Flatt, Lester (singer and musician), 180n7
Florida, 23–24, 40, 57–*58*, 77, 86, 88, 105
Foley, Ed (song writer), 89
folklore (folk culture, folklife), definition
 of, 19, 85
food, 42–48, 97–98, 173–*75*, *plate 1. See*
 also barbeque; biscuits; bourbon;
 buttermilk; candy-pulling; chitlins;
 clay eating; coffee; corn breads;
 crawfish; greens; grits; gumbo; ham;
 hog butchering; hominy; jambalaya;
 lard; moonshine; peanuts; peas,
 blackeyed; pork; pot likker; sauerkraut;
 stews; syrup, cane; tea, sweet
foundation, pier-and-sill (architecture),
 48–*49*
Fox, Nicholas (potter), *120*
Foxfire program, 134, 160, 181n21
France, influence from, 78, 102
Frank, Leo, 36, 73
"Frankie Silver" ("A Woman's Confession")
 (song), 144–48
Freeman, Elbert (musician), 14
Frontier Culture Museum (Staunton,
 Virginia), 205n65
Funkhouser, Luther (pottery retailer), *120*
furniture: bedstead, 63; bench, 63; blanket

chest, 63, 101; chair, mule-ear, 66–*67*;
 clothes press, 63; huntboard, *64*–65;
 joggling board, 65–*66*; lazy Susan
 table, 65; meal bin, 98, *100*; pie safe,
 64–65; "plain style," 62–67; sugar
 chest, 65

G
games (children's), 92, 94
gander-pulling (sport), 136–38, *137*
Gellert, Lawrence, 33
Gentry, Jane Hicks (singer), 195n76
Georgia, 3, *5*–6, 10–18, *11*, *13*, *16*, 21–22, *26*–
 29, *27*–*28*, *31*–*33*, 35–*40*, *37*, *39*, 43–*48*,
 44, *45*, 50–*56*, *50*, *53*–*54*, *56*, 58–60,
 62–65, *64*, 67–*68*, 73, 75–77, *79*, 81–*82*,
 86–88, *87*, 90–*93*, *91*–92, *95*–97, 99–*100*,
 102–4, 107, 110–*13*, *111*, *120*–22, *125*–27,
 126, *131*–*33*, 134–63, 164–67, *166*, 169–75,
 plates 1, *3*, *5*, *14*–*16*
Georgia Folklife Program, 162
Georgia Folklore Archives (GFA), 14,
 27–30, *28*, 33–34, 36–37, *50*, 73, 75–77,
 88, 90–91, *96*, *100*, 139–59, 164, 169–75,
 189n39
Georgia Sea Island Singers, 21–22, 107, 161
Georgia State University, 3, 10–11, 14, 160,
 164
"Georgia's Three-Dollar Tag" (song), 35
Germany, influence from, 14–15, 61, 101–*4*,
 103, 117, 119, 126, 128–30
Girvin, Eva (singer), 9
Glassie, Henry, 9, 11, 177
glazes, stoneware: alkaline (ash- and lime-
 based), *31*, 60–61, *94*, *103*, 110, *119*–21,
 124–25, *129*, *131*, 135, *plates 4*–*5*; Bristol,
 116–17; salt, *59*–60, *115*–20, *123*, *127*,
 plates 11–*13*
Glenn, Clifford and Leonard (instrument
 makers), 8–9
"Going to Georgia" (song), 3
Goldstein, Kenneth, 105
"Goober Peas" (song), 45–46
goobers. *See* peanuts
"Goodbye, God" (story), 164